Religious Truth
and Religious Diversity

aus
american
university
studies

Series VII
Theology and Religion

Vol. 288

PETER LANG
New York • Washington, D.C./Baltimore • Bern
Frankfurt am Main • Berlin • Brussels • Vienna • Oxford

Nathan S. Hilberg

Religious Truth and Religious Diversity

PETER LANG
New York • Washington, D.C./Baltimore • Bern
Frankfurt am Main • Berlin • Brussels • Vienna • Oxford

Library of Congress Cataloging-in-Publication Data

Hilberg, Nathan S.
Religious truth and religious diversity / Nathan S. Hilberg.
p. cm. — (American university studies. VII, Theology and religion; v. 288)
Includes bibliographical references and index.
1. Religion—Philosophy. 2. Realism.
3. Philosophical theology. I. Title.
BL51.H55   202—dc22   2008040425
ISBN 978-1-4331-0335-3
ISSN 0740-0446

Bibliographic information published by **Die Deutsche Bibliothek.**
Die Deutsche Bibliothek lists this publication in the "Deutsche
Nationalbibliografie"; detailed bibliographic data is available
on the Internet at http://dnb.ddb.de/.

The paper in this book meets the guidelines for permanence and durability
of the Committee on Production Guidelines for Book Longevity
of the Council of Library Resources.

© 2009 Peter Lang Publishing, Inc., New York
29 Broadway, 18th floor, New York, NY 10006
www.peterlang.com

Printed in the United States of America

Table of Contents

Chapter 1

Introduction

The interpretation of religion poses a dilemma: Realist interpretations of religion give rise to the philosophical problem of religious diversity and irrealist interpretations of religions are revisionary.[1] That realism and irrealism are the only two options and that they entail genuine problems will be made clear as we go. As this discussion will show, the advantage of conceiving of the world's religious landscape in this way is that understanding religion according to the parameters of this dilemma facilitates situating any interpretation of religion within it. For example, when we encounter interpretations of religion that try to avoid the charge of revisionism by offering a realist interpretation we know to be cautioned that such interpretations ultimately will confront the problem of religious diversity: that there are conflicting claims to religious truth. Similarly, we are forearmed by knowing that those who wish to avoid the difficulties facing realism by offering irrealist interpretations of religion must contend with the issue of revisionism; that is, such interpretations of religion are revisionary since they drop essential features of religion and thereby run the risk of no longer being recognizable as interpretations of religion. In this book each of the horns of this dilemma will be examined by analyzing the relevant works of authors who raise the significant issues associated with both sides of this dilemma. We will see that there are two general morals to be learned from applying this dilemma to the interpretation of religious language. First, beware of realist accounts of religion purporting to have solved the problem of religious diversity. Second, beware of irrealist accounts of religion purporting to have offered a religious perspective. Beware because whether one is a realist or an irrealist regarding religion, either comes with its costs; this is why we face a dilemma when interpreting religion. Upon having examined the costs and benefits of religious realism and religious irrealism, ultimately it will be concluded that a certain form of religious realism offers the most attractive interpretation of religion.

In the course of describing this dilemma and its implications for the study of religion some refinements regarding the conceptions of religious realism and religious irrealism that appear in the literature on the topic will be made. One of the contributions to the literature will be to address problems that have muddled the discussion of the significance of religious realism. First, in this book, religious realism describes a concern for *what it means* for a given religious belief, proposition, doctrine, etc., to be true rather than a concern for *which* religious beliefs, propositions, doctrines are true. By concerning ourselves with the former, we can track what is entailed by committing to religious realism or irrealism. By concerning ourselves with the latter, we gain nothing and add to the difficulties facing interpretations of religion. We see a concrete instance of this in Peter Byrne's treatment of realism in chapter 5; furthermore, this matter is treated in-depth in the Appendix. Second, defenders and critics of religious realism have confused matters by assuming that there is only one basic kind of opposition to realism. I argue that this is not the case and that we need to acknowledge that that there are two fundamentally different kinds of opposition to realism. When interpreting a particular instance of religious language I suggest that there are three basic options. First, religious realism describes those who hold that for a given instance of religious language there are objective truth conditions. Second, religious anti-realism describes those who hold that for a given instance of religious language these objective truth conditions do not obtain. Third, religious non-realism describes those who hold that for a given instance of religious language there are no objective truth conditions; that is, a given instance of religious language does not express a proposition.[2] Up to now, I have been using irrealism as a blanket term covering the second and third options. I will continue to do this throughout the book. When I mean the kind of thought described by the second option, I will use the term religious anti-realism, likewise with the third option and religious non-realism.

Leaving aside the matter of whether realism or irrealism offers a more accurate account of religion, my focus is on clarifying the differences between realist and irrealist interpretations of religion. We see the significance of this difference below with regard to what I call e claims. An e claim maintains that a particular religion is exclusively true and thus offers the only correct path to the ultimate reward. That conflicting e claims pose a problem is seen most starkly since the language being considered contains a religion's claim to being exclusively true. The following two examples from Christian scripture illustrate this point. First, consider "Jesus wept" (John 11:35). Next, consider "Neither is there salvation in any other: for there is none other name under heaven given among men, whereby we must be saved" (Acts 4:12). Given that this claim is made in reference to Jesus of Nazareth, Acts 4:12 poses problems that John 11:35 does not. That is, practitioners of religions other than Christianity can assent to the truth of John 11:35 without betraying fundamental tenets of their own faith. The same cannot be said of Acts 4:12. If Acts 4:12 is true, then this would be good news for Christians and bad news for non-Christians. It is bad news for non-Christians since, according to the teaching of Acts 4:12, only those who follow the way of Jesus Christ will be saved.[3] If "to be saved" means "to obtain the ultimate reward," then those who are practitioners of religions other than Christianity have good reason to be concerned if Acts 4:12 is true. Just to cite one obvious example, Muslims believe that the way to obtain the ultimate reward is to follow the ways of Islam, not the ways of Jesus Christ.

The dilemma facing religious realists and religious irrealists, as indicated above, is seen most clearly when considering e claims. However, this issue has not been written about explicitly. Another goal of this book is to fill that gap in the literature. What has been written about, though not systematically, are the ways in which realism and irrealism bear on our understanding of God's existence. Accordingly, a further goal of this book is to provide a systematic account of how realist and irrealist interpretations bear on our understanding of God's existence. This analysis of theological realism and irrealism (i.e., realism about God's existence) can be applied to the ways in which realist and irrealist construals of religious language bear on the interpretation of e claims. This analysis will constitute the body of the project. Thus, the book will be organized according to the horns of the dilemma facing interpretations of religion posited above. The first part of the book will examine issues involved in the philosophical problem of religious diversity, that is, the problem facing those who occupy the realist horn of the dilemma. The second part of the book will examine issues involved in revisionism, that is, the problem facing those who occupy the irrealist horn of the dilemma. The main body of the text will be followed by an Appendix (more will be said about this later in this introduction) in which I will examine specific philosophical concerns facing realism.

Thus, the book is organized according to a dilemma. Realist interpretations of religion give rise to the philosophical problem of religious diversity and irrealist interpretations of religion are revisionary. Accordingly, I want to make two ideas maximally clear: why it is that religious realism gives rise to the philosophical problem of religious diversity, and why religious irrealism is revisionary. After having articulated the former I will discuss the latter. Assuming that we have no way of knowing which if any of the religions of the world offers the correct path to the ultimate reward, we face a problem. One religion teaches that a particular path to righteousness is the correct one; another religion teaches something else, and so on. Considered in the light of the law of non-contradiction, we see how the world's religious landscape with its conflicting claims to ultimate truth presents a philosophical problem. According to the law of non-contradiction, not both p and not-p, if there are conflicting claims as to what constitutes the correct path to the ultimate reward, at most one claim can be correct. In other words, given that the world's religions offer different paths to the ultimate reward, at most one can be correct. Note how realism entails the law of non-contradiction. First we take a fundamental tenet of realism: "p" is true if and only if p obtains.[4] Moreover, only that p obtains can make "p" true; anything except p would make "p" not true, thus showing the intimate relation between realism and the law of non-contradiction. As we see, this has significant implications for the world's religious landscape. Invoking the law of non-contradiction implicit within religious realism, if Acts 4:12 is true, any conflicting claim must be false. That is, for the religious realist, for "there is no salvation except through Christ" to be true, it must be the case that that there is no salvation except through Christ. Moreover, for the religious realist *only* that there is no salvation except through Christ can make "there is no salvation except through Christ" true. From this we can see that the matter of religious diversity cannot be properly assessed without systematically clarifying the role of truth in religious language. My analysis of religious realism, religious anti-realism and religious non-realism will provide this assessment; this treatment will fill a gap in the literature, a gap that sorely needs to be filled.

Considering another feature of realism, one that distinguishes it from irrealism, will aid us in seeing the connection between realism and the philosophical problem of religious diversity as well as the connection between irrealism and revisionism. The philosophical problem of religious diversity is borne of the idea that given conflicting accounts at most one can be true. The idea that at most only one conflicting account can be true is unique to a realist account of truth insofar as it contains what I will call an independence condition. This independence condition is exemplified by a realist conception of truth, which maintains that "p" is true if and only if p obtains independent of what we do, say, or believe about p.[5] Irrealist conceptions of truth do not include such an independence condition. Irrealist conceptions of truth do not maintain that p's obtaining independently of "p" is a necessary condition for "p"'s being true. For example, for the realist, only that God exists independently of what we do, say or believe could make "God exists" true. For the irrealist this is not the case. For the irrealist other factors besides God's existing independently of what we do, say or believe could make "God exists" true. Some examples of this would be that affirming "God exists" means that we idealize what is most admirable about humanity (we see this in Feuerbach, to be discussed in chapter 5); another example of irrealism is to maintain that affirming "God exists" is to acknowledge that "God" has significance within well-established social practices (this will be discussed in finer detail in chapters 6 and 7 which are devoted to Wittgensteinian interpretations of religion). This lack of an independence condition, which characterizes irrealism, could possibly reconcile conflicting truth claims. These irrealist conceptions of truth would include qualifiers for how a particular state of affairs would count as a truth-maker for its corresponding proposition. The following formulation exemplifies this irrealist line of reasoning: "a is true according to such and such perspective, since their cognitive situation would dispose them to view truth along the lines of a" and "not-a is true according to thus and so perspective, since their cognitive situation would dispose them to view truth along the lines of not-a." Since factors other than that p obtains independently of what we do, say, or believe can make "*p*" true for the irrealist, we can see how putatively conflicting truth claims, religious or otherwise, constitute a problem for the realist but not for the irrealist. For the Christian realist only that the conditions described by Acts 4:12 obtain independently of what we do, say or believe can make Acts 4:12 true. If a conflicting *e* claim were true in a realist sense a serious challenge would thus be posed to the idea that Acts 4:12 were true in a realist sense. On the other hand, this would not pose a problem for irrealist interpretations of religion. That something other than the conditions described by Acts 4:12 obtain need not make the irrealist conclude that Acts 4:12 is not true. This inference simply follows from the irrealist idea, that is, its lack of an independence condition, that the obtaining of *p* independently of what we do, say or believe is not the only truth-maker for "*p*."

Having seen how the absence of an independence condition characterizes irrealist construals of religious truth, we can see that a motivation to offer an irrealist interpretation of religion could be to neutralize the problems caused by religious realism, e.g., that of religious diversity. Interpreting religion in an irrealist manner can avoid the problem of religious diversity since an irrealist construal of truth can allow for conflicting truth claims. Whatever an irrealist conception of truth might consist in, it will not have as a condition of a given "*p*" being true that *p* actually obtains; what I have just described is a realist conception of truth. In contrast to realism, which at its heart has what I have called an independence condition, irrealism takes many forms. To varying degrees, a feature of any form of irrealism, though, is that truth claims are relativized. This idea will be expanded upon later but for now it will suffice to say that some irrealist religious pluralists[6] relativize religious truth claims to their corresponding religious traditions.[7] Whatever form this relativizing takes, one can see how this relativizing maneuver neutralizes the problem of religious diversity. For the irrealist, that there are many, conflicting religious truth claims need not be a problem since for the irrealist each of these claims can be true relative to the proper context. To apply this line of reasoning, Acts 4:12 would be true for Christians but not for non-Christians. Another way to put this would be that when one's worthiness to obtain the ultimate reward would be assessed, each religious practitioner would be judged according to the standards of her or his own religion. The problem facing religious irrealism, though, illustrating why it constitutes the other horn of the dilemma I pose, is that it results in revisionism. We see this below.

A religious irrealist could maintain that Acts 4:12 applies to Christians only; that is, our irrealist would hold that there are no objective conditions whereby Acts 4:12 is true for all people including those who are not Christians. While such a move might provide comfort with regard to the problem of religious diversity, by making this irrealist, relativist move, our religious irrealist must contend with the problem of revisionism. That is, while trying to situate Christianity (in this case) within the world's religious landscape, the relativist has situated something other than Christianity. In other words, Acts 4:12, an example of Christian scripture, does not make a relative claim; it makes an absolute claim. To paraphrase Acts 4:12: if you want the ultimate reward, Jesus Christ offers *the way* to obtain it. By upholding the relative truth of Acts 4:12, one is not upholding a Christian belief. That is, to uphold a relativist interpretation of Acts 4:12 is to uphold something other than Christianity. Instead one is upholding a relativist belief that might approximate Christian doctrine. Perhaps upholding the relative truth of Christianity or any other religion is a fine move; however, by doing so, one has offered a revisionary account of religion. This is not satisfactory if our relativist's original goal was to address the problem of religious diversity. By relativizing the truth claims of the religions of the world, doctrines such as Acts 4:12 will be unrecognizable as the teachings to which religious practitioners adhere. The irrealist, by changing an absolute claim to religious truth (such as Acts 4:12) to a relative claim, has not really provided an interpretation of religion (Christianity in this case). What our irrealist has provided is an account of, say, Christianity-prime, a religion in which relative truth claims are made. By giving an account of something other than religion, this relativist, irrealist conception of religion is appropriately characterized as revisionary.

Having contended that irrealist interpretations of religion are revisionary, I can further develop the idea that revisionary interpretations of religion are problematic. When I say that the ordinary religious practitioner assents to doctrines like "God created the heavens and the earth" or "only through Christ can one be saved" what I mean is that the practitioner is affirming what she believes to be the case. That is, in so doing she affirms that "God created the heavens and the earth" accurately describes a state of affairs in which God created the heavens and the earth (and so on with "only through Christ can one be saved"...). To believe otherwise is revisionary. That is, if "x" represents a sample of religious language, the revisionist interprets "x" as meaning something other than x. Accordingly, the revisionist interpretation of "x" as something other than x will not be a religious interpretation of x. To maintain that "God created the heavens and the earth," instead of meaning that God created the heavens and the earth, means, for example, *life is worth living* or *I feel validated* or anything at all besides *God created the heavens and the earth* is to assent to something other than a standard religious interpretation of "God created the heavens and the earth." This statement exemplifies a revisionary interpretation of religion. Accordingly, a non-revisionary interpretation of religion is one that upholds the idea that when religious devotees assent to a given "p" it is p to which they assent. Note the affinity between this description of non-revisionary interpretations of religious belief and religious realism, which maintains that a religious "p" is true if and only if p. This is why I associate realism and the law of non-contradiction with a non-revisionary interpretation of religion. Here we can see that the law of non-contradiction is a condition of non-revisionary interpretations of religion. Otherwise, interpretations of a given religious "p" render "p" as meaning something other than p. While I acknowledge that symbolic uses of language are integral to religion, non-revisionary interpretations of religious language fall within limits. While I do not pretend to know the precise nature of these limits, I am confident that these limits cannot compromise the role that salvation plays in religious life. Substituting the content of Acts 4:12, "Neither is there salvation in any other: for there is none other name under heaven given among men, whereby we must be saved," for "p," we can see why allowing that anything other than p to make "p" true compromises the idea of salvation. Accordingly, I feel justified in my claim that the law of non-contradiction, and thus realism, are vital to non-revisionary interpretations of religion.[8]

Now that we are familiar with the issues raised by the dilemma I have posed, we can review the salient points thus far. I have shown why the philosophical problem of religious diversity is entailed by religious realism and why religious irrealism is revisionary. I have shown why religious diversity and revisionism are problems. Having shown the relevance of these issues to the dilemma I pose, we need to consider some broader conceptual issues associated with realism and irrealism in turn.

To this point I have used the term religious realism to describe those who hold that for a given instance of religious language there are objective truth conditions. It should be noted, though, that in this book two levels of realism are invoked. My reason for doing so is that the second level of realism, what I will be calling theoretical realism, raises conceptual problems that the first level of realism, what I will be calling ordinary realism, does not.[9] Ordinary realism underlies the practical ontologies we utilize in our everyday lives. Theoretical realism attempts to make the case that the truth of an instance of language consists in its ability to match the conditions it describes. Ordinary realism operates according to the *assumption* that "p" is true if it matches p. For our ordinary realist, it is not that she presumes realism is the correct way to think about life; she assumes that by following her realist inclinations she will manage just fine. For example, she believes her assumption that "fire burns the flesh off one's bones" matches *fire burns the flesh off one's bones* will suffice in her interactions with fire. For ordinary realism, it is *assumed* that this is a match since it offers no account of the nature of the match (giving an account of the nature of the match is the province of what I call theoretical realism; more on this follows below). Not having such an account is of no consequence in this connection, though, since our ordinary realist still manages just fine since, by the lights of ordinary realism, one is able, e.g., to avoid burning the flesh off one's bones. Notice that this description of ordinary realism invokes the law of non-contradiction in that only p and nothing other than p can make "p" true; anything other than p's obtaining will render "p" false. Ordinary realism thus entails the independence condition described above and the law of non-contradiction. Two points should be noted from this discussion of ordinary realism.

First, ordinary realism is sufficiently substantive to entail the philosophical problem of religious diversity. To see this conclusion, all we need to do is fill in an e claim for p. Recalling that the message of Acts 4:12 is "there is no salvation except through Christ" this argument follows thus: Acts 4:12 is true if and only if the conditions described by Acts 4:12 obtain. Since only those conditions would make Acts 4:12 true, any other conditions that might obtain would make Acts 4:12 not true. Second, articulating the nature of the match between "p" and p (or the nature of the match between Acts 4:12, or any e claim, and what it describes) is not part of ordinary religious realism's burden. The ordinary religious realist's burden is to address the problem of religious diversity. The portion of the main body of the text devoted to religious realism addresses precisely this problem. Attempting to address the nature of the match between "p" and p is the province of theoretical realism as discussed below.

Theoretical realism also entails the aforementioned independence condition and the law of non-contradiction; additionally, it includes a correspondence theory of truth. Theoretical realism maintains that this realist conception of truth provides the correct theory by which p should be interpreted: A given "p" should be considered to be true only if it matches p (what it describes). Accordingly, the theoretical realist owes a debt that the ordinary realist does not: to provide an account of the supposed match between "p" and p, thus showing its connection with a correspondence theory of truth. This matter will be addressed in the Appendix. Except for the Appendix, when realism is referenced throughout the body of the book I mean realism only as it bears on the issues raised by the dilemma by which this book is organized. That is, the main body of the book employs ordinary religious realism as it bears on the issues raised by the philosophical problem of religious diversity and revisionism.

Having tabled the matter of theoretical realism until the Appendix, I now turn to issues facing ordinary realism as it bears on the interpretation of religion. As indicated above, these issues are most pressing when considered in the context of e claims, e.g., Acts 4:12. Applying an ordinary realist conception of truth (and the law of non-contradiction it presumes) to, e.g., Acts 4:12, leaves us with three options. The three options are: a) that Acts 4:12, or any e claim, is false because all e claims are false, b) that one e claim is true and the rest are false, c) that more than one *e* claim is true.[10] My justification for focusing on b) in this book rather than a) or c) follows below.

The different religions of the world make truth claims that conflict with each other. Moreover, the criteria to assess the veridicality of the *e* claims of the religions of the world are not available to us. An assumption of this project, then, is that the great historical religions of the world are on a par with each other epistemically. Accordingly, we are left with the philosophical problem of trying to determine which, if any, of these claims is true. This is the philosophical problem of religious diversity. How can we sort through these conflicting claims? Realism is compatible with the idea that no religion's claim to truth objectively obtains.[11] This, option a) described above, could be exemplified by the most impassioned atheism or garden-variety indifference to religion. Realism is also compatible with the idea, described by option b) above, that at most one religion's claim to truth obtains. This scenario is exemplified by religious exclusivism, the idea that one religion is uniquely true and that other religions, insofar as they conflict with the uniquely true religion, are false. The conclusion that the *e* claims of more than one religion are true in a realist sense, the idea described by option c) above, has interesting consequences. The idea that multiple religions could maintain true *e* claims, religious pluralism in other words, could hold only if the claims to truth on the part of these multiple religions do not conflict with each other. However, if this situation indeed obtained, then there would be no religious diversity in the sense that these different truth claims would all amount to being the same. Maintaining this view could come only by revising the truth claims of the various religious traditions. For example, according to Christianity, Acts 4:12 is true. Acts 4:12, according to the other religious traditions of the world, could be true only via a highly revisionary construal of their teachings. Paraphrasing Acts 4:12 as the idea that "only through embracing Christ as your lord and savior will you be saved," this claim is incompatible with other religious traditions that do not affirm the truth of Acts 4:12. Acts 4:12 could be upheld within, e.g., a Muslim context, only if we revise the rest of the teachings of Islam which indicate that Muhammad is the ultimate messenger of Allah and that Jesus of Nazareth is not a divine being. Mutatis mutandis, Acts 4:12 will be incompatible with any non-Christian religion. In other words, pluralist interpretations of the world's religious landscape, whether they take the form that there are multiple gods or multiple religions which offer a correct account of religious truth are necessarily revisionary once we consider the conflicting *e* claims upheld by the different gods or religions countenanced within the world's religious landscape. More will be said on this in chapter 3 which is concerned with the relevant works of John Hick.

Hick's thought is important to this book conceptually as well as historically since his pluralist approach to the philosophical problem of religious diversity has provided a touchstone for other commentators on this issue. That is, commentators on this matter either agree or disagree with his ecumenical suggestion that all of the religions of the world are salvifically efficacious. Conceptually, an examination of his thoughts on the philosophical problems posed by religious diversity frames the issues involved. However, Hick does not settle these issues in a satisfactory manner. Historically, Hick's work is important in its own right; after all, an entire issue of *Faith and Philosophy* was devoted to responses to his ecumenical position.[12] A significant result of Hick's religious pluralism is that others, religious realists in particular, have continued to be compelled to construct defenses for their religious exclusivism. Hick's charge, in light of his pluralist hypothesis, is that religious exclusivism is arbitrary. Thus, the portion of the book devoted to the realist horn of the dilemma involves further discussion of religious exclusivism and the charge that it is epistemically and religiously arbitrary.[13]

Proceeding further with the description of how religious realism, religious anti-realism and religious non-realism will be employed throughout the book, a term needs to be introduced. I have described the issues involved with religious realism, which I have defined as the position that for a given instance of religious language there are objective truth conditions. Next there is religious anti-realism, which I have defined as the position that for a given instance of religious language the corresponding objective truth conditions do not obtain. Notice that religious realism and religious anti-realism are the options that answer "true" and "false," respectively, with regard to the matter of whether an instance of religious language matches its corresponding objective truth conditions. As such religious realism and religious anti-realism constitute the two cognitivist options regarding the interpretation of religious language. Introducing the idea of cognitivism will help us to distinguish between the two forms of religious irrealism: i.e., religious anti-realism and religious non-realism. Thus far we can see, then, that religious anti-realism shares cognitivism with religious realism and shares irrealism with religious non-realism. More on religious anti-realism specifically follows below.

The weakness and therefore relative inattention I give to religious anti-realism throughout the book is illustrated by the following. Religious realism and religious anti-realism are cognitivist positions which means that religious anti-realism shares the problems of religious realism without sharing the advantage religious realism has of avoiding revisionism. That is, religious anti-realism still involves the problematic idea that the truthfulness of religious language involves a match between a given instance of religious language and what it describes. Religious anti-realism just denies that there is a match between, e.g., Acts 4:12 and what Acts 4:12 describes; it should be noted, though, that this denial still constitutes a commitment as to what the nature of the match between an instance of language and what it describes would consist in. Religious anti-realism maintains that the relation between "p" and p is that there is no match; a given instance of religious language could not match its corresponding truth conditions since for the anti-realist these objective truth conditions do not obtain.

While religious anti-realism shares cognitivism with religious realism, religious anti-realism and religious non-realism, the irrealist options, share the problem revisionism. Religious anti-realism shares this problem with religious non-realism without sharing the advantage non-realism has of avoiding the philosophical problems facing religious realism, e.g., a commitment to the truth or falsity of a given instance of religious language consisting in its matching the conditions it describes. That is, religious anti-realism shares the weaknesses of religious realism and religious non-realism without sharing either of their strengths. Religious realism and religious non-realism, therefore, are the most attractive options. Though religious non-realism has significant strengths, religious realism allows for the possibility of a non-revisionary interpretation of religion. This concern triumphs because when interpreting religious language, it is crucial to do what we can to ensure that religion is what we are interpreting. Interpretations that are revisionary from the outset, such as is the case with irrealist interpretations, preclude this possibility. By promoting non-revisionary interpretations of religion, I am not advancing an essentialist approach to interpreting religion. By opting for a revisionary interpretation at the outset, we are already ensured to offer an interpretation that is something other than religious. One of my tasks throughout the book, then, is to demonstrate the revisionary character of religious irrealism. Since religious non-realism has the most promise of the irrealist options I devote much more attention to commenting on non-realist, rather than anti-realist, accounts of religion and showing why they are revisionary.

Since the second part of the book will be devoted to a detailed analysis of irrealist interpretations of religion, I will not say much about the topic here other than to indicate that the later work of Ludwig Wittgenstein figures prominently in the articulation of what I am calling non-realist ideas. Drawing from his later works, I will show that he offers compelling challenges to the idea that religious language is either true or false. Since Wittgenstein eschews the notion that religious language is either true or false, it is fairly standard in the literature for his interpretation of religion to be regarded as non-cognitivist. However, in saying that Wittgenstein eschews cognitivist interpretations of religion, we should note that it is not as though he promotes non-cognitivism since Wittgenstein does not advance one theory of religion over another.

Wittgenstein's later works indicate that he eschews all philosophical theorizing. If we think of a philosophical theory as providing a means for providing answers to questions concerning the nature of things, or as providing ultimate answers to conceptually vexing questions, perhaps Wittgenstein's theoretical quietism is appropriate. For example, if we think it is characteristic of philosophical theories to provide an ultimate answer to end a regress of "why?" questions,[14] Wittgenstein's wariness of such theories might incline us to see such chains of asking "why?" to be futile and wrong-headed.[15] Because Wittgenstein provides guidance us as to how we might avoid the pitfalls of religious realism and religious anti-realism (i.e., cognitivist interpretations of religion), his teachings are philosophically attractive. However, I will argue that his eschewing of religious realism still amounts to Wittgensteinian interpretations of religion being revisionary.

Having described how the book will be structured according to the parameters of the dilemma I have formulated, we can see the rationale for why the following chapters are arranged as they are. Following this introduction is an overview of religious realism since it occupies the first horn of the dilemma. This is followed by chapters which analyze the works of authors that bring to the fore the primary issues facing religious realism. The work of John Hick, a professed realist, illustrates the spectrum of issues that face realism regarding the philosophical problem of religious diversity; moreover, his work precedes that of others historically resulting in the fact that virtually all of the authors who write on this topic do so in response to his work. For these reasons he is the first author to whom an entire chapter is devoted. As already noted, the chief issue facing religious realists as a result of Hick's work is the charge that religious exclusivism is arbitrary. It is charged with being arbitrary since it maintains that out of all of the religions of the world with similar epistemic credentials, one religion holds the correct path to the ultimate reward. Therefore, the chapter following the discussion of Hick will include analysis of the relevant works of Alvin Plantinga and Peter van Inwagen. The former addresses the issue that religious exclusivism is intellectually arbitrary; the latter addresses the issue that religious exclusivism is religiously arbitrary.

A few comments about the relevant literature and how this book fits into it are helpful here. First, there is an asymmetry in the literature about religious realism and irrealism. According to the dilemma I formulate, religious realism gives rise to the problem of religious diversity, and religious irrealism is revisionary. Whereas religious realists acknowledge that the problem of religious diversity must be countenanced as a challenge to religious realism, religious irrealists, in contrast, generally do not acknowledge their revisionism (or, to use terms that are less loaded, they do not acknowledge that their interpretations are not of the standard variety). Regardless of the religious fallout of their irrealism, religious irrealism is typically motivated by what is considered to be the conceptual flaws of realism. For example, realist interpretations of religion are considered to be too naively literalist; furthermore, irrealists maintain that realists have been unable to give an account of what the match between language and what it describes consists in. Throughout the course of the book these general claims will be fleshed out in more detail. There is a theme, though, underlying these details. Religious realists are wary of irrealism for religious reasons; religious irrealists are wary of realism for conceptual or philosophical reasons. This is not to say, of course, that religious realists are philosophically naïve or that religious irrealists are impious. Among my reasons for treating the authors I do in this book is that each of them is very accomplished in areas in addition to philosophy of religion. While I acknowledge that realists also point out the perceived philosophical shortcomings of irrealism and that irrealists also point out the perceived religious shortcomings of realism, I will focus on the intellectual merits of religious realism and irrealism as each bears on the interpretation of religion.

Second, I want to make it clear that I am not attempting to solve the problem of religious diversity. Perhaps we can clarify the nature of this book by emphasizing what it is not. As religious conflicts have raged throughout the course of history, it would be desirable to understand the nature of the disagreement. Obviously, religion is a complex topic; any interpretation of religious conflict that does not reflect this complexity will necessarily be inadequate. In any given instance of religious conflict, so many factors are in play, it is difficult to comprehend the full array of possible issues. For example, when trying to understand the events of September 11, 2001, we might ask: Were these events the results of a clash between Christian and Muslim cultures? Is this a matter of religious conflict at all? Could it be that the events of 9/11 were purely political in nature? When trying to answer any of these questions, it is difficult to distinguish political acts from religious acts. Indeed, such a distinction seems somewhat artificial. In my efforts to analyze the philosophical problem of religious diversity, I will not be addressing such matters. Moreover, a discussion of how people treat those who hold religious beliefs other than their own would take a form very different from what I will be discussing. Among the issues I will confront in this book will be the conceptual nature of what it is that people are disagreeing about given the diverse and conflicting beliefs that comprise the world's religious landscape. While I do not pretend to offer a solution to conflicts caused by religious difference, it is important to strive for clarity regarding what it is that people are disagreeing about; in my analysis of the role of e claims in religion, this is what I will do.

Chapter 2

Overview of Religious Realism

The purposes of this overview are to discuss certain features of realism that need to be emphasized and to show their implications for the interpretation of religion. Although there certainly are other religious realists,[1] I will utilize the thought of William Alston in this overview of religious realism since he argues for a realist interpretation of religion most explicitly and most systematically. Indeed, it is the explicitness of his realism that makes the issues raised by realism so evident. As to the interpretation of religion, these issues are the philosophical problem of religious diversity and revisionism. Realism also raises more broadly philosophical issues concerning its coherence. Alston's account of religious realism indicates how religious diversity, the idea that the world's religious landscape includes conflicting truth claims, poses a problem for religious realism. Furthermore, Alston's account of realism prefaces his systematic account of the problems facing religious irrealism. In other words, a discussion of Alston's thought exemplifies the dilemma posed in the Introduction: that religious realism faces the philosophical problem of religious diversity and religious irrealism is revisionary.

While a discussion of Alston's work shows the significance of these fundamental issues, Alston himself does not address all of the religious and philosophical issues raised by religious realism. It is for this reason that I utilize the work of John Hick, Alvin Plantinga, and Peter van Inwagen in the chapters that follow to address the issues involved in the interplay between realism and the conflicting truth claims that mark the world's religious landscape. Of paramount interest is an idea associated with realism. According to the law of non-contradiction, not both *a* and not-*a*, if there are conflicting claims as to what constitutes the correct path to the ultimate reward, at most one claim can be correct. In other words, given that the world's religions offer different paths to the ultimate reward, at most one can be correct. Since we have no means available to us to assess the veridicality of the great historical religions of the world with certitude we will assume that they have similar epistemic credentials. Given this assumption, one religion's claim to being exclusively true gives the appearance of being arbitrary. A discussion of Hick's work raises this issue among many others which are also crucial to the interpretation of religion. Plantinga and van Inwagen ably respond to the charge that religious exclusivism is arbitrary; moreover, their responses raise other interesting questions for the interpretation of religion. Accordingly, the relevant works of these authors will be discussed in chapter 4.

Before moving on with these topics, though, more needs to be said about these fundamental issues concerning religious realism mentioned above. It is perhaps Alston's advocacy for realism that has him overlook one of the key problems with advancing a realist theory of (religious) language. According to Alston's conception of realism, p is true if and only if p. However, we face a problem when trying to articulate what the match between "p," an instance of language, and p, what the language describes, would consist in. As will be discussed more fully in the Appendix, Alston does attempt to address this problem. This is no insignificant matter since the idea of such a match seems to be at the heart of realism. As we will see, Alston's failure to articulate a convincing account of what such a match consists in casts a shadow of doubt on the possibility of a realist theory of language per se. However, since this difficulty faces *theoretical* realism only, this problem does not alter the composition and consequences of the dilemma by which I have organized this book since the realist horn of the dilemma is based on what I have called *ordinary* religious realism. As such, the problems facing theoretical realism need not keep us from proceeding. Accordingly, the body of the book is organized according to the issues raised by the dilemma that religious realism gives rise to the philosophical problem of religious diversity and that religious irrealism is revisionary.

In order to contextualize religious realism properly, it must be understood in relation to the other options available. Recall that there are three options when interpreting religious language: first, religious realism describes those who hold that there are objective truth conditions for a given instance of religious language; second, religious anti-realism describes those who hold that for a given instance of religious language these objective truth conditions do not obtain; and third, religious non-realism describes those who hold that there are no objective truth conditions for a given instance of religious language; that is, a given instance of religious language, e.g., an e claim, does not express a proposition. Those described by the first face the realist horn of the dilemma; those described by the second and third face the irrealist horn of the dilemma.

For a fuller description of religious realism I turn to Alston's treatment of religious language since, as indicated above, it is the most extensive and explicitly realist within the extant literature. Alston provides the following three criteria of what he calls alethic realism, realism concerning truth[2]: that the statements in question "are genuine factual statements"; that these statements "are true or false in the realist sense of those terms"; that the "facts that make true [statements] true hold and are what they are independently of human cognition."[3] Consider the statement, "God exists." Such a statement can be a genuinely factual statement (versus, e.g., an axiological claim, which might take the form "'God exists' is an expression of the worthwhileness of life'") within various theories of truth. For example, Alston allows that pragmatism, coherentism, and Kantianism all can accommodate "God exists" as a genuinely factual statement. While pragmatism and coherentism cannot accommodate the second criterion, Alston allows that Kantianism can. However, since "[c]ognition-independent realism is" incompatible with "Kantian 'transcendental idealism,'" it, Kantianism, fails the third criterion.[4] Acknowledging the nuances regarding Kant's thought, though, Alston adds that "Kantian 'partial constitutive dependence' is standardly taken to constitute a form of idealism even if Kant himself said the physical world is 'transcendentally ideal but empirically real.'"[5]

Contrasting realism with irrealism serves to illustrate what I want to emphasize regarding religious realism; understanding these contrasts will help us appreciate the issues in play. It is important to note that I am not advancing the correctness of realism as a theory. Rather, my aim is to emphasize the advantages that realist interpretations of religion have as compared to irrealist interpretations. Once we lay this groundwork concerning the differences between realism and irrealism more generally, we will be able to see how these differences bear on the advantages realism has as a way of interpreting religion.

Alston indicates that an especially important version of irrealism is that in which the non-mental is reduced to the mental such that, concerning realism, it "is independence of *mind* that is typically stressed." That is, "constitutive dependence" on mind is an important indicator of irrealism. He continues, "If physical substances, space and time, universals, or whatever, depend on a relation to mind for being what they are, for their essential character, for their constitution, then they lack the kind of independence of mind that is required for realist status."[6] However, he acknowledges that the distinction between realism and the type of irrealism typically known as idealism can be more subtle when he writes:

> Realists, so called, typically recognize the basic existence of minds; they just resist any imperialist pretensions for the mental. And idealists, so called, do not deny any reality to the physical world, abstract entities, space and time, and the like. They only insist that these items are somehow mental in nature.[7]

Expanding these ideas for realism we can say that a given instance of language is true (or false) independent of what we do, say, or believe. In contrast, for irrealism, what we do, say, and believe does bear on the veridicality of a given instance of language.

This independence condition within realism is closely related to the issues religious realism must confront. Religious realism is simply a specific kind of realism. A religious realist is a realist concerning the interpretation of religion. Thus, for the religious realist, a given instance of religious language is true if and only if the conditions described within that instance of language actually obtain independent of what we do, say, or believe. I am chiefly concerned with the implications realism has for what I have called *e* claims: instances in which a religion makes a claim to offering an exclusive path to the ultimate reward. I am chiefly concerned with *e* claims since they illustrate the realist horn of the dilemma, the philosophical problem of religious diversity, in its starkest form. In order to analyze the extant literature on religious realism, though, I need to consider what people have actually written. No one has written anything about the implications realism has for what I call *e* claims.[8] Accordingly, this book fills a gap in the literature. What *has* been written about extensively is realism concerning God. This I will refer to as theological realism, which is simply realism about God. Since it is the most widely treated topic within the general topic of religious realism, when I draw examples from other authors, I must use what they provide, and, largely, what they provide concerns theological realism. However, as we will see below, the discussion of theological realism can be readily applied to the issues by the dilemma I raise. More specifically, we can see how the concepts invoked by theological realism give rise to the philosophical problem of religious diversity. This is seen when we apply their realist concerns to *e* claims.

Regarding theological realism, Alston states straightforwardly that "most forms of theism are properly thought of as realist."[9] Once again in very plain terms, Alston states that irrealism "is subversive of the Christian faith."[10] Let us consider how irrealism might be subversive of the Christian faith with respect to *e* claims. For the religious realist, Acts 4:12 is true if and only if the conditions described by Acts 4:12 actually obtain. That is, "there is no salvation except through Christ" is true if and only if it describes a state of affairs that actually obtains: namely, that there is no salvation except through Christ. Invoking the law of non-contradiction implicit within ordinary religious realism, if Acts 4:12 is true any conflicting claim must be false. That is, for the religious realist, for "there is no salvation except through Christ" to be true, it must be the case that there is no salvation except through Christ. Moreover, for the religious realist following the law of non-contradiction, *only* that there is no salvation except through Christ can make "there is no salvation except through Christ" true.

To appreciate the significance of the above realist, non-revisionary interpretation of Acts 4:12, it is useful to contrast it with an irrealist interpretation of Acts 4:12. For the religious irrealist, the above reasoning does not apply. The religious irrealist is not bound by the same strict criteria as the realist by which "there is no salvation except through Christ" could be true. As religious irrealism would have it, there are other criteria by which "there is no salvation except through Christ" might be judged to be true. For the religious irrealist, that one feels at peace by having accepted Christ's teachings could count toward the truthfulness of "there is no salvation except through Christ." Any number of other plausible accounts could be provided here for what could make "there is no salvation except through Christ" true for the irrealist. However, and this is where the problem with religious irrealism is seen most starkly: so could any number of implausible interpretations count for the truthfulness of "there is no salvation except through Christ." If it is the case that *there is no salvation except through Christ* is not the only state of affairs that makes "there is no salvation except through Christ" true, then any state of affairs could make "there is no salvation except through Christ" true, plausible or otherwise. If the two following states of affairs, first, the White Sox are my favorite baseball team, and second, there is no salvation except through Christ could count equally toward making "there is no salvation except through Christ" true, as is the case with irrealism, this is plainly subversive of the Christian faith. Related to this point, we can see the connection between irrealism and revisionary interpretations of religion. Whatever a religious (non-revisionary) interpretation of religion might consist in, I feel confident in suggesting that the following is a revisionary interpretation of religion. It is revisionary to allow, as irrealism does, that the White Sox are my favorite baseball team could count as a truth-maker for "there is no salvation except through Christ." Again, we should note that none of this is unique to Christianity; mutatis mutandis, this line of reasoning would hold for the *e* claims of any religion.

If religious realism is necessary to interpret religion in a non-revisionary manner, one might wonder why some opt for an irrealist, revisionary construal of religion. Some might eschew (or, as we will see in Hick's case in the following chapter, temper) the religious realism I describe just so that they can avoid the problem of conflicting religious truth claims. As we will see with Wittgenstein, one might eschew (religious) realism because of its more broadly conceptual problems. Such problems will be discussed further in chapters 6 and 7, as well as in the Appendix. According to Alston, though, a key component of many prominent irrealist conceptions of deity is what he characterizes as a confusion of epistemic status with truth status.

A fundamental distinction between theological realism and theological irrealism is seen by developing the idea of the difference between epistemic status and truth status. As Alston articulates these ideas, the former can be characterized as what, under certain circumstances, we may justifiably believe and the latter as what is true. He writes, "the strength of the epistemic status of a belief has no implications at all for whether it can be given realist construal" with regard to the belief's truthfulness. Further examination will show that the "attempt to move from an epistemic assessment to an irrealist conclusion...rests on a massive confusion of truth status and epistemic status."[11] This confusion runs in two directions. Since Hick considers himself a religious realist, his thought, as will be more fully discussed in the following chapter, is particularly instructive. We can introduce Hick's conception of divinity by stating that he conflates epistemic status and truth status in that he moves from having knowledge of appearances of God (i.e., that "God exists" has positive epistemic status) to the idea that "God exists" is true in a realist sense (i.e., that "God exists" has positive truth status). He does this even though, as a Kantian, Hick would concede that we could never have noumenal knowledge of God.[12] The confusion of epistemic status with truth status also moves in another direction associated with irrealist (Christian) belief. This is the move from "God is unknowable," which seems to be the thrust of much irrealist Christian thought, to "inquiries into whether 'God exists' is true are irrelevant." This move is unwarranted. Whether God is knowable is a different question from whether God exists. God can certainly exist and be unknowable. Indeed, that is probably the standard Christian line.

Whereas realism distinguishes the epistemic status of "God exists" from the truth status of "God exists" irrealism does not. As it concerns religion, this is no mere intellectual matter. "In [the irrealist] construal," Alston writes, "we have totally lost divine-human interaction, and with it the heart and soul of the Judaeo-Christian tradition."[13] Whereas religious realism is able to retain the prospect of divine-human interaction with its insistence that *God exists* is the only state of affairs that could make "God exists" be true, this is not the case with religious irrealism. Since, for religious irrealism, states of affairs besides God's actually existing (e.g., that life is worthwhile) can make "God exists" true, we see that within religious irrealism the prospect of divine-human interaction can be lost. Thus, we see the thrust of the realist's opposition to religious irrealism: When we are considering religious language, if this language is to include the idea of God or gods *doing* things, e.g., creating the heavens and the earth, or, intervening in the course of human affairs, responding to petitionary prayer, and so on, then such a notion of deity must be understood in realist terms. A construct of my cognitive workings cannot bestow grace upon you, for example, because such a construct cannot *do* anything at all, except, of course, for the ways in which such belief might influence my undertakings. If divine action is crucial to a religious interpretation of religion, then a non-revisionary conception of deity requires a realist interpretation.

If realism is a condition of a non-revisionary interpretation of religion, why would professed Christians advance irrealist interpretations of God? Alston's diagnosis of this situation indicates that "the most common reasons for rejecting a realist construal of religious belief have consisted in metaphysical reasons for taking such beliefs to be false as so construed."[14] One reason indicated by those with irrealist inclinations is that God is believed to be so radically Other. This is manifest in the following concern: How we could even begin to assess whether our claims about God correspond to God's real existence? Claims concerning the ineffability of religious language that do not also claim the cognitive status of religious language are not my target here. However, claims concerning the ineffability of religious language are disingenuous when they, e.g., take a form in which God is claimed to be ineffable yet claims about God are also presumed to have cognitive status. This seems to be precisely the case for those such as Hick who follow the Kantian distinction between noumena and phenomena concerning God. For Hick, as long as we are referring to God as noumenal, God is ineffable and immune from intellectual scrutiny; as long as we are referring to God as phenomenal, descriptions of God can have cognitive content. A position such as Hick's enjoys having a robust sense of God, a God who *does* things: intervenes in the course of human affairs, makes commandments, bestows grace, etc., while not having to be accountable for providing any epistemic reasons or arguments for believing in God. [15] Such an understanding defines God in such a way that it cannot be determined what could be counted as evidence for or against the existence of God. Despite this, Hick still claims to be a religious realist.

Though more will be said about Hick and his Kantianism in the following chapter, my aim in contrasting Alstonian realism with Hick's critical realism has been to illustrate the import of what I call ordinary religious realism. For the ordinary religious realist, a given instance of religious language is true or false regardless of what we do, say or believe. That said, more light can be shed on the horn of the dilemma facing religious realism: the philosophical problem of religious diversity. In that it maintains that for any instance of religious language there are objective truth conditions, religious realism is impacted by the philosophical problem of religious diversity, i.e., that the world's religious landscape includes conflicting *e* claims, in obvious ways. A feature of *e* claims (e.g., Acts 4:12) is that to be true, an *e* claim must be *uniquely* true, invoking the law of non-contradiction I have associated with ordinary religious realism. Following this line, when there are conflicting truth claims *at most only one* can be true. Accordingly, religious exclusivism, the idea that a particular religion contains the unique path to the ultimate reward, is central to the religious realist's response to the horn of the dilemma she faces: the problem of religious diversity, which can also be glossed as the problem of conflicting *e* claims.

To summarize this overview of religious realism, I suggest that the most fundamental difference between realism and irrealism can be characterized as an independence condition, present in realism but not in irrealism. That is, to be true in a realist sense, an instance of language must match what it describes independently of what we do, say, or believe. This independence condition, characteristic of realism, also figures in the philosophical problem of religious diversity. Hick's citing of Alston in the following illustrates this concept. Another reason why I have utilized Alston's thought to describe religious realism, in addition to the explicitness with which he argues for it, is due to his prominence in the field. John Hick acknowledges this prominence when he indicates that it is broadly agreed, with Alston, "that the most viable defense of religious belief has to be a defense of the rationality of basing beliefs on religious experience." However, as Hick acknowledges, once we take that route we are faced with the problem of conflicting accounts of religious experience and the corresponding conflicting truth claims which originate from different religious traditions.[16] This dynamic exemplifies the idea that religious realism and religious irrealism each have their tradeoffs. Following the logic of the dilemma by which this book is organized, the cost of irrealism is that it results in revisionism. While Alston's religious realism enables him to avoid revisionism, the cost of his religious realism, as he acknowledges, is that he faces the problem of religious diversity. That is, the realist who holds that one religion is correct faces the issue of similarly credible but conflicting truth claims put forth by other religions of the world. For Alston, what makes this a *philosophical* problem is that the world's various religious traditions have similar epistemic credentials. He writes, "The existence of a plurality of religious communities…is hardly a crucial epistemological problem unless there are substantial grounds of belief within each community."[17] Alston acknowledges that this is the case. For him, the nature of the problem is

since the participant of one religious DP has no non-question-begging reason to suppose herself in a superior epistemic position to her competitors, she is not justified in supposing that it is her DP that is the reliable one...Religious diversity is a reason for *doubting* the reliability of any particular religious doxastic practice.[18]

If the practitioners of the world's religions are in similar epistemic positions, Alston acknowledges that they have reason to doubt the certainty with which they might hold their own religious beliefs insofar as they conflict with the well-established beliefs of other religions.

Hick acknowledges that the religious realism recommended by Alston gives rise to the philosophical problem of religious diversity. With this in mind, we now turn to a more detailed discussion of Hick's thought. His approach to the issues entailed by the dilemma I pose is especially significant in that he tacitly acknowledges the situation I have described confronting the interpretation of religion. He acknowledges the importance of religious realism in avoiding revisionism; he also acknowledges that religious realism leaves one with the philosophical problem of religious diversity. Hick's problem, as we will see, is that in confronting the philosophical problem of religious diversity (i.e., that of conflicting *e* claims) he undermines his claim to being a religious realist.

Chapter 3

A Realist Interpretation of Religious Diversity

John Hick's work figures prominently in any discussion of the philosophical problem of religious diversity. His work provides a scholarly treatment of what seems to be the most obvious objection to the idea that there is a problem of religious diversity. This objection is that, despite their apparent differences, the various religions of the world essentially share the same core values, e.g., treat your fellow humans as you would like to be treated yourself. However, as an interpretation of religion, this objection is not without its own problems. Another reason that Hick is a prominent figure in any discussion of the philosophical problem of religious diversity is that much of the work that has been done in this field is an explicit response to his pluralist hypothesis. Following the publication of John Hick's *An Interpretation of Religion*,[1] the philosophical literature on religious diversity has had the prevailing theme of recommending how to deal with the problem of religious diversity.[2] Because of the central role his thought has in the literature on this topic, it is necessary to address his work early in the project. This placement is justified conceptually since assessing his pluralistic hypothesis serves to introduce the problems that loom for any treatment of religious diversity; Hick's work serves as a microcosm for the issues in play regarding the philosophical problem of religious diversity. As mentioned above, placing my discussion of Hick here also makes sense from a historical perspective since the authors discussed in the following chapters write in response to him. Therefore, this chapter also serves as an introduction to the ideas in play in the philosophical problem of religious diversity, the problem specifically facing those on the realist horn of the dilemma I have formulated.

Hick's case is especially interesting within the framework of my argument since he claims to be a realist and to have avoided the problem of religious diversity by way of his pluralist hypothesis. According to the dilemma by which I have framed these issues, the problem of conflicting truth claims from the various religions of the world is entailed by committing to religious realism. As we will see, his claim to realism, especially when considered in the context of his claim to offer a religious interpretation of religion, suggests quite strongly that he is trying to avoid the charge of revisionism. For example, he writes, "A non-realist" or, in my terminology, an irrealist, "interpretation [of religion] is in contrast [to his own purportedly realist interpretation of religion], radically revisionary."[3] From Hick's purported realism, it follows that the three options available to him regarding the matter of religious diversity would be that, first, no religion is true (e.g., atheism), second, one religion is true (exclusivism), and, third, some religions are true (e.g., polytheism). Hick would contend that none of these labels fits his work. He considers himself a realist and a pluralist; however, as we will see below, Hick rejects polytheism. He does claim, though, that all of the great axial faiths of the world do truly have a transcendent referent and are equally salvifically efficacious. According to the dilemma I have posited, it follows that the only way to be a realist and a pluralist is to offer revisionary interpretations of *e* claims. This scenario indeed applies since, within a realist framework, if we are faced with more than one *e* claim and these *e* claims conflict, at most one *e* claim can be correct. This situation must obtain unless we revise the meaning of these *e* claims such that they are construed in a way so that they do not conflict. However, Hick claims to be a realist, a pluralist,[4] and to offer a non-revisionary interpretation of religion. In short, Hick's work ostensibly poses a counterexample to the dilemma I argue faces interpretations of religion.

The most obvious reason why the present discussion of Hick's work is placed here, along with other treatments of religious realism, is that Hick considers himself to be a religious realist. The need for the systematic treatment of religious realism, anti-realism, and non-realism is seen when we consider the opposing features within Hick's account of religious diversity. The assessment of him as a religious irrealist need not worry us yet but the reasons for this assessment will be spelled out subsequently. First, though, let us consider Hick's claim to being a religious realist. Hick's approach to the problem of religious diversity needs to be understood within the context of his claim to realism. For Hick, a realist conception of a transcendent Real is what differentiates religious from revisionist interpretations of ostensibly religious phenomena; as such, realism is central to all that Hick has to say about religion.[5]

Given that realism is central to Hick's pluralist interpretation of religion, it is important to consider how realism and religious pluralism relate to each other. Thus, there are two ways in which one can be a pluralist concerning *e* claims. One way is just to be an outright revisionist and hold that *e* claims from different religions only seem to conflict since they are not really making exclusivist claims but are in fact providing different paths to the same ultimate reward. Though Hick would probably disagree with this characterization of his work, this conclusion is unavoidable. The other way to be a pluralist concerning *e* claims would be, insofar as affirming an *e* claim entails theism, to embrace polytheism.[6] That is, since we would have different *e* claims attributable to different deities, the stage for polytheism has already been set. This approach to the problem of religious diversity in effect just rearticulates the same problem: we still have competing *e* claims; it's just that within a polytheistic context, each *e* claim would have divine sanction. Hick, appealing to the principle of parsimony, does not opt for a polytheistic account of religious pluralism.[7] Thus, a problem arises with the two ways I propose of conceiving of being a pluralist concerning e claims as they bear on Hick's case. Hick opts against the polytheistic way and he opposes the idea that his pluralistic hypothesis is revisionist in character. A more detailed discussion of the roles that realism and pluralism play in Hick's thought will shed light on how this tension in his interpretation of religion reveals itself.

As stated above, Hick's claim to realism must be placed within the context of his pluralistic hypothesis which he describes as follows. "In Kantian terms, the divine noumenon, the Real *an sich*, is experienced through different human receptivities as a range of divine phenomena, in the formation of which religious concepts have played an essential part."[8] Hick appeals to a unified religious realism to warrant the credibility of seemingly diverse religious traditions; additionally, Hick postulates that a realist interpretation of the divine noumenon, i.e., the Real *an sich*, is a condition of the possibility of salvation. He writes, "Each of the great post-axial streams of religious experience...all affirm a transcendent Reality in virtue of which [salvation or liberation] is available to us."[9] So, as we can see, Hick sees realism as a pre-requisite for his pluralistic hypothesis. That is, he postulates a noumenal Real which underlies its various phenomenal manifestations as experienced in the religions of the world. To see the role the noumenal/phenomenal distinction plays in Hick's conception of realism, we need first to consider its Kantian origins.

I begin this discussion of the Kantian origins of the phenomenal/noumenal distinction by situating it within the historical context within which Kant wrote his *Critique of Pure Reason*. In the first *Critique* Kant indicates that his philosophical stance is between the emphasis on a priori mental spontaneity of the Rationalists and the emphasis on sensory experience of the Empiricists with his famous passage: "Thoughts without content are empty, intuitions without concepts are blind."[10] In this passage, Kant shows how his thought avoids what he saw as the pitfalls of both Rationalism and Empiricism. Kant's thought challenged the notion that the only two types of intelligible judgments are analytic judgments, known a priori, and synthetic judgments, known a posteriori. "Hume's Fork" famously expresses this thought that Kant was challenging. I quote the relevant, classic passage from Hume:

> Does it [a book, given thought, judgment, expression, etc.] contain any abstract reasoning concerning quantity or number [analytic truths]? No. Does it contain any experimental reasoning concerning matter of fact and existence [synthetic truths]? No. Commit it then to the flames, for it can contain nothing but sophistry and illusion.[11]

The way in which Kant responds to "Hume's Fork" with a counterargument for the synthetic a priori nature of time and space allows for the Rationalist possibility that time and space, as a priori categories, operate within our understanding as the condition of the possibility of having experience but acknowledges Empiricist skepticism by prohibiting the metaphysical pretensions of the Rationalists. Elucidating this idea, Donald Palmer writes that upon Kant's postulation of the phenomenal/noumenal distinction

> [t]raditional metaphysics was impossible because it was always the result of illegitimately applying notions of space, time, and causality to the noumenal world when in fact these concepts can only be applied to the observable world.[12]

With the phenomenal/noumenal distinction Kant was able to save what he saw as the necessity of mental generativity (that we can spontaneously produce ideas independent of sensory experience), a concern of the Rationalists, while addressing the concerns of the Empiricists as represented in Hume's Fork.

Kant articulates this distinction as follows:

> [I]f we entitle certain objects, as appearances, sensible entities (phenomena), then since we thus distinguish the mode in which we intuit them from the nature that belongs to them in themselves, it is implied in this distinction that we place the latter, considered in their own nature, although we do not so intuit them, or that we place other possible things, which are not objects of our senses but are thought as objects merely through the understanding, in opposition to the former, and that in doing so we entitle them intelligible entities (noumena).[13]

The above passage is not intended to provide an argument to warrant the distinction between phenomena and noumena but merely to introduce the parameters of the division Kant wants to present: the term *phenomena* shall refer to the appearance of things as they present themselves to us sensibly, and the term *noumena* shall refer to the being of things themselves as they would be known intelligibly. To this point, Kant distinguishes between phenomena and noumena, put simply, as the former being objects of sensibility and the latter being objects of intelligibility. Further into his discussion of these terms, however, he defines them more precisely, which shows that he employs the term *noumenon* negatively, as a qualification that specifies that which we cannot know.

Further clarifying the roles of the faculties of sense and reason, Paul Guyer suggests that, according to Kant,

> we must distinguish between appearance and reality. He [Kant] then equates this distinction with one between that which is passive and that which is active in ourselves, which he in turn equates with the distinctions between sensation and reason.[14]

For one, this passage would indicate the active role which Kant sees reason holding. Furthermore, from Frederick C. Beiser we see that the "form of

sensibility consists in two a priori forms of intuition: space and time."
Moreover, reason "consists in certain a priori concepts that are necessary
conditions of thinking any object whatsoever; namely existence, necessity,
substance, and cause."[15] Beiser states the more general connection of sensibility
to phenomena and reason to noumena when he writes that "sensibility gives us
knowledge only of how things appear to us; reason provides us with knowledge
of things as they are in themselves."[16] Albert W.J. Harper describes the
distinction between phenomena and noumena in a more specific sense as what
Kant refers to as the "negative" function of noumena. Harper writes that the
Kantian sense of phenomenon as appearance means "nothing in itself beyond
our mode of representation concerning it."[17] He continues, the noumenon "is
entirely outside the space-time manifold; we can have no knowledge of its
properties or relations, it cannot be predicated of and no synthetic propositions
are able to be formulated about it."[18]

Things-in-themselves and noumena are synonymous.[19] "Things-in-
themselves are never objects of our senses, but are thought as objects through
the understanding and are called intelligible entities to distinguish them from
intelligible objects."[20] This terminological distinction anticipates the more
specific negative sense of noumenon: the thing-in-itself is noumenal; in
addition, it signifies that which we cannot know directly. There is a world "out
there" to be known objectively; however, it is precisely this noumenal aspect of
the thing-in-itself that we cannot know. The phenomenal/noumenal distinction
helps us to understand the conditions under which, according to Kant, we are
able to have knowledge. Articulating the difference between phenomena and
noumena thus reflects the transcendental nature of Kant's philosophy, which,
accordingly, has as its goal to describe the conditions of the possibility of sensory
experience and knowledge generally. Noumena, Beiser writes, "are not a type of
existing thing, but simply the forms or structures to which any existing or
possible thing must conform." Since "the laws of reason do not refer to any
existing thing...Kant is not worried about the problem of their verification or
application in experience."[21]

Kant himself defines noumenon as "a thing which is not to be thought as
object of the senses but as a thing in itself, solely through a pure
understanding..."[22] Furthermore, the concept of the noumenon is "to show
that [sensible knowledge] cannot extend its domain over everything which the
understanding thinks."[23] This passage is possibly ambiguous, for from it one
could arrive at the conclusion: while knowledge derived sensibly cannot
comprehend the noumenon, the understanding can. I do not take Kant to be
holding this position. Rather, it is the thing itself that cannot be known; there is
a limitation on our ability to know things in themselves, period. This limitation
consists of two qualifications. We cannot know the world in itself; rather, we

can only know how the world represents itself (first qualification) to us (second qualification) according to rules which Kant holds to be absolute, applying to all knowers.

Next, Kant introduces the negative aspect of the noumenon:

> If by 'noumenon' we mean a thing so far as it is *not an object of our sensible intuition,* and so abstract from our mode of intuiting it, this is a noumenon in the *negative* sense of the term. But if we understand by it an *object* of a *non-sensible intuition,* we thereby presuppose a special mode of intuition, namely, the intellectual, which is not that which we possess and of which we cannot comprehend even the possibility. This would be 'noumenon' in the *positive* sense of the term.[24]

In the (not altogether illuminating) passage above, Kant delineates the difference between the "negative" and "positive" senses of noumenon. Now we shall see that Kant's presentation of noumenon as a negative concept supports my interpretation of the ambiguous passage from A 255 above. Kant underscores the importance of the negative sense of noumenon in the following passage:

> [B]ut our concepts of understanding, being mere forms of thought for our sensible intuition, could not in the least apply to (intelligible entities to which our sensible faculty of intuition has no relation whatsoever). That, therefore, which we entitle 'noumenon' must be understood as being such only in a *negative* sense.[25]

Kant further highlights the negative significance of the noumenon when he writes,

> the concept of a noumenon is necessary, to prevent sensible intuition from being extended to things in themselves...The concept of a noumenon is thus a merely *limiting concept,* the function of which is to curb the pretensions of sensibility; and it is therefore only of negative employment.[26]

Up to this point it could be possible to interpret Kant's presentation of the noumenon as a limit on sensible knowledge only; however, in the following passage Kant gives a comprehensive prohibition:

> What our understanding acquires through this concept of a noumenon, is a negative extension; that is to say, understanding is not limited through sensibility; on the contrary, it itself limits sensibility by applying the term noumena to things in themselves (things not regarded as appearances). But in so doing it at the same time sets limits to itself, recognising that it cannot know these noumena through any of the categories, and that it must therefore think them only under the title of an unknown something.[27]

For Kant, then, the noumenon limits what we can know about a thing in itself with respect to any and all forms of knowledge. Philip J. Rossi provides a useful summary on Kant's conception of the noumenon. Rossi writes:

> The notion of noumenon is thus negative; it serves to bar us from making claims that objects have, in themselves, "intelligible" grounds, i.e., grounds whose exhibition in concepts bears no reference to an ordering of time or in space. The notion of noumenon thus serves as a reminder that human reason, properly aware of its own limitations in its theoretical use, has no right there to make a positive characterization of whatever might link a realm of objects to their "intelligible ground."[28]

According to the passages above, it is the negative sense of noumenon that suggests that we cannot know a thing-in-itself. More specifically, we have epistemic access to something only as it presents itself to us, mediated by the various contingencies of experience.

That we cannot know a chair, for example, as it exists in itself and thus must know it as it presents itself to us mediated by experience in no way calls into question the existence of the chair. From "we cannot know the chair-in-itself" it does not follow that "the chair, therefore, does not exist." Nor does it follow that "the chair's existence (whether it exists), therefore, is unimportant." The only conclusion that can be drawn with respect to the chair's existence from Kant's negative sense of noumenon is that this chair, whose phenomenal existence we can know with some empirical certainty, cannot be known as it exists in-itself.

I offer Terry Godlove's interpretation of Kant's epistemology in an effort to clarify the above. While I cannot know the chair-in-itself I can have knowledge of this chair as it appears to me. This approach might sound like subjectivism. However, Godlove vigorously opposes this interpretation of Kant's teaching. Kant's mission is to describe the conditions of the possibility of human knowledge as such. In other word, if Kant's epistemology is subjectivist in nature then it describes a subjectivism shared by all knowing humans given the way their cognitive faculties work. This scenario hardly describes subjectivism. If my knowledge of the chair is particular to me, then it is a particularity which is underwritten by the conditions of the possibility by which humans know things. If subjectivism is the proper term for this process, then it should also apply to respiration since *I*, the subject, breathe. That is, my breathing, the condition of the possibility of which is provided by the processes by which humans generally breathe, is particular to me. However particularly I might breathe or cognize, the conditions under which I do them constitute in part why I qualify as a human. While this might describe a less than comprehensive epistemic agenda, it does not describe subjectivism.[29] For Kant, the objective existence of the chair in itself is not irrelevant. Rather, his position is that we do not have direct access to this noumenal knowledge. It is simply an expression of modesty about what we can know.

Kant states exactly this point in reference to his critique of the ontological argument. Kant's argument that we cannot prove the existence of God merely by thinking of the highest being assumes the phenomenal/noumenal distinction. Thinking God, even if God does exist, does not mean that we know God-in-itself; indeed, it is precisely this noumenal knowledge that Kant's phenomenal/noumenal distinction shows us that we are denied. Kant's thought (e.g., in reference to his criticism of the ontological argument) shows the limits of reason. Kant indicates the impermissibility of using reason to "prove" that something, in this case God, exists in the external world when he writes in reference to his own thought, namely, that it "serves rather to limit the understanding than to extend it to new objects."[30]

A revisionary feature of Hick's approach to religious realism manifests itself in his employment of the phenomenal/noumenal distinction. We see this aspect of Hick's interpretation of religion by referring back to Kant who held that what I am calling theological realist efforts to establish God's existence were mistaken. His critique of the ontological argument exemplifies what Kant regarded as a mistaken understanding of metaphysics and as such did not establish that God exists. Rather than simply ally himself with rationalist or empiricist metaphysics, Kant excises from each what seems to him to be correct while leaving behind the errors of each. This interpretation leaves us with Kant's well-known teaching that our knowledge of the world is empirically real yet transcendentally ideal. Indeed, this approach could very well be a satisfactory way of sorting things out when we, say, try to comprehend the physical world. As Alston puts it, "So long as the pattern of our sense experience is what it is, we can, perhaps, (following the Kantian line) adjust to the metaphysical downgrading of trees and houses to systems of phenomena."[31] However, the traditional understanding of God within Western theism cannot accommodate an analogous interpretation and retain its integrity. For example, God cannot be omnipotent if God is in any way dependent on human cognitive machinations for God's being. Such a reduction of God's being simply cannot be assimilated to traditional theistic belief, if such belief includes God's attributes being "omni…" anything, since God's being whatever God is would be dependent somehow on human cognitive workings.

Having seen the origin of the phenomenal/noumenal distinction in Kant, along with some of its wider intellectual ramifications, we are better equipped to discuss and assess Hick's employment of this distinction. The phenomenal/noumenal distinction plays a role in what he calls his critical realism and his pluralistic hypothesis. In contrast to naive realism (the belief that the external world is just as we perceive it to be), Hick advocates critical realism, which involves "taking account of the conceptual and interpretive element within sense perception."[32] The Kantian character of Hick's conception of realism is evident in Hick's solution to the problem of religious diversity which is predicated on this view of realism. Hick addresses this problem by

> appealing to the distinction between God/the Ultimate/the Real/the Transcendent *an sich* and that ultimate reality as variously humanly conceived, and thus variously humanly experienced, and hence variously humanly responded to in historical forms of life. Such a recognition of variety in our human response to the Transcendent depends upon the epistemological principle propounded by St. Thomas, 'Things known are in the knower according to the mode of the knower,' and developed in the modern world by Kant in a way that has affected nearly all western philosophy since.[33]

When Hick writes, "the distinction between God/the Ultimate/the Real/the Transcendent *an sich* and that ultimate reality as variously humanly conceived, and thus variously humanly experienced," he is referring to the Kantian distinction between noumena and phenomena. The Real *an sich*, i.e., the Real in-itself, means the noumenal Real. The phenomenal Real is the Real as it is humanly experienced. Here again, Hick is articulating his pluralistic hypothesis. A feature of his pluralistic hypothesis is that our cognitive input as it bears on our knowledge of the divine noumenon is culturally determined. We see this when Hick writes, "In the case of religion the mode of the knower, i.e. the conceptuality in terms of which the divine presence comes to consciousness, differs as between different human religious cultures and epochs."[34] It is for this reason, according to Hick, that Christians encounter the divine noumenon as the Holy Trinity, Muslims encounter it as Allah, and Hindus encounter it as, e.g., Shiva, and so on.

Again, Hick presumes a realist interpretation of religious experience when he writes, "the Real *an sich* is postulated by us as a pre-supposition, not of the moral life, but of religious experience and the religious life..."[35] For Hick, realism is a pre-requisite for many aspects of his interpretation of religious language. First, realism is a pre-requisite for there to be a God who exists independently of us, which is, in turn, a pre-requisite for there to be a God who acts upon us. Hick also maintains that there is a transcendent reality (which Hick glosses as non- or supra-natural) which impinges upon us. All this requires a realist interpretation to support the belief in interaction with a personal God. Additionally, Hick states that "the cosmic optimism of the great world faiths depends absolutely upon a realist interpretation of their language."[36]

For Hick, then, we can see the different religions of the world "as different forms of the more fundamental conception of a radical change from a profoundly unsatisfactory state to one that is limitlessly better because rightly related to the Real." He continues, "I suggest that these different conceptions of salvation are specifications of what, in a generic formula, is the transformation of human existence from self-centeredness to a new orientation, centered in the divine Reality." He then glosses salvation as "an actual change in human beings from self-centeredness to a new orientation centered in the ultimate divine Reality."[37] Whether or not Hick is correct that the above issues depend on a realist interpretation of religious language is one matter; the matter I intend to address, however, is whether Hick is indeed true to the realism he professes.

Hick's claim to realism is tenuous. Alston, who does not view Kant's thought on this matter as being fully realist,[38] writes the following on Hick's Kantianism.

> Just as Kant took theoretical knowledge to be restricted to the *phenomenal* world, the system of the ways reality appears to our senses, and not to penetrate to that reality itself, so Hick considers the objects of worship in a given religious tradition to have phenomenal rather than noumenal reality.[39]

Alston continues by indicating that, as Hick applies it to religion,

> the Kantian scheme becomes relativized. Instead of a single human schematization of the manifold of sensation by a unique set of categories, we have different interpretations of the Real as it appears to people in different religious traditions...(The status of the) modes of appearance of the Real in a given religious tradition...is that of a mode of appearance rather than the independent reality of that which is appearing.[40]

In the above passage, Alston argues that the relativism which Hick derives from Kant's distinction between phenomena and noumena does not meet realist criteria. Hick's Kantian approach, by utilizing the distinction between a phenomenal understanding of God (which we can have, according to Kantian teaching) and a noumenal understanding of God (which we cannot have, according to Kantian teaching), tries to have the best of both worlds. By "best of both worlds" I mean that Hick claims to be a theological realist, but charges himself with having to account for only a phenomenalist understanding of God.[41] We will see below why, according to Alston, such phenomenalism does not pass realist criteria.

As we have seen, Hick relies on the phenomenal/noumenal distinction to address the problem of religious diversity. That is, according to Hick, there is the divine noumenon which underlies and transcends the diversity of religious phenomena. Thus we see one side of the "best of both worlds." Hick wants the theological robustness, exemplified in his conception of salvation and the sacred unity behind religious diversity, that comes with a realist conception of the divine noumenon. The other side is that, via the Kantian distinction between phenomena and noumena, Hick holds himself responsible for having to show only that the divine noumenon can be demonstrated phenomenally since it is a given that nothing can be known noumenally. That x has phenomenal existence reports nothing to us about the existence of x in-itself. That is the Kantian doctrine. Stated in terms of our topic, appearances of Elvis count no more toward the truth of "Elvis is alive" than hierophanies should count toward the truth of "God exists," unless there is some way of connecting the phenomenal appearance of x to the noumenal x in-itself. However, as we shall see, this is precisely where Hick runs into trouble.

Any arguments which take the form: "'God exists' is true because there are manifestations of God," have the same problem. They confuse epistemic status with truth status. That is, just because x has positive epistemic status does not mean that x is true. Consensus is an example of a determinant of epistemic status but not necessarily of truth status. Obviously, just because a critical mass of people agree that x is true does not make x true. Similarly, following Hick's use of the phenomenal/noumenal distinction: just because people can point to cases where "God exists" *appears* to be true, that is, we have before us some earthly, phenomenal manifestation of God, does not mean that "God exists" *is* true. The case that Alston makes is that "God exists is true" must be given a realist interpretation in order for traditional Christian doctrine to retain ideas like, e.g., "God created the heavens and earth." Such an act, or any act, cannot be attributed to a God the truth of whose existence depends on such notions as consensus or appearance. After all, the consensus as to the truth of "God exists" could change as could the notion of x counting as an appearance of God without any of this having any bearing on the truth of "God exists." So while Hick is able to cite phenomenal manifestations of God's existence (which might give "God exists" positive epistemic status), this does nothing to show the existence of God in a realist sense. As such, his claim to being a realist concerning the interpretation of religious language is seriously called into question.

On the face of it, it would seem that Hick's insistence on a realist interpretation of religious language in conjunction with his pluralist sensibilities would lead him to polytheistic conclusions. While Hick does not see himself as a polytheist,[42] one must ask how Hick could maintain his pluralism in the face of conflicting e claims from the various world religions. How can each e claim be true if one e claim conflicts with another? Hick's way of answering this question heralds his revisionism. That is, his revisionism follows from his irrealist leanings, leanings which show that Hick's work does not constitute a counterexample to the dilemma by which I have framed this project. That he tries to avoid the philosophical problem of religious diversity (i.e., the horn of the dilemma facing religious realists) via his pluralist hypothesis comes with the

33

cost of his giving revisionary accounts of religion (i.e., the horn of the dilemma facing religious irrealists).

Hick addresses this issue by calling for interpretations of religious language that flatten the differences between conflicting religious claims until they are no longer differences.[43] For Hick, the key to unifying the seemingly conflicting *e* claims of the different religions of the world is that they are each salvifically efficacious. He describes what he must regard as minor differences across religions since he recommends that they not distract us from what he regards as the important issue, the common soteriological efficacy of the world's great religions. He writes, "when the Indian religions affirm and the Semitic religions deny [the temporal infinity of the universe], this is not a dispute affecting the soteriological efficacy of either group of traditions." In a similar vein, he dismisses "the question" of the nature of the afterlife since it "is not soteriologically vital." With this statement he summarily concludes that there "are many…disputed trans-historical beliefs. However it is not necessary to list… examples since I want to make the same points about them all…that such 'knowledge' is not necessary for salvation/liberation."[44]

Having thus seen the central role that Hick considers soteriological efficacy to hold, he commends us to see the matter of religious truth with some subtlety. He suggests that mythological truths do not "conflict" with other mythological truths when he writes, "none of [the competing religious claims] constitutes an absolutely pure example of truth-claims conflict. Religious history is more complexly shaded."[45] Nevertheless, Hick goes on to list the kinds of religious phenomena that should be understood mythologically, that is, phenomena where conflicting accounts across religions are tolerable since such differences do not, as he puts it, impact on the soteriological efficacy of any of the religions. Moreover, these differences lose their poignancy when, as Hick recommends, we interpret them mythologically. According to Hick, the following account should be interpreted as being mythological and not factual in nature; therefore, these elements of the religions of the world should not be seen as really being in conflict with each other.

Within the Hindu tradition these include the Vedic stories of the gods, the doctrine of the devas and the many heavens and hells, and the idea of reincarnation. Within Judaism: Israel as God's chosen people, the numerous anthropomorphic rabbinic stories about the Lord, and the ideas of the ups and downs of Jewish history as divine rewards and punishments. Within the Buddhist tradition: the idea of rebirth, the Jakata [sic] tales of the Buddha's previous lives, and discourse about the heavenly Buddhas. Within the Christian tradition: the stories of Jesus's virgin birth, bodily resurrection and ascension and of Mary's immaculate conception and bodily assumption into heaven; the doctrine of divine incarnation, the satisfaction and penal-substitutionary conceptions of atonement, and the ontological doctrines of the Holy Trinity; the image of the church as the body of Christ, and the doctrine of transubstantiation…[46]

For a final clarification, Hick indicates that such beliefs as the above "may well be true or false myths rather than true or false factual assertions."[47] It is at this point that Hick runs into difficulty. If "true" and "false" are the proper terms to describe myths as well as factual assertions, what then is the difference between myths and factual assertions? It is not clear what this differentiation settles. For example, living a good Christian life bears different fruits than does living a good Jewish, Muslim, Buddhist, and so on, life. For example, the former could well involve proselytizing and the latter (e.g., Judaism) would not. Is this difference between Christianity and Judaism reconciled by calling it "mythical?" Hick plays upon the ambiguity within his pluralist hypothesis to argue for two separate concerns that seem to me to be in tension with each other: The first one I will call the universalist premise, that all of the religions of the world access the noumenal Real. He maintains the universalist premise because of his pluralism. The second one I will call the particularist premise, that each of the religion's claims to truth is authentically true (despite the appearance that they might significantly conflict with one another). He maintains the particularist premise because of his desire to be seen as treating each religion's claims to truth seriously. After all, the idea that he offers a religious interpretation of religion permeates his work.[48]

Hick's way of managing this difficulty is to treat the conflicting elements of religious life as being mythical (i.e., non-factual) in character. As indicated above, he contrasts mythical truths with factual truths. According to Hick, the mythical character of conflicting religious claims renders an evaluation of their veridicality a futile undertaking. Then why even use the terms *true* and *false* as ways of describing instances of mythical language at all? It seems that Hick's point in allowing the possibility of the so-called myths of individual religions to be true is so that he can uphold the idea that each religion is authentically true. That being said, it still is clear that his emphasis on the universalist premise comes at the expense of the particularist premise.

Ultimately, Hick's way of settling the question concerning the veridicality of a religion comes to this: He writes, "truth or validity or authenticity of such [diverse] manifestations" as they are experienced in the religions of the world "lies in their soteriological *effectiveness* (emphasis added)."[49] The following examples illustrate three instances of Hick emphasizing the universalist premise at the expense of the particularist premise. First, there are "important ideas within the different traditions which…can be seen…to be different expressions of the same more fundamental idea: thus the Christian concept of salvation and the Hindu and Buddhist concepts of liberation are expressions of the more basic notion of the realization of a limitlessly better possibility for human existence." Second, the "Real in itself is the noumenal ground of both of these ranges of phenomena (whether the most Real is held to be personal or impersonal)." Third, we "have to learn to live with [conflicting historical beliefs], tolerating the varying interpretations imposed by different faith-perspectives."[50]

In each of these instances it is clear that Hick is emphasizing the universalist premise at the expense of the particularist premise. In the first example, Hick emphasizes the "more basic notion of the realization of a limitlessly better possibility for human existence." What is it that "a limitlessly better possibility for human existence" is more basic than? Hick's conception of salvation/liberation is, as he sees it, more basic than the particular tenets of Christianity, Hinduism or Buddhism, particularly when these tenets diverge. Regarding the second example, according to Hick, the idea of a divine noumenon is more fundamental than whether one regards it as a personal or impersonal being. Perhaps he is right about this, but he would be unable to persuade me that to the religious devotee, particularly, say, one engaged in prayer, that it is not utterly fundamental that God is a personal being. In other words, maintaining that the divine noumenon is more basic than whether it is experienced as personal or impersonal hardly seems like a religious interpretation of religion. Regarding the third example, it is preposterous to suggest that one is interpreting religion religiously while also holding that we "have to learn to live with [conflicting historical beliefs], tolerating the varying interpretations imposed by different faith perspectives." Christians maintain the historical belief that Jesus Christ was a divine incarnation; within Judaism and Islam such belief would be regarded as blasphemous. While I would agree with Hick that we should tolerate our Christian, Jewish, and Muslim neighbors, it hardly seems to be in the spirit of getting along with each other to gloss over core differences, regarding them as less important than the religions' common salvific efficacy. It seems that what Jews, Christians, and Muslims care about is not that they are all going to get the ultimate reward despite their doctrinal differences; what they cling to dearly is the belief that it is precisely because of their adherence to their particular doctrines that they will obtain the ultimate reward.

Leaving little doubt that Hick promotes the universalist premise at the expense of the particularist premise, he affirms this emphasis in a later work as well. According to Hick, we can see the different religions of the world "as different forms of the more fundamental conception of a radical change from a profoundly unsatisfactory state to one that is limitlessly better because rightly related to the Real." Again: "If salvation is taking place, and taking place to about the same extent, within the religious systems presided over by these various deities and absolutes, this suggests that they are different manifestations to humanity of yet a more ultimate ground of salvific transformation."[51]

At this point I want to make it clear that my intent is not merely to find what I consider to be flaws within Hick's pluralist argument. Indeed, it is an enlightened position, and he argues for it admirably. However, Hick's pluralist hypothesis serves as a cautionary tale for anyone who advocates an ecumenical position. While there is nothing inherently wrong with promoting a universalist position (the idea that the religions of the world are all true in some significant respect), anyone who promotes the truth of all religions cannot simultaneously proclaim the truth of each individual religion without radically revising (especially) the *e* claims of each religion. This is so since the *e* claim of one religion inherently entails the falsity of rival *e* claims. Is accounting for such exclusivity fundamentally at odds with ecumenism? That is the question I pose and that Hick's work fails to answer because it programmatically dismisses exclusivist claims. It bears repeating that I grant that such dismissal is not in itself a misstep; such dismissal, though, I contend, is inconsistent with a religious interpretation of religion.

Returning to Hick's solution to the problem of conflicting *e* claims, we see that the idea is to interpret away the differences until the *e* claims no longer conflict. Since such a solution seems to be revisionary in character, we must acknowledge Hick's stated opposition to revisionism, whether in its reductionist or naturalist forms. As he sees it, by siding with theological realism, he is opposing reductionism. According to him, the current debate between realists and irrealists simply revisits the age-old debate between religious and naturalist interpretations of the universe. As Hick sees the issue, all variations of the debate reduce to religious or naturalist terms.[52] Hick maps his critical realism as it pertains to the interpretation of religious language onto the following way of formulating the issue. If there is no transcendent, noumenal ground of the Real, there can be no authentically religious interpretations of ostensibly religious language. Restricting interpretations to the realm of phenomena limits us to naturalist interpretations of ostensibly religious language. Hick expresses this idea as stated below:

> the reality or non-reality of the postulated noumenal ground of the experienced religious phenomena constitutes the difference between a religious and a naturalistic interpretation of religion. If there is no such transcendent ground, the various forms of religious experience have to be categorized as purely human projections.[53]

Hick's stated intent is to interpret religion religiously; he has also stated his opposition to naturalist reductionism, a form of revisionism. That he proposes such revisionary interpretations of religious diversity, as seen in the suggestion that we interpret away the differences between conflicting claims until they no longer conflict, gives one pause.

In the following passage, he seems to acknowledge the problem posed by conflicting *e* claims but then just brushes aside whatever problems there might be. He writes, "[The religions of the world] cannot all be wholly true; quite possibly none is wholly true; perhaps all are partly true." However, given what he sees as their seemingly similar salvific efficacy, we would "do well to learn to tolerate unresolved, and at present unresolvable, differences concerning these ultimate mysteries."[54] To put Hick's words in the language of this book, he appears to acknowledge that the religions of the world cannot *all* be true due to their conflicting *e* claims; however, rather than acknowledge this situation as a problem, he recommends that we tolerate these differences. This is the most attractive rendering I can put on Hick's pluralist hypothesis. The less attractive, and it seems to me more accurate, gloss of his pluralist hypothesis is that he suggests we interpret away the differences between religions until they are no longer differences.

While Hick's plea for tolerance might indeed be admirable, such pleas do not change the fact that *e* claims are held to be *uniquely* true. Though certainly aware of Acts 4:12 (an example of an *e* claim), Hick nevertheless overlooks the idea that it makes a claim to being uniquely true. He even references Acts 4:12 explicitly. "We are all familiar with such New Testament texts as 'There is salvation in no one else [than Jesus Christ], for there is no other name under heaven given among men by which we may be saved' (Acts 4:12)."[55] Hick even acknowledges that, insofar as one embraces pluralism, one must reject exclusivist (i.e., *e*) claims. However, he provides no reason for us to believe that he sees the inherently revisionist character of rejecting *e* claims when he writes: "Insofar, then, as we accept that salvation is not confined to Christianity we must reject the old exclusivist dogma." Such "old dogma" as Acts 4:12 (or fill in any *e* claim) is central to religious life. If embracing pluralism means rejecting such *e* claims, Hick opens himself to a "so much the worse for pluralism" response from ordinary religious practitioners. Not that Hick needs to please all possible detractors, but asking religious people to reject *e* claims does not seem to square with fostering a religious interpretation of religion.

The problems facing Hick's pluralist hypothesis can be summed up in that the following three features of his interpretation of religion are in tension with each other. First, there is his realism concerning the interpretation of religious language; second, there is his religious pluralism; third, there is his emphasis on a religious interpretation of religion. Each of these three features, though perhaps intellectually sound on its own, cannot be simultaneously held together with the other two. The first two features give rise to polytheism. Although polytheism is not itself a problem, once one adds to that the non-revisionist character of the third feature of his pluralist hypothesis, we are faced with irreconcilable problems concerning Hick's interpretation of the monotheistic traditions. That is, there is no non-revisionary interpretation of polytheism within a monotheistic context.[56] The combination of the first and third features seems fine. However, once one adds the second feature, we are faced with the problem of conflicting e claims wherein, according to the law of non-contradiction entailed by the realism in the first feature, at most one e claim can be true. The combination of the second and third features could conceivably be acceptable, if one gives an irrealist construal to the divergent claims entailed by the second. So, obviously, once one includes the realist interpretation within the first feature to this combination, we are faced with the same insurmountable problem described above: The law of non-contradiction entailed by realism disallows the possibility that more than one conflicting e claim can be true. Thus, Hick's work cannot escape the dilemma facing the interpretation of religion. Try as Hick might to avoid the problem of religious diversity facing religious realists, his irrealist tendencies result in revisionary interpretations of religion.

In the context of the world's religious landscape, ordinary religious realism leads to the conclusion that, insofar as these beliefs conflict, at most one religion can maintain the truth. Thus, we see the religious exclusivism that comes with realism. Being a religious exclusivist is one way to deal with the problem of religious diversity. When confronted with a situation wherein other reliable, well-established beliefs run counter to one's own, dealing with this by believing that "I'm right and the rest of you are wrong" has a certain appeal. However, once we acknowledge the apparent justifiability of religious beliefs other than our own, it might seem that religious exclusivism is somewhat arbitrary. This issue has received the attention of two prominent religious realists. Alvin Plantinga and Peter van Inwagen acknowledge that their (Christian) exclusivism is predicated on their religious realism; they do so in a manner that addresses the issue of whether (Christian) exclusivism is arbitrary. Accordingly, the next chapter is devoted to these two authors who address this matter facing those who occupy the realist horn of the dilemma. Plantinga examines the matter of whether Christian exclusivism is rationally arbitrary; van Inwagen considers the question of whether Christian exclusivism is religiously arbitrary.

Chapter 4

Religious Exclusivism: The Problem of Being Arbitrary

The focus on religious exclusivism is due to its being the only realist option that is not revisionary. This conclusion becomes apparent by defining religious exclusivism as acknowledging the truth of one and only one e claim. If no religions contain true e claims, then the problem of conflicting religious truth claims is simply undermined since none of the religions provides correct e claims. The preceding is not a religious interpretation of the situation in that the meanings of putatively religious claims are changed. If more than one of the religions of the world hold correct e claims, the problem of conflicting religious truth claims is just glossed over. In this scenario the problem is not acknowledged because many (or perhaps all) of the religions provide correct e claims. However, this is not a non-revisionary interpretation of the situation either. As we have already seen, the truth of one e claim entails the falsity of conflicting e claims. The philosophical problem of religious diversity arises most starkly when we have exclusivist interpretations of the religious landscape.

The discussion of the relevant works of Alvin Plantinga is squarely situated within the realist horn of the dilemma by which this book is organized. According to the dilemma, realist construals of religion must contend with the philosophical problem of religious diversity and irrealist interpretations are revisionary. As one who maintains that Christian e claims can be true in a realist sense, Plantinga acknowledges the presence of the conflicting e claims of other religions. This stance poses a problem in that, via the law of non-contradiction, at most one of these conflicting e claims can be true. If these conflicting e claims have similar epistemic credentials, then Hick's charge that it is arbitrary to maintain that one religion's e claims are exclusively true seems reasonable. Therefore, it is appropriate to discuss Plantinga at this point: He is the author who most explicitly and systematically defends religious exclusivism and the realism which underlies it from the charge of being irrational or arbitrary. The goal of the discussion of Plantinga's works treated here is to shed light on his idea that by being an (in Plantinga's case, Christian) exclusivist one is not being intellectually arbitrary. Accordingly, one of the goals of this chapter is to acknowledge and address one of the implications of the chief problems facing those on the realist horn of the dilemma: that by being committed to the idea that their religion is exclusively true, they are being intellectually arbitrary.

In his defense of Christian exclusivism, Plantinga articulates his stances on rationality and warrant generally and as applied to the philosophical problem of religious diversity. In the course of discussing Plantinga's religious epistemology, his account of what knowledge consists in as applied to religious belief, we will see that according to Plantinga, the religious exclusivist violates no epistemic duties and is thus cleared of the charge that religious exclusivism is epistemically (and morally) arbitrary. In his reply to Hick's pluralist hypothesis, he gives an overview of his position on the philosophical problem of religious diversity. Plantinga enunciates the cognitivist, realist character of his position, Christian exclusivism, in that he considers there to be a truth of the matter, a truth of the matter to be determined by conditions other than what we merely say, do, or believe. He writes, "I believe that Christians are epistemically fortunate in a way in which those who disagree with them are not."[1] In response to Hick's charge that such exclusivism is arbitrary, Plantinga indicates that this would be arbitrary if "nonChristian views are epistemologically just as well based as Christian beliefs…" Regardless of the soundness of this statement, with it Plantinga expresses his view regarding the cognitive nature of religious language in that he allows for the possibility that there could be a truth of the matter. That is, according to Plantinga, exclusively holding certain religious beliefs is not arbitrary if these beliefs are epistemically superior to competing beliefs. Moreover, he sees no compelling reason to concede that Christian beliefs are undermined by competing beliefs. Additionally, by adhering to Christian beliefs at the exclusion of other beliefs, Plantinga allows that he is "perhaps *mistaken*, but not arbitrary," as Hick charges.[2] That is, Plantinga holds that epistemic warrant could settle the matter of the diversity of religious truth claims and he believes that Christians are warranted in their beliefs. By virtue of such warrant, Christian belief would not be arbitrary. Although Christian belief would not be arbitrary by this account, Plantinga's realism allows that it could be incorrect.

By holding to this position, we see that Plantinga regards religious belief as having cognitive content. That is, Plantinga maintains that religious beliefs can be properly described by the adjectives "true" and "false." Furthermore, Plantinga differentiates true belief from merely prudential belief. Specifically, he writes, it is possible that "the great religions…all have things literally wrong, even if many are salvifically effective."[3] Implicit in Plantinga's response to Hick here is the idea that prudential considerations (e.g., that beliefs are effective as opposed to being true) are inadequate when it is an issue of epistemic warrant that confronts us. Moreover, since Plantinga sees religious life as consisting of, inter alia, holding right beliefs, we need to examine how Plantinga conceives of warrant with regard to Christian belief.

A discussion of relevant passages from Plantinga's recent book will help to illuminate his conception of warrant and truth as these concepts relate to religious epistemology. This discussion will make Plantinga's religious realism evident. In turn we will see how his religious realism gives rise to his religious exclusivism, an exclusivism that calls for a defense from the charge that it is arbitrary. He sets up the topic by describing what he opposes, which is "the attitude expressed in 'Well, I don't know whether Christian belief is *true* (after all, who could know a thing like that?), but I do know that it is irrational (or intellectually unjustified or unreasonable or intellectually questionable)" – that attitude, if I am right, is indefensible."[4] For Plantinga, this is indefensible due to the connection he sees between truth and rational belief. That is, if Christian belief is true, in the sense that Christian belief consists of true propositions, it certainly is not irrational to hold Christian beliefs. I will address this matter by discussing Plantinga's responses to what have been regarded as crucial problems facing theology.

One of the themes Plantinga cites as a supposed problem facing theological realism derives from the legacy of Kant. That is, even if the omnipotent, omnibenevolent, omniscient God of traditional Western theism does exist, we cannot refer to God. Plantinga responds to this notion by suggesting that "there is really nothing in Kant to suggest that in fact we can't think or talk about God."[5] What we can draw from Plantinga's suggestion is the possibility that theological irrealists have misattributed their irrealism to Kant. In other words, they have taken Kant's ban on making assertions concerning the noumenal Real as sanction for their views that all language about God cannot be literally true. "God created the world," on this account, cannot be literally true since, as they see it, Kant showed that any factual discourse we undertake must concern phenomena, not noumena. Whether or not Kant is correct about this (or whether or not Plantinga is correct in attributing significant strands of theological irrealism to Kantianism), this much is clear. The attitude expressed by "of course I'm critical of theological realism, I'm a Kantian…" is one that should be viewed with suspicion. Kant's thought is much too complex and multi-faceted for such characterizations to hold. As such, a detailed examination of the significance of Kant's role in philosophy of religion is beyond the scope of this book.

Plantinga cites another approach that is taken to be a challenge to the realism he advocates. This challenge is related to the Kantian line discussed above in its emphasis on human cognitive input into knowing that which is known. This approach is seen in Walter Kaufman's anti-realist revisionism; Kaufman's anti-realism takes the form that theological language is not literally true. We see the form Kaufman's theological anti-realism takes in the following passages. Kaufman writes,

> God symbolizes that in the ongoing evolutionary historical process which grounds our being as distinctively human and which draws (or drives) us on toward authentic human fulfillment (salvation)…

42

'God' is the personifying symbol of that cosmic activity which has created our humanity and continues to press for its full realization…'God' is a symbol that gathers up into itself and focuses for us all those cosmic forces working toward the fully human existence for which we long.

The Christian image/concept of God, as I have presented it here, is an imaginative construct which orients selves and communities so as to facilitate development toward loving and caring selfhood, and toward communities of openness, love, and freedom.[6]

Plantinga objects to Kaufman's theological anti-realism for its inherently revisionary character. Plantinga argues that Kaufman's

rehashing of secularity under the guise of 'reconstructing' Christianity encourages dishonesty and hypocrisy; it results in a sort of private code whereby one utters the same phrases as those who accept Christian belief, but means something wholly different by them…Wouldn't it be vastly more honest to follow the lead of, e.g., Bertrand Russell, A.J. Ayer, or Daniel Dennett, or Richard Dawkins, or even Madalyn Murray O'Hair, declaring forthrightly that there is no God and Christianity is an enormous mistake?[7]

Plantinga's point is that theological anti-realism is tantamount to atheism and Christian atheism, as it were, is an oxymoron. The revisions Kaufman proposes render Christian beliefs such that they lose any resemblance they might have to Christian beliefs understood in a traditional or ordinary manner.

With regard to the theological realist/anti-realist/non-realist schema I have been employing, it should be clear that Plantinga's theological realism differs from Kaufman's theological anti-realism. This difference consists in Kaufman's regarding theological language as being literally false; Plantinga allows for the possibility that religious language can be literally true as well as false.[8] Whereas Plantinga allows for the possibility that, e.g., "God created the world," is literally true, Kaufman construes theological language as being literally false in the sense that, e.g., "God created the world" for Kaufman does not mean, literally, that God created the world. Rather, for the likes of Kaufman, "God created the world" means something like "the world has intrinsic worth."

In the context of Plantinga's theological realism, that he would find Kaufman's theological anti-realism to be objectionable is a fairly straightforward matter. There are, of course, more complicated cases. Hick's works on religious diversity provide one such example. Assessing Hick's interpretation of religious language is somewhat more complicated in that, we will recall, he purports to be a religious realist but his application of Kantian thought undermines his claim to realism. Plantinga treats the difficulties facing Hick as a matter of the latter waffling regarding the cognitive character of religious language. To use the example Plantinga cites, it is either true or false that God's attributes are purely formal.[9] Either way, a dilemma faces Hick's conception of the Real. In other words, "God attributes are purely formal," according to Plantinga, is a statement that is either true or false. For Plantinga it is the bivalence of this statement (i.e., that it is either true or false) that poses a dilemma for Hick. Hick conceives of the formal nature of God's attributes as follows: "purely formal and logically generated properties such as 'being a referent of a term' and 'being such that our substantial concepts do not apply'."[10] By applying Hick's use of the phenomenal/noumenal distinction to his articulation of God's formal attributes we see the dilemma facing his conception of God. If we conceive of God's properties (whether they are formal or not) strictly phenomenally, there is no way of connecting them to God noumenally. This simply follows the ban Kant places regarding noumena: we cannot say anything positive about them. If we conceive of God's properties strictly noumenally, similarly, we have no way of knowing which phenomena, if any, are manifestations of divine noumena. This dilemma facing Hick maps onto the philosophical problem of religious diversity directly. The essence of Hick's pluralist hypothesis is that the various forms that deities take throughout the world are all phenomenal manifestations of the noumenal Real. However, we see that the dilemma facing Hick is that, on the one hand, we have no way of knowing that, e.g., Shiva, Buddha, Yahweh, the Trinity, Allah, and so on, are phenomenal manifestations of the noumenal Real. On the other hand, if there is a noumenal Real, the Kantian ban on making substantive assertions about noumena prohibits us from connecting the aforementioned list of theistic forms to the noumenal Real. This leaves us with a situation wherein all manifestations of deity are equally (dis)similar regarding their connection to the noumenal Real.

That this problem is inherent within Hick's approach to the philosophical problem of religious diversity has the effect of Hick, as it were, "hedging his bets." That is, he has set up the issue in such a way that it is hard to imagine how he could be wrong about it. It is difficult (impossible?) to prove that a particular religious phenomenon is not a manifestation of the noumenal Real. Plantinga's realism involves no such hedging. Plantinga allows that his realist construal of the religious situation could be wrong. It is this presumption that there is a fact of the matter about which we can be right or wrong that distinguishes Plantinga's religious realism from Hick's. Plantinga writes,

> If the nominalists are right, all of us realists are wrong...Why should it be different in religion? The idea that in religion we must all be equally right and all equally wrong (as Hick's assessment would have it) seems no more compelling than the idea that in thinking *about* religion we must all be equally right and equally wrong.[11]

Plantinga sees no reason why religious language should be set apart from any other kind of language regarding the assessment of its truth or falsity. It need not be insulated from such assessments due to its putatively ineffable character. Plantinga is open to the possibility that religious language is false as the following passage indicates: "the religious life is a venture; and foolish and debilitating error is a permanent possibility. (If we can be wrong, however, we can also be right)."[12] Plantinga characterizes his religious realism in connection with the idea that the religious life can be right or wrong. That is, religious life can be based on beliefs that can be described by the adjectives "true" or "false." For Plantinga, that a particular instance of religious language (e.g., "God exists") is true means that it is true in what I have been calling a realist sense. That is, for Plantinga, "God exists" is true if and only if it is the case that God exists. Having seen Plantinga's commitment to the prospect of religious realism, we now examine more closely what form this takes in his treatment of the philosophical problem of religious diversity.

As a realist, Plantinga is committed to the idea that only p could make "p" true. Filling in *only Christian teaching is ultimately correct* for p, we see the connection between ordinary religious realism and religious exclusivism. As a Christian exclusivist, or, to put it in our terms, one who holds that Christian e claims are uniquely true, Plantinga believes "both (1) The world was created by God, an almighty, all-knowing, and perfectly good personal being (one that holds beliefs; has aims, plans, and intentions; and can act to accomplish these aims), and (2) Human beings require salvation, and God has provided a unique way of salvation through the incarnation, life, sacrificial death, and resurrection of his divine son."[13] These two statements evince the exclusively Christian character of Plantinga's stance regarding the matter of religious diversity. That is, Plantinga's response to the horn of the dilemma facing religious realism, the philosophical problem of religious diversity, is to be a Christian exclusivist.

That Plantinga holds these beliefs to be uniquely true, to the exclusion of conflicting religious beliefs (conflicting e claims in particular), is regarded by Hick (*qua* religious pluralist) as morally and epistemically arbitrary. In the context of discussing moral objections to exclusivism, Plantinga first sets out to specify what he means by exclusivism. "[A]n exclusivist, as I use the term, not only believes something like (1) or (2) [from above] and thinks false any proposition incompatible with it; she also meets a further condition C." Condition C includes three conditions: "being rather fully aware of other religions, knowing that there is much that at the least looks like genuine piety and devoutness in them, and believing that you know of no arguments that would necessarily convince all or most honest and intelligent dissenters of your own religious allegiances."[14] These clarifications to Plantinga's Christian exclusivism enable us to see why he objects to Hick's construal of the problem of religious diversity. As Plantinga sees it, pluralists, "like John Hick, hold that [some religious] propositions…are literally false although in some way still valid responses to the Real."[15] For Plantinga, this situation is untenable. For

Plantinga, the only valid responses to the Real would be those that reflect true beliefs about the Real. Moreover, according to Plantinga's realism, there is a truth of the matter about which one can hold beliefs that are either true or false.

Before going further into Plantinga's response to Hick's charge that exclusivism is arbitrary, it is noteworthy to consider the three options Plantinga cites with regard to holding an exclusivist belief: first, continue to hold it; second, withhold belief; and third, accept its denial.[16] What is noteworthy about these three options is that Plantinga continually refers to Hick as an example of the second option. As Plantinga sees it, the form his own religious belief takes is not rendered less sound simply because it has a distinctively Christian character. Accordingly, Hick's position is not rendered more sound simply by virtue of, as Plantinga sees it, Hick's withholding belief.

Let us take stock of the relevance of the groundwork we have laid. Having established Plantinga's religious realism we see his relevance to the discussion of the realist horn of the dilemma by which this book is organized. Plantinga's religious realism, by way of the law of non-contradiction which characterizes it, gives rise to his religious exclusivism. That is, if there are conflicting accounts of religious truth, at most one can be correct. Plantinga has opted for the idea that there is one correct account of religious truth, the Christian account. Now we are prepared to discuss his response to one of the problems facing religious realism: that by opting for religious exclusivism, and the religious realism such exclusivism entails, the religious exclusivist is intellectually arbitrary. As Plantinga puts it, "the claim is that as an exclusivist, he [*qua* exclusivist] holds unjustified beliefs and/or irrational beliefs."[17] According to Plantinga, one who objects to exclusivism might see this matter as follows: Given the presence of numerous religious beliefs, many of which differ from the beliefs one might oneself hold, it is arbitrary or unjustified/irrational to maintain that one's own beliefs are uniquely true; though such a stance might be a faithful one, "rational" is not the proper term to describe it. Plantinga addresses this charge, that exclusivist beliefs are not rational, by considering the matter of warrant. If the exclusivist's beliefs are warranted, then, according to Plantinga, the exclusivist's belief can properly be described as rational. Moreover, if these beliefs are rational, then they are not arbitrary.

Plantinga conceives of warrant as: "that property, whatever precisely it is, that distinguishes knowledge from mere true belief..."[18] The distinction between knowledge and merely true belief is significant. For example, if I believe that someone in China is eating a meal right now, that belief is probably true. However, my belief, though probably true, hardly counts as an instance of what we would typically call knowledge. In order for my belief to count as knowledge would require some kind of warrant, e.g., that I am watching someone in China eating a meal right now.

In keeping with his penchant for discussing rationality, justification, and warrant together, Plantinga further develops these ideas when he writes, the "central core of [justification]...is the notion of *being within one's intellectual rights*, having violated no intellectual or cognitive duties or obligations in the formation and sustenance of the belief in question."[19] The religious exclusivist is charged with having violated an intellectual duty by virtue of holding beliefs which are inappropriate to the relevant evidence. Plantinga characterizes this charge against the exclusivist as follows. According to critics of exclusivism, the exclusivist violates "a duty to proportion degree of belief to (propositional) evidence from what is *certain*, that is, self-evident or incorrigible, as with [e.g.] Locke...."[20] John Locke, accordingly, is a propagator of the legacy that we have a duty to proportion belief to the available evidence for that belief. To address the charge above, Plantinga states the following in the exclusivist's defense: "But at present there is widespread (and, as I see it, correct) agreement that there is no duty of the Lockean kind."[21] That is, evidentialism is no longer assumed to be the only (or proper) way to conduct epistemology.[22]

Since the evidence supporting one religion seems to be no better (or worse) than the evidence supporting another, Plantinga directly addresses the matter of whether religious exclusivism is arbitrary. As he puts it, a typical charge is

> that exclusivism is intellectually *arbitrary*. Perhaps the idea is that there is an intellectual duty to treat similar cases similarly; the exclusivist violates this duty by arbitrarily choosing to believe [exclusively Christian beliefs] in the face of the plurality of conflicting religious beliefs the world presents.[23]

Plantinga defends exclusivism from this charge in an elaborate manner. He argues, "you do not violate [the idea expressed in the charge above] if you nonculpably think the beliefs in question are *not* on a par...What would be relevant here," he continues, "would be *internal* or internalist epistemic parity: parity with respect to what is internally available to the believer."[24] He then goes on to characterize what is internally available to the believer as follows: "detectable relationships between the belief in question and other beliefs you hold" and "the *phenomenology* that goes with the beliefs in question."[25] This includes the sensuous and nonsensuous elements involved in holding a certain belief. Plantinga continues with this illustration of what he means when he offers the example of

> the belief's just having the feel of being *right*...[F]urthermore, if John Calvin is right in thinking that there is such a thing as the Sensus Divinitatis and the Internal Testimony of the Holy Spirit, then perhaps (1) and (2) [the exclusivist Christian beliefs cited earlier] are produced in me by those belief-producing processes, and have for me the phenomenology that goes along with them; the same is not true for propositions incompatible with them.[26]

Plantinga's invoking of the *sensus divinitatis* here provides an example of a treatment of epistemology that is not evidentialist in character. That is, while there is no evidence to support the notion that one has a *sensus divinitatis*, if a *sensus divinitatis* is part of our cognitive equipment, one is epistemically deprived if one does not acknowledge the beliefs that would be the outputs of a *sensus divinitatis*. While Plantinga might not have evidence that there is such a thing as a *sensus divinitatis*, there is no evidence to the contrary. Plantinga's point is that evidentialism goes awry here; the Christian exclusivist has violated no epistemic duty by believing the outputs of the *sensus divinitatis*. Accordingly, having violated no epistemic duty, it is hard to see the validity behind charging the religious exclusivist with being intellectually arbitrary.

Before we return to Plantinga's response to the charge that religious exclusivism is intellectually arbitrary, it should be noted that Plantinga's employing of the *sensus divinitatis* is not without critics. Though Richard Gale is among these critics, his criticisms follow a discussion of what he sees as the compelling aspects of Plantinga's account of the role of the *sensus divinitatis* in his epistemology. In the trilogy culminated by *Warranted Christian Belief*, according to Gale, Plantinga argues

> with considerable force in *Warrant: the Current Debate* and *Warrant and Proper Function* that what warrants a "basic belief," a belief that is not based on or inferred from another belief, is that it results from the proper functioning of one's cognitive faculties in the right kind of epistemic environment according to a design plan successfully aimed at truth.[27]

In addition, for Plantinga, the *sensus divinitatis* is part of one's cognitive faculties. Continuing with his discussion of Plantinga's epistemology, according to Gale, the former argues that

> it is possible that theistic, and in particular Christian, belief have warrant in an analogous way to that in which sensory and memory beliefs, etc., do. If theism is true, then God would want to reveal himself to created persons. Toward this end he implanted in them as part of their original cognitive equipment, along with the cognitive faculties in the standard package [basic beliefs that arise from our senses, memory, introspection, and a priori reason], a *sensus divinitatis* that would enable them to form true noninferential beliefs about God's presence and intentions upon having certain experiences, such as reading the Scriptures, seeing a beautiful sunset, feeling guilt, and so on.

Moreover, provided "their *sensus divinitatis* is functioning properly" these experiences would lead to warranted theistic beliefs.[28]

Though Gale presents Plantinga's account of the cognitive function of the *sensus divinitatis* in a favorable light, ultimately he is critical. Gale argues that the analogy Plantinga draws between the standard package and the *sensus divinitatis* fails. Gale writes,

> there are agreed upon objective tests for a cognitive faculty in the standard package being in a state of dysfunction, malfunction, pathology or disorder. But it is obvious that there are no agreed upon objective tests for a person's *sensus divinitatis* suffering from dysfunction, malfunction, pathology or disorder.[29]

Gale's point seems to be that since we cannot know when the *sensus divinitatis* is working improperly, we cannot truly know when it is functioning properly. This inability to appraise the deliverances of the *sensus divinitatis* contrasts with how we can assess the standard package; for the most part we are able to tell when it is functioning (im)properly. Thus, it seems the analogy between the standard package and the *sensus divinitatis* fails.

Having refined our understanding of Plantinga's religious epistemology, I should note that whether or not he is successful in his argument for the cognitive function of the *sensus divinitatis*, his point concerning religious exclusivism is well taken. Plantinga's point is that one can hold beliefs that others do not without being intellectually arbitrary. That is, even if Plantinga has not succeeded in demonstrating the cognitive function of the *sensus divinitatis* it still is not clear that the exclusivist has violated any epistemic duties such that by virtue of her exclusivism she is being intellectually arbitrary. That others hold beliefs that conflict with mine does not thereby render my beliefs arbitrary. My belief which opposes the idea of white supremacy is not rendered an arbitrarily held belief by virtue of the fact that there are people who do believe in white supremacy. By noting that exclusivism is no more arbitrary than pluralism in this case, Plantinga heralds the point that perhaps avoiding arbitrary beliefs is not really the issue. Perhaps that one can have correct (or incorrect) beliefs is the issue. On this, Plantinga writes,

> But couldn't I [*qua* exclusivist] be wrong? Of course I could! But I don't avoid that risk by withholding all religious (or philosophical or moral) beliefs; I can go wrong that way as well as any other, treating all religions, or all philosophical thoughts, or all moral views, as on a par. Again, there is no safe haven here, no way to avoid risk.[30]

Indeed, perhaps arbitrariness is not the issue here. Taking a stand regarding the matter of religious diversity does not necessarily commit one to being arbitrary. As Blaise Pascal might put it, this is a matter about which we are "embarked." Even if we withhold from making a commitment regarding our stance concerning religious diversity, this still has the effect of taking a stance. In addition, as Plantinga notes, withholding belief is "incompatible with some [beliefs] adopted by others."[31] Thus, the presence of incompatible beliefs seems to be inevitable. For Hick, the mere presence of incompatible beliefs seems to render arbitrary the idea of holding to one belief exclusively. The moral to be drawn here is that mere incompatibility of a belief with beliefs held by others does not seem to be a good reason not to hold that particular belief. Therefore it seems that exclusivist belief should not be disqualified as irrational merely by virtue of its incompatibility with beliefs held by others.

Having addressed the idea that religious exclusivism is arbitrary because others hold beliefs that conflict with one's exclusively held beliefs, we now move to a more detailed analysis of Plantinga's treatment of rationality per se. My goal is to show that Plantinga's conception of rationality, though it offers a largely compelling response to the charge that religious exclusivism is intellectually arbitrary, leaves intact my claim that religious exclusivism is still subject to the dilemma I have posed. That is, religious exclusivism, and thus the religious realism by which it is entailed, still faces the philosophical problem of religious diversity.

Aiming to dispel the idea that religious exclusivism is arbitrary because it is irrational, Plantinga offers five different conceptions of rationality and argues that exclusivism violates none of them. First, there is what he calls *Aristotelian Rationality*, which, according to Plantinga,

> is the sense in which man is a rational animal, one that has *ratio*, one that can look before and after, can hold beliefs, make inferences, and is capable of knowledge. [This sense of rationality] is also, presumably, irrelevant in the present context; at any rate, I hope the objector does not mean to hold that an exclusivist will by that token no longer be a rational animal.[32]

Next, Plantinga considers what he calls *The Deliverances of Reason*, which he characterizes as follows.

> An important use of 'rational' analogically connected with the first has to do with reason taken in this more narrow way. It is by reason thus construed that we know *self-evident* beliefs – beliefs so obvious that you can't so much as grasp them without seeing that they couldn't be false. These are among the *deliverances of reason*...a belief is *rational* if it is among the deliverances of reason and irrational if it is contrary to the deliverances of reason.[33]

The third sense Plantinga calls *The Deontological Sense*, about which he offers the following:

> Irrationality in this sense is a matter of failing to conform to intellectual or epistemic duties...But we have already considered whether the exclusivist is flouting duties [in discussing the first two senses of rationality]...As we saw, the exclusivist is not necessarily irrational in this sense either.[34]

The exclusivist is irrational by the standards of the first three senses of rationality only if "there is a good argument from the deliverances of reason to the denials of what he believes. I myself do not believe there are any such arguments. Presumably, the same goes for the pluralist objector."[35] That is, the religious exclusivist is no more intellectually arbitrary by the lights of these first three conceptions of rationality than the religious pluralist would be. Thus the standards of these first three senses of rationality would seem not to disqualify the exclusivist as irrational. Next, what Plantinga refers to as "*Zweckrationalität*...is means-end rationality."[36] Is the exclusivist irrational according to this fourth sense of rationality? That depends on the exclusivist's goals. If, for example, orthodox belief is the exclusivist's goal, then it is not implausible that exclusivist belief is a rational means. Thus, the exclusivist is not necessarily irrational as defined in this fourth sense, either. Plantinga calls the fifth and final conception of rationality he considers *Rationality as Sanity and Proper Function*. In this case, he indicates that "'rationality' means absence of dysfunction, disorder, impairment, pathology with respect to rational faculties. So this variety of rationality is again analogically related to Aristotelian rationality..."[37] Thus, Plantinga reasons, since the exclusivist was not thereby disqualified by the standards of Aristotelian rationality, so the realist is not thereby disqualified by the standards of rationality as sanity and proper function. At this point, Plantinga's argument is apparent. None of the standards of rationality available to us has been able to disqualify the religious exclusivist's claim to rationality. Accordingly, we have no reason to regard the religious exclusivist as irrational. As such, the charge that the religious exclusivist is intellectually arbitrary loses its force.

Having addressed the matter of whether the religious exclusivist is to be considered irrational, Plantinga next considers the final epistemic objection he sees facing the exclusivist: that "the exclusivist doesn't have warrant, or anyway *much* warrant (enough warrant for knowledge), for his exclusivistic views."[38] To assess the merits of this charge, Plantinga first addresses it in the context of what he cites as "the two main internalistic accounts of knowledge: the justified true belief account(s) and the coherentist account(s)."[39] According to Plantinga, exclusivists do not lack warrant according to the justified true belief account since if (1) and (2), the two statements of Plantinga's exclusivist Christian belief,[40] "are true, then clearly accepting them has great aptness for the fulfillment of that duty."[41] Moreover, exclusivists do not lack warrant according to the coherentist account since, Plantinga states, "surely a coherent set of beliefs could include both (1) and (2)..."[42]

Next, Plantinga considers the exclusivist's prospects in the light of what he offers as the two "main externalist accounts [of warrant]": reliabilism and proper functionalism.[43] With regard to reliabilism, Plantinga contends that the exclusivist does not lack warrant in this sense since "if (1) or (2) *is* true, it could be produced in me by a reliable belief-producing process."[44] Furthermore, the exclusivist does not lack warrant in the proper functionalist sense since we could "suppose (1) is true. Then it is surely possible that God has created us human beings with something like Calvin's Sensus Divinitatis, a belief-producing process that in a wide variety of circumstances functions properly to produce (1) or some very similar belief."[45]

Thus, Plantinga concludes, the objection that the exclusivist could not possibly be warranted is unfounded. The exclusivist's beliefs could quite plausibly occur within the parameters of the standards of rationality and warrant discussed above. Furthermore, it should be noted, that these are standards employed by friends and foes of religious exclusivism. It is significant that the religious exclusivist is not found to be in violation of these standards. It is an important element of the exclusivist's epistemic credentials. Having shown that the fact of religious diversity does not necessarily undermine the religious exclusivist's truth claims, Plantinga has accomplished what he set out to do. By having shown that the religious exclusivist is not thereby irrational and has violated no epistemic duties, Plantinga does serious damage to the charge that the religious exclusivist is intellectually arbitrary.

It is a significant conclusion within the framework of this project if religious exclusivism is not intellectually arbitrary. The problem facing the realist horn of the dilemma is that, via the law of non-contradiction, at most one of the many conflicting *e* claims within the world's religious landscape can be correct. Religious exclusivism, entailed by ordinary realism's association with the law of non-contradiction, is the name given to the idea that only one religion contains true *e* claims. Given the presence of many conflicting *e* claims within the world's religious landscape, it is a reasonable concern that the religious exclusivist is being intellectually arbitrary by maintaining that, of all of the variety of *e* claims there are, *hers* is the only one that is true. Though Plantinga has done an admirable job of arguing that religious exclusivism is not intellectually arbitrary, a problem must remain for our realist exclusivist. Otherwise, if the realist exclusivist did not face a problem, the dilemma by which this book is organized would not be genuine.

What Plantinga has done, in effect, is to acknowledge the situation of there being multiple and conflicting *e* claims within the world's religious landscape without acknowledging that this is a *problem*. He has described this situation without acknowledging it as constituting a problem by arguing that adherents of particular *e* claims are not in an intellectually arbitrary position provided they have not violated any of their epistemic duties as enumerated by Plantinga. However, a cornerstone of his defense of religious exclusivism relies on the idea of the proper function of the *sensus divinitatis*. If Plantinga's Christian exclusivism is correct that God created and sustains the world via divine providence and that Christ is required for salvation, then perhaps we can grant to Plantinga that he has provided a plausible account of Christian epistemology. However, with regard to the philosophical problem of religious diversity, whether an *e* claim, e.g., Plantinga's (2), is true is precisely the issue at hand. By parity of reasoning a Buddhist apologist for religious exclusivism could provide the same account, mutatis mutandis, for the *sensus Buddhatatis*. This idea could be applied to all of the religions of the world. However, the problem remains which, if any, similarly plausible *e* claim is correct. *That is* the philosophical problem of religious diversity. Though Plantinga has argued admirably for the idea that (Christian) exclusivism is not necessarily arbitrary intellectually, he has brought us no closer to a resolution regarding the philosophical problem of religious diversity. Defenses of exclusivism justified along the lines articulated by Plantinga are available to religious practitioners of all stripes. Accordingly, we see that religious exclusivism still faces a problem: that there are conflicting *e* claims with similar epistemic credentials. The presence of conflicting *e* claims with similar epistemic credentials remains a problem for the religious exclusivist even if the religious exclusivist has violated no epistemic duties in adhering to a particular *e* claim. Having addressed the intellectual side of the charge that religious exclusivism is arbitrary, we now proceed to Peter van Inwagen's discussion of the idea that exclusivism is religiously arbitrary.

Since this book is envisioned to be a contribution to the literature in the field of philosophy of religion, one can see why we are concerned with whether religious exclusivism is intellectually arbitrary (thus addressing the philosophical concern) and whether it is religiously arbitrary (thus, naturally, addressing the religious concern). Having just discussed the issue of whether religious exclusivism is intellectually arbitrary we now consider the issue of whether it is religiously arbitrary. Plantinga's stature in philosophy generally and in philosophy of religion specifically makes his inclusion in a segment devoted to prominent Christian exclusivists replying to the philosophical problem of religious diversity a natural fit. In contrast, Peter van Inwagen, a unique sort of Christian exclusivist, explicitly challenges the idea that there even is a philosophical problem of religious diversity. The distinctive tone of his thoughts on this matter also challenges our understanding of religion. Indeed, van Inwagen indicates that he does not expect his approach to what is known as the philosophical problem of religious diversity "to recommend itself to anyone who is not a traditional, orthodox Christian."[46] Even so, there is still something to learn from his work whether or not one fits that description. He does neither approach this issue emphasizing the epistemic parity of the beliefs within each religious tradition nor does he see it as a matter of equitable salvific efficacy across the various religious traditions. Van Inwagen sees the so-called problem of religious diversity as being based on a dubious premise because he rejects the idea that Christianity is one religion among other religions and that all religions are similarly attuned to divine reality. He reminds us that all religions, including Christianity, by definition, are entirely human constructions; as such, the problem of religious diversity is one that is entirely the creation of humans.

"Christianity," van Inwagen notes, is a compression term, a semantic convention used to place particular kinds of phenomena (in this case, Christian phenomena) under one umbrella term. He illustrates this point by noting that people typically do not think of themselves as being members of a religion. For example, one is not a member of Christianity; one is a member of, say, the Roman Catholic Church. What is the significance of this distinction? If one is a Christian who is concerned with salvation, instances of *e* claims such as Acts 4:12 should get one's attention. It reads, we will recall, "Neither is there salvation in any other: for there is none other name under heaven given among men, whereby we must be saved."[47] So the significance of the distinctions to which van Inwagen calls our attention is great. If we do not adhere to the right *e* claim properly, the stakes could involve one's ultimate reward, one's eternal salvation.

With this particular instance of an *e* claim in mind, let us call the following the "salvific formula": only and all those who do or believe *e* will gain the ultimate reward. If we see Christianity as a humanly contrived abstraction and thus one of the "religions of the world," sharing the stage with other such religions as the drama of the problem of religious diversity is played out, we can appreciate the distinction van Inwagen makes.[48] Seen in this context, we can address the question: Of what consequence is van Inwagen's distinction between the Roman Catholic Church and Christianity? When it comes to assessing whether one has followed the Christian version of the salvific formula as it is articulated in, e.g., Acts 4:12, van Inwagen is undeniably correct when it comes to successfully being an adherent of a given *e* claim, the terms "members of the Roman Catholic Church" and (as it were) "members of Christianity" do not describe the same group. In this case, the difference between referring to a discrete community as opposed to a humanly constructed abstraction is manifest. This is not to say that van Inwagen (or anybody) knows that the former group is "in" and that the latter group is "out." When he writes, "That is God's business and not ours," it is an expression of appropriate modesty.[49] A lesson we can learn from van Inwagen for our specific purposes is that exclusivism is inherent not only within what we normally call religions but also within what we normally call denominations. However, to appreciate more fully the perspective that van Inwagen brings to this issue, we need to consider his argument in greater detail.

One of the chief objections to religious exclusivism is that it presumes divine favor for the religion being referenced. Not making such a presumption, van Inwagen notes that God's ways are inscrutable and thus appeals to faith. He writes,

> What is a part of my faith is that God is a righteous Lord and a loving Father, and, therefore, whatever plans He has made for involuntary non-Christians, they will involve no injustice; and not only will they involve no injustice, but they will be the work of a love that surpasses human comprehension.[50]

Within this context, we are better situated to understand van Inwagen's position that, not only is Roman Catholic exclusivism permissible, it is the only attitude that includes no pretense to know God's ways. In response to the charge that exclusivism is arbitrary, van Inwagen, acknowledging that God exceeds our comprehension, demurs in the passage already cited above: "That is God's business and not ours."[51] In response to the question: "May it not be that all the world's religions are instruments of God's salvation?"[52] van Inwagen remains agnostic. That is, perhaps all the world's religions are equally salvifically efficacious, but this is beyond our ken. The importance of submitting to faith is underscored by van Inwagen when he notes that "I have no way to prove that this [the idea that all the world's religions are instruments of God's salvation] is false. If I had, I should be living not by faith but by sight."[53]

Before delving further into van Inwagen's unique perspective on the problem of religious diversity, I should make some comments to help guide this discussion. That van Inwagen is a religious exclusivist is certainly not unique. Moreover, that he provides religious justification for his religious exclusivism by deferring to God is not unique, either. However, his way of articulating the relation between God and "religion" certainly is (more on why I place "religion" in scare quotes follows below).

We see that for van Inwagen, exclusivism is inherent within Christian life. He writes, "the Church is a unique instrument by which Christ and the Holy Spirit are working to bring us to the Father."[54] The attitude to be adopted by the individual person regarding this relation between God and the Church is indicative of the exclusivism van Inwagen sees as being inherent within Christian life. He writes, "I don't see how I could coherently give up this belief (that Christianity exclusively is true) other than by ceasing to [be] a Christian."[55]

Religious pluralism is often presumed to be a less arbitrary, more tolerant, inclusive, open-minded, and (dare I say) politically correct alternative to religious exclusivism. This is not how van Inwagen sees it. His opposition to this presumption about religious pluralism introduces the significance of his observation that religion is a humanly constructed abstraction. He writes, "'Religious pluralism' is not the contradictory of religious exclusivism, but one more case of it."[56] As van Inwagen sees the matter, a pluralistic approach to the world's religions that suppresses their unique claims to truth for the sake of highlighting their ostensible commonalities is at least as arbitrary and even more arrogant than exclusivism. What shall count as a religion? This question is itself exclusionary. We can illustrate the problem van Inwagen sees here by imagining an ecumenical council. Who gets invited? This question raises the problems van Inwagen sees when we try to conceive of the world's religions as humanly contrived abstractions. The idea that something can or cannot count as a religion and thus will or will not receive an invitation to our council is, as noted above, itself a form of exclusivism. Moreover, the pluralist attitude of embracing all those who embrace pluralism excludes those who renounce pluralism, namely exclusivists.

However, this particular point about the exclusionary character of religious pluralism is not van Inwagen's emphasis. Rather, he calls our attention to the fact that the "world religions, insofar as they have any reality at all, are human creations…their existence and properties are not part of God's plans for the world."[57] Van Inwagen states this within the context of his argument that the very idea of "world religions" is a product of the Enlightenment and that the Enlightenment agenda "is to direct the attention of people away from the Church and to focus it on the abstraction 'Christianity,' which is the sort of thing that can be compared and contrasted with other abstractions like Buddhism and Islam."[58]

Thus we see van Inwagen's idea that the issue of religious diversity is based on what he considers a dubious premise. If we accept his idea that it is not unreasonable to regard the Catholic Church and Israel as the only two divinely inspired human creations,[59] comparing, e.g., the Catholic Church, with Islam would be an instance of comparing radically disparate institutions. Comparing Christianity with Islam, on the other hand, is an instance of comparing like institutions: both are entirely human-created abstractions, "compression terms," van Inwagen calls them. However, this kind of comparison, according to van Inwagen, distracts us from what is truly of spiritual importance. As van Inwagen sees the issue, "no religion is a divine creation."[60] That the truth claims of entirely human-created institutions conflict with each other is neither surprising nor a matter of spiritual significance. For van Inwagen, in matters of spiritual importance we should be concerned not with human creations but with divinely inspired creations.

Whether or not he is factually correct in his assertions and observations about divine inspiration, religion, and religious diversity, van Inwagen must be credited for attending to matters that in his view are of true spiritual import as they pertain to our relation to divine providence. In doing so, he aims to make the case that religious exclusivism is no more arbitrary than religious pluralism.

He sees the problem of religious diversity in that it involves comparing entirely human-created institutions, as distracting us from divine providence. As such, van Inwagen stops the debate over religious diversity before it can start. Rather than treating the ostensible problem of religious diversity at face value, van Inwagen indicates that the real issue concerns who shall receive salvation. For him, the idea that some may receive salvation and some may not (that is, a way of construing the problem of religious diversity) is not a matter of fairness, or competing truth claims from epistemically equally well-situated but conflicting socio-historical practices (a.k.a., religions); rather, for van Inwagen, these matters are God's business and not ours. As such, according to van Inwagen, those concerned with the philosophical problem of religious diversity are simply spinning their wheels. Even so, achieving clarity about the terms of the debate (even if the debate does consist in so much wheel-spinning) is a goal worthy of our attention if we wish to have an understanding of the world's religious landscape, even if that landscape is a human contrivance.

The clarity we gain by considering van Inwagen's account is the insight that we need not regard the religious exclusivist and the religious pluralist as being diametrically opposed, one (the exclusivist) seemingly arbitrary and arrogant, the other (the pluralist) seemingly open-minded and tolerant. If we regard the religions of the world as human constructions, being open to the truthfulness of all of them is no less arbitrary than being open to the truthfulness of just one of them. Indeed, according to the law of non-contradiction, being open to the truthfulness of all of the religions of the world when their truth claims conflict, is not only arbitrary, such religious pluralism is incoherent.

Having argued that his affirming of particular Christian beliefs is no more arbitrary than is assenting to religious pluralism, van Inwagen has addressed the charge that religious exclusivism is religiously arbitrary. Combined, Plantinga and van Inwagen have formed a credible response to the concern that religious exclusivism is arbitrary. This is significant in that exclusivism has a compelling response to its chief criticism. However, in forming his response to this concern, van Inwagen is no less subject to the horn of the dilemma facing religious realists.

The philosophical problem of religious diversity is still a problem for van Inwagen in that at most one of the conflicting e claims of the religions of the world can be true. As he acknowledges, he has no more evidence that Christian truth claims are correct than do adherents of other religions. This fact is indeed problematic for the idea that one religion's e claims are uniquely true. Belief despite this lack of evidence is what faith consists in, though. Criticizing such an appeal to faith by calling it arbitrary seems to miss the mark. Assenting to the truth of what one believes, despite the fact that others assent to other equally credible but conflicting beliefs, seems to be at the heart of religious life.

Acknowledging this truism, though, raises an important issue. To say that religious devotees assent to the truth of what they believe does not strike one as a controversial statement. The issue that arises, then, is how one is employing the concept of truth. Since considering alternatives to realist conceptions of truth is one of our goals, we turn now to our treatment of religious irrealism.

Chapter 5

Overview of Religious Irrealism

The purposes of this overview are to discuss certain features of irrealism that need to be emphasized and to show their implications for the interpretation of religion. To this end, it is useful to recall how religious irrealism is situated within the larger context of this book. When interpreting a particular instance of religious language there are three basic options. First, religious realism describes those who hold that for a given instance of religious language there are objective truth conditions; second, religious anti-realism describes those who hold that for a given instance of religious language these objective truth conditions do not obtain; and, third, religious non-realism describes those who hold that for a given instance of religious language there are no objective truth conditions; that is, a given instance of religious language does not express a proposition. So far, irrealism has served as a blanket term covering options two and three and will continue to do so. The term *religious anti-realism*, describes the kind of thought described by option two; *religious non-realism* is the term for option three. In addition to describing the salient features of religious irrealism by citing illustrative examples, this overview has two further goals. The first addresses the reasoning for why the focus is on religious non-realism, as opposed to religious anti-realism, for the portion of the book below. The second main purpose of this overview is to demonstrate that religious irrealism is subject to the dilemma articulated in this book by showing how irrealist interpretations of religion are inherently revisionary.

The chief feature distinguishing religious irrealism from religious realism is an independence condition that is present in realism and absent in irrealism. For the religious irrealist, then, what makes a given religious "*p*" true is not that "*p*" describes some state of affairs *p* that obtains independently of what we do, say, or believe concerning "*p*." For the religious irrealist other criteria besides a match between "*p*" and *p* can count for the truthfulness of a given religious "*p*." The thought of Ludwig Feuerbach epitomizes this concept.[1] Since Feuerbach provides a paradigmatic case of religious irrealism, I will devote some attention to a discussion of his thought. Moreover, since his thought provides a classic case of religious *anti*-realism specifically, this discussion will serve to show why in the second portion of this book, there is much more attention to the *non*-realist aspect of religious irrealism.

Considering Feuerbach's thought in greater depth is useful for another reason. Discussing a difference I have with Peter Byrne over the interpretation of Feuerbach's thought will highlight the distinction between religious realism and religious anti-realism. This distinction will be made more evident by our discussion of Feuerbach since the disagreement between Byrne and myself concerns whether Feuerbach's interpretation of religion is properly realist or anti-realist in character.

Feuerbach's role in the present discussion becomes even more prevalent when contextualizing his thought within the wider intellectual landscape. John Hick does so by citing the thought of Feuerbach as the historical turning point with respect to the presumption of realism about God.[2] In other words, before Feuerbach's thought became part of this intellectual landscape, when "God" was referenced, it was taken for granted that "God" was to be understood in a realist sense. Regardless of the historical accuracy of Hick's claim, its intent is significant. Feuerbach, a nineteenth-century writer typically attributed with being the father of modern atheism, wrote much about God; however, when Feuerbach wrote of God, he was not referring to the God typically associated with the Western theistic tradition: the Creator of the heavens and the earth, for example. Rather, by "God," Feuerbach was describing a projection of our species-consciousness.[3] Thus, we see Hick's point concerning Feuerbach's thought as marking an historical turning point concerning the presumption of realism in the conception of God. That is, prior to Feuerbach, it was taken for granted that when "God" was the object of a particular belief – *God*, the being described by traditional Western theism, was the object of that belief. Contrasted with this presumption, Feuerbach offers a systematic account of what else reference to God might mean.

It is in this vein that *The Essence of Christianity* expresses what Feuerbach describes as the "true anthropological essence of Christianity" and the "false theological essence of Christianity." The former indicates the idea that insofar as religious language attributes our highest ideals, love, will, and reason to humans, it is true. The latter indicates the idea that insofar as religious language attributes these ideals to God, and thus not to us, it is false. The focal point here is that, for Feuerbach, when language about God is true, it is ultimately about humans. In other words, "God exists," for example, is false if by God we mean a personal being who fits the description of traditional Western theism. That is, by "God" Feuerbach does not mean the God as described within traditional Western theism who exists independently of human cognitive undertakings. Rather, by "God" Feuerbach is describing a human projection. It is for this reason that Feuerbach's thought serves as a prime example of religious anti-realism. Theological realism describes those who hold that for "God exists" to be true the corresponding objective state of affairs must obtain. In contrast, theological anti-realism describes those who hold that these objective conditions do not obtain. If the objective conditions that must obtain for "God exists" to be true include that God be the personal being who created the heavens and the earth, it is clear that Feuerbach is an anti-realist since he holds that these objective conditions do *not* obtain.

Feuerbach indicates that for him, "God" refers to something other than the God of traditional Western theism when he writes, "God as God – as a purely thinkable being, an object of the intellect – is nothing else than the reason in its utmost intensification become objective to itself." Again, "God springs out of the feeling of a want; what man is in need of, whether this be a definite and therefore conscious, or an unconscious need – that is God."[4] Since Feuerbach would agree that "God exists" constitutes a human projection, this exemplifies what I call theological *anti*-realism precisely because it expresses the position that "God exists" is false since it does not refer to a state of affairs independent of human cognitive undertakings.

Peter Byrne disagrees with the above characterization of theological anti-realism and Feuerbach as illustrative of it. He argues that the mere extra-mental existence of God is not enough to establish God's existence in a realist sense. After all, according to Byrne, even Feuerbach allows that God exists extra-mentally and clearly the atheist Feuerbach would not be properly characterized as a theological realist. The crux of the difference between Byrne's position and mine concerns whether, as Byrne puts it, the "facets of human nature" described by Feuerbach concerning God as a projection of our species consciousness consist of "extra-mental things."[5]

Byrne's point about Feuerbach is as follows: He asserts that religious realism must involve more than the mere extra-mental existence of God. That is, a customary characterization of religious realism would have it that for "God exists" to be true, it must be the case that God exists independently of our cognitive undertakings. As Byrne would have it, God as construed along Feuerbachian lines does exist extra-mentally -- as a projection of our species consciousness. Byrne finds this situation objectionable since it allows Feuerbach, the "father of modern atheism" to qualify as a religious realist! To address this situation, Byrne adds the following criterion for religious realism: "[religious realism] is no more, and no less, than the view that there is a sacred, transcendent reality."[6]

Byrne's concern is misplaced. The manner in which Byrne construes Feuerbach's interpretation of God's existence still would not qualify Feuerbach as a theological realist. First, the idea that God exists extra-mentally for Feuerbach, as Byrne contends, is quite dubious. Feuerbach's construal of God as merely a projection of "species *consciousness*" hardly qualifies as *extra*-mental existence since it is clear that he does not allow that God exists independently of the sphere of human cognitive activity. After all, according to Feuerbach, God is a human projection. Thus we see the heart of the matter concerning how theological realism has been presented throughout this book: that "God exists" is true or false independent of what we believe, say, or do. Contrary to

Byrne, for Feuerbach, "God exists" is true *only* to the extent of what we believe; that is, God does not exist independently of human cognitive activity.

There is a further problem with Byrne's characterization of theological realism as the view that "there is a sacred, transcendent reality." What are we to do with the likes of Bertrand Russell (who seems to be best understood as a realist atheist)? Alston articulates the problem I am describing aptly when he writes in reference to Russell that he "takes there to be to an objective reality by reference to which our religious statements, as well as others, are true or false." This seems to be a clear-cut case of realist atheism since Russell takes it to be the case that "this reality contains no supreme personal deity."[7] For Russell, for "God exists" to be true, it must be the case that God exists, accordingly, Russell exemplifies realism. In that, for Russell, God does not exist, Russell exemplifies atheism. In other words, it seems entirely possible that one can be a realist concerning how to assess the truth of "God exists" and not, as Byrne would have it, have to commit oneself to the idea that there is a sacred, transcendent reality. The challenge that Russell's realist atheism poses to Byrne's formulation of religious realism indicates that perhaps we should be wary of Byrne's conception of religious realism. That is, trouble looms for those who would associate realism with a commitment to which sentences are true. One obvious advantage to the definition of realism promoted here, which includes a commitment to what it means for a given "p" to be true, is that we can articulate what such commitment entails. The same cannot be said of Byrne's conception of religious realism which entails a commitment to which religious "p"s are true. Without some special knowledge for determining the truth or falsity of such instances of religious language, agnosticism about such matters seems to recommend itself. Even if we cannot know which religious "p"s are true, we can still attain clarity regarding what is entailed by committing to their truth or falsity. That is the aim of the conception of realism articulated here.

Regardless of where one stands concerning the details of my disagreement with Byrne, it has the following significance for our topic. According to Byrne, Feuerbach does not qualify as a religious anti-realist as I construe these matters; I am confident that I have shown that Feuerbach is best described as a religious anti-realist by virtue of his position that the objective truth conditions for "God exists" do not obtain. Whether Feuerbach's interpretation of religion is properly considered to be anti-realist in character matters within the context of the dilemma formulated here. It also matters for historical reasons since, as Hick indicated, Feuerbach's thought is an historically significant exemplar of the move away from the presumption of realism concerning the existence of God. If Feuerbach's thoughts about religion, and those interpretations of religion which echo the idea that God is a human projection, are properly regarded as anti-realist, according to the dilemma by which this book is organized, we should be suspicious of their revisionary character. We should be suspicious since religious language purports to be religious by virtue of its reference to that which is sacred independent of what we do, say, or believe. According to religious anti-realism, religious language derives its meaning precisely *because* of what we do, say, or believe. The revisionary character of religious anti-realism is seen in that the truthfulness of anti-realist interpretations of religion is based entirely on what we do, say, or believe. For example, for religious anti-realism, language about God is not true with respect to anything about God; rather, such language is true dependent on what we do, say, or believe with respect to God. Making God's very existence contingent on what we do, say, or believe drops essential features from traditional Western theism, e.g., God's omnipotence. Thus we see the revisionary character of religious anti-realism.

After describing Feuerbach's religious anti-realism, it is necessary to reinforce how it is that religious anti-realism shares the weaknesses of religious realism and religious non-realism without sharing either of their strengths. This is why, with the exception of the preceding discussion of Feuerbach, religious anti-realism does not get much attention in this project. As mentioned in chapter 1, religious realism and religious anti-realism are cognitivist positions, which means that religious anti-realism shares the problems of religious realism without sharing its advantage of avoiding revisionism. That is, religious anti-realism still involves the problematic idea that the truthfulness of religious language involves a match between a given instance of religious language and what it describes. Religious anti-realism just denies that there is a match between, e.g., Acts 4:12, and what Acts 4:12 describes; it should be noted, though, that this denial still constitutes a commitment as to what is involved in the nature of the match between an instance of language and what it describes. Religious anti-realism maintains that the relation between "p" and p is that there is no match; a given instance of religious language could not match its corresponding truth conditions since for the anti-realist these objective truth conditions do not obtain.

Religious anti-realism shares cognitivism and its attendant difficulties with religious realism. Religious anti-realism and religious non-realism, the irrealist options, share the problem of revisionism. Religious anti-realism shares this problem with religious non-realism without sharing the latter's advantage of avoiding religious realism's problematic commitment to the truth or falsity of a given instance of religious language consisting in its matching the conditions it describes. That is, religious anti-realism shares the weaknesses of religious realism and religious non-realism without sharing either of their strengths. It is for these reasons that in the portion of the book that follows this overview, the portion devoted to the irrealist horn of the dilemma, I focus on religious non-realism rather than religious anti-realism.

Having framed how religious irrealism and its component parts, religious anti-realism and religious non-realism, fit into the organization of the larger project, we can examine in more depth why I see revisionism as the most significant feature of religious irrealism. Now we are better situated to see why it is that revisionism is a problem when interpreting religion. More specifically, we can see why revisionism is a problem facing those who occupy the irrealist horn of the dilemma in particular. According to the definition of realism used here, "p" is true if and only if it matches p. As discussed below, the revisionary nature of irrealist interpretations of religion consists in their maintaining that "p" means something other than p. For example, for the religious realist, for "God exists" to be true, it must be the case that God exists. For the religious realist "God exists" means God exists. This logic follows for other statements that could be made of God, e.g., "God created the heavens and the earth" means God created the heavens and the earth and as such exemplifies a religious interpretation of religion. Seemingly in agreement with the religious realist, the religious irrealist also might maintain that "God exists" is true. However, by "God exists" the irrealist means something other than God exists if by "God exists" we mean a state of affairs that actually obtains, namely, that God exists. Rather, the irrealist might interpret "God exists" as meaning that life is worthwhile, the world has value, or that by assenting to "God exists" one is evincing commitment to a certain way of life. While these are interpretations with which the religious realist might very well agree, essential features of theistic doctrine are lost if "God exists" does not also mean that God exists. Any theistic doctrine is either lost or significantly modified within an irrealist interpretation of religion.

Though in the following chapters I will undertake a detailed analysis of the revisionary character of the work of irrealist authors who are especially relevant to this book in order to illustrate the revisionary character of religious irrealism, I need to address preemptively what I regard to be the most significant counter to my argument that religious irrealism is revisionary. This is the idea that one could give an irrealist interpretation "all the way down." To illustrate this idea consider some of the beliefs central to Christian faith: God created the universe; God is providential; God reveals divine commands; God offers forgiveness to those who obey these commands; and God grants salvation to those who accept Jesus Christ as their savior. In order for the beliefs in the preceding list to be true, "God exists" must also be true. Thus, if "God exists" is false, i.e., if the objective truth conditions for "God exists" do not obtain, then these other central tenets of the Christian faith must also be false. How might a religious irrealist respond to this?

Consider the following as an example of an irrealist interpretation of religion: "'God' symbolically refers to our highest moral ideals"; affirming

"God's existence" is simply an affirmation of the value of these ideals. If one favors an irrealist interpretation of "God exists" such as the one above, then our irrealist would likely resist the contention that the truth of, e.g., "God grants salvation" depends on the truth of "God exists." One could be an irrealist "all the way down," as it were; that is, one could offer a comprehensively irrealist interpretation of religion. For example, if "God exists" is interpreted as "'God' symbolically refers to our highest moral ideals," then "God grants salvation" could be interpreted along similar lines, say, as "affirming such moral ideals is enriching" whether or not "God exists" is true in a realist sense. Interpreting religious language in a comprehensively irrealist way poses a putative counterexample to my claim that, e.g., for "God grants salvation" to be true, "God exists" must also be true. For the comprehensive irrealist, it could be granted that for "God grants salvation" to be true, "God exists" must also be true. What our irrealist challenges is the idea that for "God exists" to be true, it must be the case that God actually exists. In other words, what makes our comprehensive irrealist so is that she reinterprets what it would mean for "God grants salvation" and "God exists" to be true. Now we can appreciate the revisionary character of religious irrealism more fully. While it may indeed be the case that our irrealist has committed no epistemic misstep and is a fine person who lives a morally upstanding life, the point is that religious life does not seem to be *merely* about the affirmation of moral ideals. Indeed Christian language includes moral ideals, but Christian theistic language is also about *God*. Irrealist interpretations allow truth conditions other than that God exists to verify the truthfulness of "God exists." As such, irrealist interpretations are revisionary.

One could contend that my argument that religious irrealism is revisionary employs circular logic. That is, by assuming that Christian (or any theistic) language must be about God, it could be said that I am begging the question I mean to be asking: *Is* religious language about God? By begging this question instead of asking it, it could be said, I have defined religious irrealism in an uncharitable manner. I submit that this is not the case. I am entirely open to the prospect that the irrealists might be correct about the question of God's existence, but that is beside the point. The point is that if one has realist expectations concerning, e.g., being granted salvation by God, then "God exists" must be true in a realist sense. Stated somewhat differently, if one does not embrace the proper e claim in a realist sense one is denied realist expectations of the ultimate reward. Moreover, irrealist construals of the ultimate reward are revisionary.

My contention is that realist expectations concerning an ultimate reward are denied to those who do not embrace the appropriate e claim in a realist sense. Having laid this groundwork, I can address the criticism that no such realist expectations need to be in place for one expecting an ultimate reward. Such a critic could hold that one's beliefs (or expectations) could be irrealist, as I have put it, "all the way down." For example, one's understanding of "heaven," as an example of a possible ultimate reward, could consist of the peace of mind that comes with having lived a morally good life as opposed to having an understanding of "heaven" that consists of a bodily resurrection and/or strumming harps with one's fellow angels. The following is in response to such an irrealist critic to show some possible consequences of realist versus irrealist beliefs.

The following constitutes an argument for the inevitably revisionary consequences of religious irrealism. In other words, this argument indicates why only religious realism can avoid offering revisionary interpretations of religion. Not out of hubris but for ease of reference I call this argument "Hilberg's Wager." Let us suppose for a moment that God does exist, and that God wants us to have true, realist beliefs about God. Let us also suppose, merely for the purposes of verbal economy (since this case could be extended to any theistic religion), that God wants us to have Christian beliefs about God. Among the Christian beliefs to be upheld is the belief that God is a personal being who is accessible to ordinary believers via, e.g., prayer, ritual, or contemplation. Suppose we have a person who in all other respects lives a good Christian life, *except* that this person is a religious irrealist and so understands Christian doctrine along the lines of, say, that described above: our hypothesized Christian practitioner understands "God" as a *merely* symbolic representation of our highest moral ideals. According to the conception of God I describe above, this person would be in trouble for having held irrealist beliefs about God when, according to the parameters of this scenario, realist beliefs were the correct beliefs to hold. Although this person may live a good life, this person holds incorrect beliefs about God and thus would be subject to unfavorable divine judgment. That is, this scenario depicts a situation in which there is an identifiable loss for having held irrealist beliefs. On the opposite side, there is no parallel loss. That is, if one incorrectly held realist beliefs about God (in other words, if the objective truth conditions for "God exists" do not obtain) there is no loss since there would be no God to cast judgment for one's having held the wrong beliefs about God. Another consideration is that we could speculate that God exists and would command us to have non-cognitive beliefs (i.e., beliefs that are neither true nor false) about God (e.g., "'God' is love" might be a candidate for such a belief). However, that is not coherent since there would be at least one true (and therefore cognitive) belief that we are required to hold concerning God: that we are to have non-cognitive beliefs about God. Thus, the incoherence of a mandate to have non-cognitivist beliefs about God comprehensively ("all the way down") is patent.

Both forms of religious irrealism, religious anti-realism and religious non-realism, fare poorly with respect to Hilberg's Wager. If God were to command us to have anti-realist beliefs in religious matters, then we would have an odd scenario on our hands. For if religious anti-realism describes those who hold that for a given instance of religious language (in this case, "God exists") the relevant objective truth conditions (in this case, that God exists) do not obtain, then it is not at all clear who could be issuing such divine commands if the objective truth conditions for "God exists" did not obtain. For if it were the case, as religious anti-realists maintain, that "God exists" be objectively false, then surely God could not be commanding us to hold anti-realist religious beliefs since in this scenario God would not exist. Religious non-realism describes those who hold that there are no objective truth conditions for "God exists." That is, for religious non-realism, "God exists" is neither true nor false; this is what non-cognitivism consists in. As such, the incoherence involved in God commanding us to hold non-realist religious beliefs was described in the preceding paragraph.

On the matter of religious non-realism and the cognitivity of religious language, that religious language includes truth claims seems to be evident. When we are told that there is no salvation except through Christ, this is either true or false. It is either true or false that one must accept Christ in order to gain the ultimate reward, say, eternal life. Perhaps the irrealist might counter that the ideals Christ symbolizes, e.g., peace and compassion, are intrinsically worthy and should be embraced to live a fulfilled life. If all we mean by the dictum, "there is no salvation except through Christ" is the irrealist interpretation that the ideals Christ symbolizes, e.g., peace and compassion, are intrinsically worthy, then the dictum that we must embrace Christ is false since one can be peaceful and compassionate without embracing Christ. Conversely, if it is the case that there is an eternal reward, obtainable only by those who have accepted Christ, the dictum in question is true. In either case, "there is no salvation except through Christ" is a cognitive statement: one that is either true or false.

Perhaps emphasizing the revisionary character of religious irrealism can be illustrated most starkly in the case of theistic language. To avoid revisionism, "God commands us to believe x," for example, must be true in a realist sense. This must be the case since on a non-revisionary interpretation, for God to command us to do anything, "God exists" must be true independent of what we do, say or believe, i.e., in a realist sense. A consequence of Hilberg's Wager is that the irrealist theist faces a regress: at what point does one stop the sequence of irrealist beliefs? As long as one believes that religious language is, inter alia, about a God who exists independently of human experience, at least one belief must be held to be true in a realist sense. I suppose that one could stop the regress of irrealist interpretations at any point. However, it seems that the regress *must* stop with at least one realist belief by at least this point: theistic religious language is about God if by "God" we mean a being who exists independently of human experience.

Throughout this book I have emphasized key features of religious realism and religious irrealism by contrasting them with each other. A key feature of realism is what I have called an independence condition: In order for "*p*" to be true, *p* must obtain independently of what we do, say or believe. Within this definition of realism a key feature of irrealism is revealed: for irrealism, the truth of a given "*p*" *is* dependent on what we do, say or believe. It is this lack of an independence condition that ultimately renders irrealist interpretations of religion revisionary. For the irrealist, something other than *only through Christ can we be saved* can make "only through Christ can we be saved" true. This statement exemplifies what the revisionary character of religious irrealism consists in.

When considering an instance of religious language, e.g., "only through Christ can we be saved," it is easy to regard such language as being either true or false. If it were true that religious language is either true or false that would leave realist and anti-realist interpretations of religious language as the only options. However, as indicated in the Introduction, the later work of Wittgenstein teaches us to avoid such conclusions. When such conclusions are rejected by a philosopher of Wittgenstein's stature, the need for a thorough treatment of his thought on this matter is evident. Chapters 6 and 7 will accordingly be devoted to a discussion of Wittgensteinian thought as it pertains to the interpretation of religious language, what I have called religious non-realism.

Chapter 6

Religious Non-realism: Neither Realist Nor Anti-realist

Although Wittgenstein never wrote anything on religion that was intended for publication, he did say enough regarding the relevant concepts such that we can consult what has been published to construct a Wittgensteinian critique of the dilemma I have posed for the interpretation of religion. More to the point, while Wittgenstein himself might not have any published remarks on the interpretation of religion, he did have something to say about the conception of realism by which I have framed the dilemma I see facing the interpretation of religion. Given these parameters, the first goal of this chapter is to achieve maximal clarity with regard to a critique of religious realism which can plausibly be attributed to Wittgenstein. Though Wittgenstein's critique of realism is penetrating, his interpretation of religion faces problems as well. The logic of the dilemma by which this book is organized dictates that this be so. Wittgensteinian non-realist interpretations of religion, a kind of religious irrealism, are revisionary in character. Thus, the second goal of this chapter is to show how Wittgensteinian non-realism results in revisionary interpretations of religion.

It might seem that religious language should be either true or false. Such a formulation simply follows the law of the excluded middle: either p or not-p. Following the law of the excluded middle, a given instance of religious language should be either true or false. Thus, it would seem that there should be only two different positions: those who maintain that religious language is true and those who maintain that it is false. However, the matter is not that simple. Using "God exists" to exemplify this point, a review of the literature will show that we must acknowledge three distinct approaches to the question of God's existence. Adapting (i.e., making more specific) our understanding of the issues involved concerning religious realism to "God exists," we have the following: First, theological realism describes those who hold that for "God exists" there are objective truth conditions. Second, theological anti-realism describes those who hold that for "God exists" these objective truth conditions do not obtain. Third, theological non-realism describes those who hold that for "God exists" there are no objective truth conditions; that is, "God exists" does not express a proposition. Again, when appropriate, the term irrealism is used as a blanket term covering the second and third options. This schema needs to be as clear as possible since it is crucial to interpreting Wittgenstein's thought on this matter properly. A typical misunderstanding of Wittgenstein's thought casts it as anti-realist in character. However, Wittgenstein found realism and anti-realism to be equally misguided. As such, Wittgenstein's thought is best characterized by what has been referred to above as non-realism; I describe Wittgenstein's thought in this manner to make clear that while it eschews realism it also eschews anti-realism. That is, Wittgensteinian non-realism is not a theory about how language does relate or needs to relate to reality; rather, Wittgensteinian non-realism is not a theory at all. I use the term non-realism to show its relation to realism and anti-realism; it isn't either and it eschews both.

This discussion begins by drawing attention to two matters with regard to third approach, theological non-realism. The first matter is that it is seemingly in violation of the law of the excluded middle. My treatment of Wittgenstein on the question of God's existence will show how we can make sense of this. The second matter is that *non*-realism is different from *anti*-realism. As is evident throughout this chapter, the present treatment of Wittgensteinian interpretations of religion has interesting ramifications for his place within the literature. Recent commentators on this topic, though trying to argue to the contrary, actually illustrate the need for the distinction between religious anti-realism and religious non-realism. Michael Scott, having overlooked the differences between Wittgenstein and those who fit the description of anti-realism provided here, mistakenly interprets Wittgenstein in a straightforwardly non-cognitivist light. The trichotomy proposed above facilitates a more subtle perspective. Brian Clack argues that it is mistaken to characterize Wittgenstein as offering a non-cognitivist interpretation of religion. Though Clack's argument for this interpretation misfires he is right when he argues that Wittgenstein does not promote non-cognitivism in that Wittgenstein does not promote any philosophical theories at all. However, by eschewing realism, Wittgenstein still, in the end, offers an interpretation of religion that is revisionary. In addition, although Wittgenstein does not *promote* a non-cognitivist interpretation of religion, Clack's Wittgenstein still offers interpretations of religion that *amount to* being non-cognitivist. As I will show, these interpretations of Wittgenstein's thought suffer from misunderstandings of crucial features of his treatment of realism. In the trichotomy presented here, the schema by which we distinguish Wittgensteinian non-realism from realism *and* anti-realism, there is a means to alleviate these misunderstandings that plague the literature.

Dogmatic, absolute statements – "in order for there to be such and such then thus and so must obtain" – are among the kinds of (would-be) statements of which Wittgenstein is quite wary. I say "(would-be) statements" since I want to leave open the question of whether such a string of words is indeed a statement. Calling this string a statement implies that it indeed makes sense; whether it makes sense is the issue to be explored. In this vein, those who assent to the comprehensive applicability of the law of the excluded middle must contend with important challenges when faced with Wittgenstein's criticisms of realism. The following passages from Wittgenstein indicate his views on the law of the excluded middle and its relation to a realist conception of truth as they impact on the topics I am addressing. He writes, "The law of excluded middle says here: It must either look like this or like that."[1] As Jeffrey Price puts it, Wittgenstein finds the picture presented by the law of the excluded middle "to be itself a picture, whose accord with the reality is precisely the issue. Wittgenstein thus opposes a double confusion; it is a particular picture of reality that leads us to assume that pictures are adequate to reality."[2] In this case, Wittgenstein does not oppose employing pictures per se but the idea that the picture presented by the law of the excluded middle is adequate to reality. For example, the law of the excluded middle seems to offer an exhaustive account of what is the case: Either p or not-p.

Wittgenstein challenges the notion that the law of the excluded middle is exhaustive. The assumption that our conceptual pictures can be adequate to reality is just the kind of Tractarian doctrine that the later Wittgenstein repudiated. That Wittgenstein disavowed the notion that the truth or falsity of a would-be proposition is to be determined by whether or not it matches up with a picture within some external reality is clear in sections 519–523 of *PI*. Instead of the idea that such pictures are to be seen as telling us which propositions are true or false, Wittgenstein writes, "I should like to say that 'what the picture tells me is itself.'"[3] The tentativeness with which Wittgenstein offers this understanding of a picture is instructive. He is not giving us a theory of meaning or a theory of anything. However, from his indicating his view that "what the picture tells me is itself," we can see what pictures do *not* tell us. Pictures do not tell us which propositions are true or false. Applied to our topic, we can glean the following moral. For Wittgenstein, the notion that certain objective conditions must obtain in order for "God exists" to be true can lead us into confusion. We can be led to believe that in order for a negation to be meaningful, we must assume some sort of substantiality of that which is to be negated.

Applying this idea to the question of God's existence is illustrative. Following this line that God is a substance, the question of God's existence would be determined by whether this substance exists or not. That is, to deny that God exists presumes that God is a being which exists or not. Wittgenstein would contend that such a denial, in an anti-realist vein, runs into the same kind of metaphysical difficulties as does affirming that God exists in a realist sense. Both the theological realist and the theological anti-realist are committed to a picture, which is assumed to be adequate to assess the truth or falsity of claims regarding an objective state of affairs. The picture to which the theological realist is committed is that the objective conditions by which the truth of "God exists" would be verified must obtain. The picture to which the theological anti-realist is committed is that the objective conditions by which the truth of "God exists" would be verified must obtain but do not. Wittgenstein denies that either picture is adequate to reality. That is, the Wittgensteinian theological non-realist holds that it is not the case that these conditions must obtain. Price expresses this when he indicates that "Wittgenstein questions the value of such a picture (one in which it is assumed, e.g., that God either exists or not) because it fails 'to determine what we have to do, what to look for, and how...'"[4] James Conant also comments on the role of pictures within Wittgenstein's work when he writes, "We need...to distinguish between two pictures: the picture implicit in our practice and the filled-in version of the picture."[5] By respecting the former we begin to know what to do, what to look for, and how. By being suspicious of the latter, we can avoid imposing hidden metaphysical requirements on ourselves of which we might not even be aware. Accordingly, we would be less prone to confusion.

Wittgenstein lists some examples of the futility of trying to determine the truth or falsity of seeming propositions which thus would seem to admit of being subject to the law of the excluded middle. Wittgenstein questions the sense of the idea that we can understand whether "a deaf-mute...talks to himself inwardly in a vocal language..." or whether it makes sense to say that it is "5 o'clock on the sun" (based on what time zone?). He questions what it would mean to say that people on the North and South poles are "above" or "below" the Earth.[6] Finally, Wittgenstein offers the following regarding the inconclusiveness of the law of the excluded middle:

> The reason why the use of the expression "true or false" (that is, *must* be true or false, according to the law of the excluded middle) has something misleading about it is that it is like saying "it tallies with the facts or it doesn't", and the very thing that is in question is what "tallying" is here.[7]

According to this interpretation of Wittgenstein, assuming the comprehensive applicability of the law of the excluded middle allows confusion. Most relevant to our topic is the confusion brought about by the following notion: By allowing the negation of X, we allow that X is something that can indeed be negated. It is precisely this confusion, which such applications of the law of the excluded middle can promote that Wittgenstein would have us avoid. In reference to the law of the excluded middle, Wittgenstein had put to him the would-be proposition: "Either God exists or God does not exist." To this, Wittgenstein responded, "Couldn't he half exist?"[8]

Whatever Wittgenstein might mean by this cryptic remark, he does *not* mean that "God exists" is either true or false. It seems that Wittgenstein eschews such cognitivist understandings of religious language. In eschewing cognitivist interpretations of religious language, though, it is not that Wittgenstein promotes a non-cognitivist interpretation of religious language. However, it seems that a non-cognitivist interpretation is an inevitable consequence of a Wittgensteinian interpretation of religious language.

The reason that a Wittgensteinian, non-realist critique of (religious) realism constitutes a "third" option relates to the non-cognitivist interpretation of religious language with which Wittgenstein seems to leave us. This is a matter to be considered with some subtlety. By using the term *non-realism* I do not mean that Wittgenstein promotes a theory of religious language called "non-realism." Wittgenstein eschews all philosophical theories. My choice of this term is simply to show the relation of Wittgenstein's non-realist option to the realist and anti-realist options. That said, by eschewing realist and anti-realist interpretations of religious language, Wittgenstein nevertheless seems to leave us with no other option than the idea that religious language is neither true nor false. It seems that Wittgenstein challenges both religious realism, which describes those who hold that for a given instance of religious language there are objective truth conditions and religious anti-realism, which describes those who hold that for a given instance of religious language these objective conditions do not obtain. Challenging the intelligibility of both, Wittgenstein's thought seemingly exemplifies a third option. The first two options above constitute the two cognitivist approaches to "God exists." To wit: First, theological realism: for "God exists" to be true, it must be so independent of human experience, and, second, theological anti-realism: it is false that "God exists" independent of human experience. Eschewing these two approaches, Wittgenstein's thought can thus be seen as a third, non-cognitivist option. It is for this reason that I am compelled to stress the distinct character of Wittgenstein's theological *non-realism*. I use this terminology to distinguish Wittgenstein from realists *and* anti-realists since he maintains that the metaphysical assumptions underlying realism and anti-realism are confused. P. M. S. Hacker puts this aptly when he writes, "Wittgenstein was not siding with one philosophical theory (e.g., anti-realism) as opposed to another (e.g., realism), but diagnosing the intellectual diseases that inform both."[9]

As we have seen, by presenting a "third" option as described above, Wittgenstein seems to leave us with the idea that it is neither true nor false that "God exists" independent of human experience. If it is neither true nor false that "God exists" independent of human experience, then is "'God exists' independent of human experience" even a meaningful combination of words? If not, then Wittgenstein indicates that meaningless combinations of words should not be understood as meaning something meaningless, rather, such a "combination of words is being excluded from language, withdrawn from circulation."[10] If that is the case, then, for: "'God exists' must be true (in a realist sense) for there to be, e.g., a Christian understanding of salvation," which word(s) are to be withdrawn from circulation? If "God exists" is a meaningless combination of words, then it seems that Wittgenstein must be suggesting an alternative understanding to the question "Does God exist?" besides "true" or "false." Otherwise, he would not really be providing a "third option" as contrasted with the realists and anti-realists. For if "God exists (in a realist sense)" were indeed the kind of sentence that could be true or false, then either the realists or anti-realists would be correct, and that would be that. There would be no call for a third, Wittgensteinian option. As Wittgenstein himself has indicated, he does not believe "God exists (in a realist sense)" is the kind of string of words that can be assessed as true or false. If language concerning God's existence is, by Wittgenstein's lights, neither true nor false, or, to be "withdrawn from circulation" then just what is the nature and meaning of religious language for Wittgenstein? The following passage sheds light on how we should *not* understand religious language on a Wittgensteinian view.

> There is nothing wrong with theology, precisely because it consists of a set of rules for the proper employment of religious terms. Things would go wrong if the theologian thought he was making true factual claims about God. Doing so would turn him into a metaphysician who had confused grammatical and factual investigations.[11]

Interpretations that assume that religious language entail metaphysics, according to Wittgenstein, lead to confusion. In order to understand the nature of this confusion and how Wittgenstein would have us avoid it requires further discussion of this distinction between grammatical and factual concerns.

It would seem, according to Wittgenstein, that our religious realists and anti-realists have confusedly occupied themselves with factual concerns in that they regard "God exists" as admitting of truth or falsity. By the non-realist and non-cognitivist line left to us by Wittgenstein, "'God exists' independent of human experience" is not the kind of expression that admits of truth or falsity. Thus Wittgenstein's thought stands in contrast to the cognitivist (i.e., realist and anti-realist) contention that for "God exists" to be true, certain objective conditions must obtain, which, according to the Wittgensteinian, commits the realist (and anti-realist) to nonsensical metaphysical theses. For the Wittgensteinian, laying down requirements for what objective conditions must be in place for "God exists" to be true is a dubious undertaking. We will deepen our understanding of Wittgenstein's teaching, though, by asking: Why should that be? I do not know whether the sentence "Someone in a Chinese village is eating breakfast right now" is true. However, I certainly do know what conditions must be in place for that sentence to be true. Why should predicating true or false statements of God be any different? One prominent line of thought has it that predicating of God poses special difficulties because any reference we make to God cannot be entirely successful.[12] Using one of the customary divine attributes, this point can be illustrated by considering the statement "God is all-powerful." This statement cannot literally be true according to this line of thought since the concept of power would inevitably be constrained by our human understanding of power. Stated more generally, if God is ineffable, or transcends description, or cannot be literally predicated of, and so on, nothing we say about God can be literally true.[13]

However, this is not what Wittgenstein has in mind when he eschews both realist and anti-realist accounts of religious language. Understanding Wittgenstein in terms of his treating religious language as neither true nor false because it is indeterminate constructs a "straw-man" version of Wittgenstein's thought. Such a conception of Wittgenstein casts him in a logical positivist light, a description the later Wittgenstein was clearly at pains to avoid. By engaging the as it were "positivist Wittgenstein" it seems to me that one is engaging something other than Wittgenstein of his later work particularly.[14] By engaging Wittgenstein's thought where it is most penetrating I believe we can also see how his teaching can be most helpful in our understanding of religious language. Moreover, when I make a case for how Wittgenstein is situated within the dilemma I have formulated, I want to be situating the most attractive, and thereby the most likely to be accurate, interpretation of his work possible.

The supposed indeterminacy of religious language can, at best, only partially explain why (the later) Wittgenstein eschews religious realism and religion anti-realism. I offer another reason why, for Wittgenstein, "God exists" might be the kind of string of words that is neither true nor false independent of human experience, that is, does not conform to the law of the excluded middle. For Wittgenstein, "God exists" is not a factual proposition at all, but is rather a rule regulating practice within a religious language-game. Wittgenstein writes, "'You can't hear God speak to someone else, you can hear him only if you are being addressed'. – That is a grammatical remark."[15] As a grammatical remark, it is not true (or false) in the same way an ordinary factual propositional statement would be true (or false). For example, Hacker indicates that for Wittgenstein "it is not a fact of nature, but a grammatical truth, i.e. a rule of grammar, that white is lighter than black."[16] An ordinary propositional statement, "My chair is black," is true if my chair is black and is false if my chair is not black. This is different from saying that "white is lighter than black." "White is lighter than black" expresses a grammatical rule for what we mean by "black" and "white." As a grammatical remark expressing a rule for the usage of "white" and "black," it is not possible that "white is lighter than black" be false without significantly changing what we mean by "black" and "white." It is in this sense that grammatical remarks express rules and as such are not true or false in the same way that factual propositions would be true or false. Assuming that our understanding of "white" and "black" is in place, if someone stated that this printed page you are reading does not consist of black ink on a white page, the means for checking the factual accuracy of such an assertion would be fairly straightforward. If someone stated that "white is not lighter than black," however, we might wonder whether this person understands how to use these words. That is, we might wonder whether this person grasps the rules for the usage of "white" and "black." Grammar tells us how terms, for example "true" and "false," shall be employed. In this vein, "God exists," for instance, describes a rule for practitioners of a particular language-game. According to this Wittgensteinian understanding, religious practice, in order as it is, is not undertaken because people believe that "God exists" expresses a true factual proposition. Rather, living one's life as though God exists constitutes what we mean by living a religious life (at least within a theistic context).

By Wittgenstein's lights "God exists" is not a true proposition along the lines of other true propositions, e.g., "you are reading these words right now" (of course, "God exists" is not a false proposition for Wittgenstein, either). Rather, "God exists" is one of the rules for playing a (theistic) religious language-game. "Bishops move diagonally" is similarly a rule for playing chess; *qua* rule, it is neither true nor false. Moving a bishop sideways would not constitute the falsehood of "bishops move diagonally;" rather, such a move would be in violation of the rule. Similarly, atheism, say, does not constitute the falsehood of "God exists;" rather, atheism is an illegitimate move in language-games in which the rule "God exists" is relevant. We might say of a Christian atheist (for lack of a better term, since I do not know what else to call someone who seems to be a practicing Christian but who denies that God exists) that she is playing the Christian language-game in an odd way, i.e., violating the rule "God exists." A garden-variety atheist would then be said not to be playing the Christian language-game at all. Whereas theological anti-realism holds that the objective conditions whereby "God exists" would be true do not obtain, this is not what the Wittgensteinian, theological non-realist maintains. Thus, what I am calling theological anti-realism and theological non-realism involve very different ideas regarding the meaning of "God exists." Significant confusion is avoided if we keep the distinction between theological anti-realism and theological non-realism in mind. Before I turn to some particular cases where confusion is avoided if we remember the distinction between anti-realism and non-realism, I need to make one more clarification regarding Wittgensteinian non-realism more generally.

Once more, for emphasis, I am not recommending that we understand Wittgenstein as promoting a theory called non-realism. Since what the later Wittgenstein teaches us is not a theory at all, it is misleading to say "Here are the features of a theory of interpretation we can draw from Wittgenstein's later work." In this vein, though some appeals have been made to the later

Wittgensteinian idea of "language-games," it is not as though he promoted, as it were, a "theory of language-games." That said it is still useful to have some sense of how the later work of Wittgenstein employs this crucial idea of language-games.

The features associated with Wittgenstein's conception of language-games make his criticisms of metaphysics apparent. Given the later Wittgenstein's disinclination to set out a theory of language (or of anything), commentators "have complained that Wittgenstein gives no criteria of identity for language-games."[17] So the following are not intended to be criteria of what is essential to a language-game, but I offer these simply as features typically associated with language-games:

a. Like a game, language is rule-governed.
b. Rules determine which moves make sense.
c. The meaning of the word is determined by the rules of the game.
d. There is an irreducible multiplicity of language-games.
e. The idea of a language-game does not have an essential definition but is a family-resemblance concept.
f. Using the rules of one language-game to assess another invites confusion.
g. Language-games are connected with practice.
h. Language-games do not require justification by external sources.
i. Language-games are rooted in our natural activities.[18]

These features are listed here to illustrate the function of language in the later thought of Wittgenstein. One benefit of Wittgenstein's language-game approach is that it provides a well-grounded understanding of where language gets its meaning: from practice. By virtue of this approach we avoid problems concerning how language links up with the world outside of language. Does "Hustle" refer to the name of a dance or is it a command that might be directed at a loafing football player? In the sections beginning the *Philosophical Investigations*, Wittgenstein avoids such problems by commending us not to understand words as deriving their meaning in terms of their referring to the external world. Rather, language gets its meaning from use. Which of the above meanings of "Hustle" is appropriate? That depends on whether one is playing, as it were, the "disco language-game" or the "football language-game." I do not mean to trivialize the matter of what scope a language-game shall have with this example. Asking, "How significant should a human activity be before it counts as a language-game?" ultimately is asking, "What shall count as a language-game?" Wittgenstein does not countenance such questions as being legitimate. Which activities count as games? These are family-resemblance concepts. I have significant things in common ("family-resemblances") with my cousins that I do not have in common with other people. However, we would be at a loss to describe these commonalities exhaustively. This does not bear unfavorably on the meaning of "cousin." We still employ this concept successfully. Rather than trying to define what shall count as a language-game, Wittgenstein takes the attitude that these practices are undertaken and are in place as they are. Theories of reference, in contrast, by laying down the requirements for what must be the case in order for a given word to "match" with its corresponding object in the extra-linguistic world, offer a confused account of the nature of language, according to Wittgenstein. Rather, for Wittgenstein, grammar provides rules by which certain moves within language make sense; expecting more, e.g., for language to match up with a metaphysically independent reality, betrays a misunderstanding of how language works.

The role of language-games in Wittgenstein's later thought further reinforces the idea that Wittgensteinian non-realism is distinct from anti-realism. Unlike non-realism, anti-realism *does* involve a metaphysical commitment to what is the case. We see this below. Keeping in mind the distinction I make between anti-realism and Wittgensteinian non-realism helps us to avoid confusions. One such confusion is that Wittgensteinian thought promotes relativism. If we see relativism as a kind of anti-realism, we will see how characterizing Wittgenstein as a relativist is misguided. In the following, Patrick Sherry expresses a typical realist understanding of a Wittgensteinian construal of religious belief:

> Wittgenstein's followers wish to claim that religion has its own standards of truth and rationality, and yet at the same time to avoid what Winch calls a 'Protagorean Relativism'. There is no point in claiming that God has His own kind of reality or religion its own kind of truth unless there is at least some similarity between these and other kinds of reality or truth; otherwise…we are merely using the words to mean whatever we choose to mean by them.[19]

The above passage is indicative of a not uncommon realist misinterpretation of Wittgenstein: one that casts Wittgensteinian thought as relativist. Wittgenstein is not a relativist, if we think of relativism as a form of anti-realism. Relativism can be seen as a form of anti-realism in that it describes the position that the objective conditions which would render the proposition "x is absolutely true" true do not obtain. This characterization of relativism shows that it entails a metaphysical commitment. Wittgenstein opposes metaphysics of any kind. Therefore, characterizations of Wittgenstein as a relativist miss the mark and will lead to misinterpretations of his thought. Thus, the Wittgenstein treated throughout this book is not a straw-man, misrepresented as an anti-realist of a relativist stripe. Indeed, confusion ensues when Wittgensteinian thought is miscast as anti-realist. In keeping with the logic of the dilemma by which the issues involved in this book have been framed, Wittgensteinian non-realist interpretations of religion are revisionary. Even so, the goal here is to present his thought on religion in a maximally attractive way. I now turn to a discussion of a recent example of such an error: a treatment that presents Wittgenstein in an unfavorable light, though this is not the stated purpose of the article, because the author does not see the distinction I recommend between anti-realism and non-realism. A goal of the following discussion is to show that even when more appropriately cast as *non*-realist (versus *anti*-realist), Wittgensteinian interpretations of religion are still revisionary.

An article by Michael Scott facilitates the untangling some of the issues facing Wittgensteinian interpretations of religious language. In it he argues that "it is incumbent on religious realists and non-realists to provide an account of the nature of truth in religious discourse, or provide some other explanation of how to frame the realism question." He also poses the questions, "what content does the question about whether God really exists have and what evidence is relevant in deciding an answer to it? More generally, on what substantive philosophical issues do religious realists and non-realists disagree?"[20] I concur that his charge is well founded and it is this matter that I intend to address. Scott is quite right that the debate over theological realism has been and continues to be messy. One side talks past the other while the issues over which they dispute remain to be settled or remain to be seen as to whether they are legitimate issues or not. However, before we can even begin to try to address these questions, we must first differentiate within the group that Scott lumps together as "non-realists." We must do this because it is clear that theological realists would have different disagreements with anti-realists as opposed to non-realists. For instance, theological realists and anti-realists could disagree on *whether* "God exists" is true or false; theological non-realists would challenge the idea that it even makes sense to conceive of "God exists" in terms of truth or falsity.

Scott gives us the task of describing what exactly it is that people disagree about regarding theological realism. Now, with this background, it is evident that the nature of the disagreement depends on who is doing the disagreeing. Theological realists will disagree with anti-realists regarding the truth or falsity of "God exists." More precisely, theological realism describes those who hold that for "God exists" there are objective truth conditions. Theological anti-realism describes those who hold that for "God exists" these objective conditions do not obtain. However, since both agree that "God exists" is either true or false, they maintain a cognitivist view of religious language, at least in this case. The nature of the disagreement between theological realists and anti-realists, however, is fundamentally different from the disagreement between theological realists and non-realists. This is because non-realists maintain that "God exists" is neither true nor false due to its lack of factual content. Clearly, theological anti-realism and theological non-realism, as I am presenting them, involve very different positions regarding the meaning of "God exists."

In many cases in the literature on theological realism, including the article in question by Scott, the terms realism, anti-realism, non-realism, and irrealism are neither used with particular consistency nor with any particular concern about how they might correspond to different approaches to the question of God's existence. These terms are used interchangeably, sometimes innocuously, but sometimes masking substantive differences and confusions. Scott contributes to the problem by failing to distinguish between two discernibly different ways of approaching the question of God's existence. I propose to set this matter aright by offering a way in which we can more appropriately understand the different approaches to the question of God's existence, thus clearing away unnecessary confusion. Achieving clarity on the questions raised by Scott will not only help us understand the issues involved regarding theological realism, an analysis of the questions raised by Scott will enhance our understanding of Wittgensteinian interpretations of religious language.

My use of Wittgenstein's thought to illustrate theological non-realism, which maintains that "God exists" is neither true nor false, is directly relevant to Scott's argument. I would characterize Scott's approach in "Framing the Realism Question" as employing a Carnapian version of Wittgenstein's thought to attempt to show that theological language lacks factual content. We see this in Scott's approving use of the following passage from *Zettel*:

> One man is a convinced realist, another a convinced idealist and teaches his children accordingly. In such an important matter as the existence or non-existence of the external world they don't want to teach their children anything wrong. What will the children be taught? To include in what they say 'There are physical objects' or the opposite?...But the idealist will teach his children the word 'chair' after all, for of course he wants to teach them to do this and that, e.g. to fetch a chair. Then where will be the difference between what the idealist educated children say and the realist ones? Won't the difference only be one of a battle cry?[21]

Scott offers the following commentary on this passage. "Talk about physical objects, it seems, does not depend on ontological commitments to their existence."[22] So the conclusion that Scott wants to draw from the above, adapting it to the terminology we are using here, is that there is no practical difference between those who have realist belief and those who have anti- or non-realist belief. If, following this line, one lives one's life as though "God exists" is true, it makes no difference whether one construes the meaning of

"God exists is true" along realist lines or not. Scott continues, "While Carnap's conclusion is similar to Wittgenstein's [the one he draws in the above passage from *Zettel*], he [Carnap] reaches it through an analytically more satisfactory route." This route is more satisfactory since, according to Scott, via Carnap's thought

> The realist/non-realist is presented with a dilemma. Either the question is particular and resolvable with the procedures of logical or empirical investigation admissible within the framework, or it is general and its answer will trivially follow from more specific claims made about the existence of members of the class of entities in question.[23]

This argumentation leads Scott to the following conclusion, "Carnap's account seems to undermine any attempt to make sense of the philosophical existence question, i.e. whether the subject matter of a framework really exists prior to adopting that framework."[24]

I offer two responses to Scott's conclusion above. First, this conclusion strikes me as an adaptation of Hume's fork. From this adaptation of Hume's fork, Scott draws the further conclusion that theological language lacks cognitive content. Second, the above passage from Scott also resembles instrumentalism as this term is used in philosophy of science. On the first topic, here again is the relevant, classic passage from Hume:

> Does it [a book, given thought, judgment, expression, etc.] contain any abstract reasoning concerning quantity or number [analytic truths]? No. Does it contain any experimental reasoning concerning matter of fact and existence [synthetic truths]? No. Commit it then to the flames, for it can contain nothing but sophistry.[25]

In Scott's passage cited above, he indicates that he sees a dilemma facing theological realism: a dilemma that approximates Hume's fork (that a judgment is either analytic and verifiable by logical means or synthetic and verifiable by empirical means, or "illusion"). The dilemma is that either 1) the question "is particular and resolvable with the procedures of logical or empirical investigation admissible within the framework," or 2) "[the question] is general and its answer will trivially follow from more specific claims made about the existence of members of the class of entities in question."

Horn 1) resonates with Hume's description of what we typically call a synthetic undertaking. Had Scott not included "logical" investigation, this comparison would be even closer. However, by qualifying this as logical investigation "admissible within the framework," this brings Scott's description closer to that of a synthetic undertaking; that is, Scott's description would seem to curb a priori judgments since the investigations Scott recommends would take place within a presumably extant framework. Horn 2) calls to mind Hume's description of what we typically call analytic truths. For example, "All bachelors are unmarried men" does not provide us with any new information about the world (i.e., it is not a synthetic truth); rather, the predicate ("are unmarried men") trivially follows from the subject ("All bachelors"). That is, "All bachelors are unmarried men" expresses an analytic truth. By saying, "its answer will trivially follow from more specific claims made about the existence of members of the class of entities in question," Scott appears to have glossed this horn of the dilemma in analytic terms. So it appears that Scott has taken an adaptation of Hume's fork and used it to argue for the non-cognitivity of the string "God exists." That is, since "God exists" qualifies as neither, as it were, synthetic nor analytic, this expression, supposedly lacking meaningful, factual content, shall be cast to the flames as sophistry and illusion.

Hume's fork, despite Hume's philosophical stature, has not avoided significant criticism; moreover, one could argue that "God exists" could withstand Hume's fork. Generally speaking there is, of course, Kant's argument for the viability of synthetic a priori judgments, which Hume's fork would not allow. More specific to the present context here one could ask: How would Scott's apparent neo-Humeanism deal with an argument for the existence of God based on experience as William Alston does in *Perceiving God*? In other words, we should not take for granted that "God exists" could not qualify as a legitimate synthetic proposition in this case. As Alston argues, we have no more reason to discount the prima facie reliability of beliefs formed by mystical perception than we do for those formed by sensory perception since there is no non-circular way to justify beliefs in either case.[26] The significance of this is that Hume's fork would allow sensory perception as a means of justifying synthetic judgments but would not allow perceptual experience of any sort to justify the judgment that God exists since belief in God was one of the beliefs presumably to be cast to the flames.

Scott's passage above also calls to mind instrumentalism, as this term is used in philosophy of science. Instrumentalism treats unobservables as instruments that do not have an independent reality in their own right but are simply tokened as an expedient in order for us to be able to refer to them.[27] Treating unobservables (whether at the "micro" level, e.g., quarks, or at the "macro" level, e.g., God) merely as instruments, we can say that this is a useful theory in that it provides us with a way to talk about things we cannot see. In addition, it does not commit us to the possibility of having an inflated ontology by which we assert the existence of things whose being we cannot verify. This approach to unobservables might have some promise. Perhaps it can appease the likes of Alston by giving us an intelligible way to talk about, e.g., God, in that we acknowledge that tokens like "God" have a legitimate role in our language. Perhaps these tokens can even have some degree of predictability, i.e., something that lends credibility within a scientific idiom, about them. On the instrumentalist account we can have some reasonable grasp of the conditions under which unobservables tend to present themselves. Moreover, by referring to them as instruments, we can say that this nomenclature gives us a way of talking about that which cannot be observed but which seems to have an impact on the lives we live. At this point, however, we can see where this instrumentalist view shares a defect with the view Scott espouses above. Views which assert that entities within a framework can only be made sense of (i.e., tokened) within that framework (as Scott would have it) cannot countenance novelty. This is the case insofar as they entail an "I wouldn't have seen it if I didn't believe it" attitude. That is, they cannot account for newly discovered entities that do not already fit the established framework. As Stathis Psillos argues, only a realism that allows for the independent existence of the external world, and the entities that inhabit it, can accommodate novel findings.[28] Indeed, the idiom of "discovery" is unintelligible within such a framework model. If entities within a framework make sense only within that framework, then all so-called novelty is "invention" in that we can token "new" entities only insofar as they make sense within the accepted framework.

We need to be aware of these problems raised by this Humean view of belief discussed above in order to see the significance of Scott's argument. He exemplifies the Humean character of his argument when he approvingly states that, for Carnap, "the question of God's existence, as raised by philosophers, must be a pseudo-question, for there is no agreed framework in which it can be posed and argued about."[29] That is, since, recalling the Humean character of the language Scott uses, the question of God's existence can be framed neither empirically (i.e., as a synthetic judgment) nor logically (i.e., as an analytic judgment), Scott concludes that "Does God exist?" must be a pseudo-question. My point is that Scott's Humean approach relegates questions about God's existence to the non-cognitivist dustbin of concepts that ostensibly lack meaningful, factual content. As such, Scott's insistence on a non-cognitivist interpretation of religious language overlooks the three fundamentally distinct ways of assessing the truth of "God exists" I have presented. This oversight leads to confusion in Scott's approach to the question of God's existence.

This brings us back to our central issues: What are the substantial issues facing theological realism? How many ways of assessing the truth of "God exists" are there? My response to these questions is to propose that there are three ways in which the question of God's existence can be posed and argued about: 1) theological realism 2) theological anti-realism, and 3) theological non-realism. Two of these three ways, 1) and 2), agree that there is a substantive matter about which to disagree: 1) describes those who hold that for "God exists" there are objective truth conditions; 2) describes those who hold that for

"God exists" these objective conditions do not obtain. By virtue of their holding that it is "true" and "false" that these objective conditions obtain, theological realism and theological anti-realism respectively represent the two cognitivist options regarding the question of God's existence. The approach that Scott recommends to us, utilizing the thought of Carnap, as we have seen, is a non-cognitivist approach to the interpretation of "God exists." Due to this non-cognitivist approach, Scott simply dismisses what I have been referring to as theological realism and anti-realism. Moreover, and this is where the inadequacy of Scott's insufficiently nuanced approach can be seen readily, he conflates what I have been calling anti-realism and non-realism.[30]

We see Scott's non-cognitivism when he approvingly cites what he takes to be Carnap's similarity to Wittgenstein regarding theological issues. He writes, "if Carnap is right, then these claims cannot be taken at face value, as asserting ontological propositions about the existence of God. Rather, they will have to be interpreted as expressing a commitment to a theistic framework."[31] Scott continues,

> it appears that Carnap is successful in giving prima facie cause for doubt that the ontological question addressed by realists and non-realists has content, or that ontological assertions do more than express attitudes towards the framework under discussion.[32]

This is a standard non-cognitivist line and by adopting it, Scott misrepresents the literature under consideration. He conflates anti-realism (a cognitivist stance) with non-realism (a non-cognitivist stance). Theological realism simply has different responses to anti- and non-realism. Perhaps it is this difference that Scott construes as incoherence on the part of theological realists.

Next we see a concrete example wherein Scott's misrepresentation of the issues involved regarding theological realism gives rise to an identifiable error. He cites D. Z. Phillips as a critic of theological realism, and while I certainly agree that Phillips is a critic of realism, Scott's misrepresentation of the issues involved causes him to misconstrue the nature of Phillips's critique.[33] He does so by conflating what I am calling options 2) and 3), theological anti- and non-realism. This conflation prompts Scott to characterize Phillips as taking a cognitivist, anti-realist approach when Phillips's avowed Wittgensteinianism, as I will show, makes him a *non*-cognitivist (and *non*-realist) regarding religious language.

Scott writes, "As we have seen, Phillips proposes that the question of God's reality can be thought of as similar to that of the reality of physical objects."[34] Presumably we can ordinarily discuss whether it is true or false that physical objects exist. Thus Scott seems to cast Phillips's thought as taking a cognitivist view of religious language. As I will show, this is plainly wrong. Phillips is at pains to show that he, following Wittgenstein, is not a (theological) anti-realist; that is, relevant to our purposes here, Phillips does not maintain that "God exists" is false. Rather, Phillips's Wittgensteinianism makes him a non-realist, that is, one who maintains that God's existence is not properly thought of in terms of truth or falsity. More in-depth analysis of Phillips's thought as it relates to our topic will follow in the next chapter in the segment devoted to him, but the following will suffice to illustrate this particular point.

Phillips writes, "What Wittgenstein is trying to do is not to get the realist to embrace non-realism. Rather, he is trying to get him to look in a certain direction, to our actions and practices, where religious belief has its sense."[35] The above terminology is unfortunate; but in this case the context makes it clear that what Phillips means by "non-realism" here is what I am calling "anti-realism." That is, neither Phillips nor Wittgenstein want to convince the realist that the objective conditions by which the truth of "God exists" would be assessed do not obtain, the position that describes what I am calling anti-realism. Rather, contrary to Scott's characterization that Phillips construes God's existence along the lines of physical objects, the Wittgensteinian Phillips wants the realist to see that religious language does not admit of truth or falsity. Instead, for Phillips, religious language indicates a commitment, a way of orienting one's life.

Phillips affirms this approach to religious life, that religious belief and language are indicative of a commitment to live one's life a certain way, in the following passage. He opposes those who assume "that the dispute between the believer and the unbeliever is over *a matter of fact*." He continues, "it *makes no sense* to say that God might not exist."[36] This, according to Phillips, is so since God's existence is not a matter of fact. Finally, Phillips makes it perfectly clear that he sees no analogy between God and physical objects when he argues that "it may be said that the word 'God' does not refer" since "finding God is not a matter of 'finding out' at all; it cannot be the subject of any quasi-empirical enquiry. Finding God is a spiritual matter."[37] These passages should show that Phillips, following Wittgenstein, is *not* an anti-realist. Ultimately, the disagreement between realists and anti-realists *is* over a matter of fact: Theological realism describes those who hold that for "God exists" there are objective truth conditions; theological anti-realism describes those who hold that for "God exists" these objective conditions do not obtain. Theological *non*-realists, like Phillips and Wittgenstein oppose theological realism as well as theological anti-realism. They argue that realists and anti-realists both, by virtue of their assessing it in terms of truth or falsity, misunderstand the nature of religious language. It is little wonder Scott sees the question of God's existence as being muddled, since he overlooks the distinction between anti- and non-realism. His treatment of Phillips shows this.

I suggest that Scott's misrepresentation of Phillips's thought is a reflection of his mischaracterization of the question of God's existence. Had Scott acknowledged the distinction between theological anti- and non-realism, perhaps he could have framed the debate over God's existence, and Phillips's place in it, more appropriately. Such being the case, we conclude our discussion of Scott by addressing one of his original points. He maintains that "it should be possible to understand what religious realism consists in, and where it differs from non-realism, independently of the question of whether God exists in the spatiotemporal framework." I agree with Scott; it should be possible. The goal here, by proposing a more precise way of understanding the options available regarding the interpretation of religious language and thus the question of God's existence in particular, is to help show how this can be more appropriately undertaken. That is, the first step in showing the substantive differences between theological realism and non-realism is to show how non-realism differs from anti-realism and then to show how theological realism differs from each, respectively. This objective has been accomplished by showing a) that theological realists and anti-realists would disagree over one fundamental issue, whether the objective conditions by which the truth or falsity of "God exists" would be assessed do indeed obtain, and b) that theological realists (as well as anti-realists) and non-realists would disagree over a different fundamental issue: theological non-realism maintains that "God exists" is neither true nor false (indicating that non-realism holds that both realists and anti-realists are confused).

Scott has not shown the incoherence of theological realism; rather, Scott's article adds to the confusion by not having framed the issue properly. Contrary to Scott, who countenances only two approaches (which, as I have shown, are effectively non-cognitivism and non-sense), there are three distinct approaches to the interpretation of religious language: 1) religious realism, 2) religious anti-realism, and 3) religious non-realism. Keeping these distinctions in mind will help us to avoid the confusion, conflating options 2) and 3), which I have shown to have befallen Scott. Seeing that there are three fundamentally distinct approaches to interpreting religious language will help us in more adequately framing what Scott calls the realism question.

Regardless of the adequacy of Scott's presentation of what he calls the "realism question," the non-cognitivist interpretation of religion he recommends is still subject to the dilemma facing interpretations of religion by which this book is organized. Therefore, even though I have showed that Wittgensteinian interpretations of religion are most properly understood as being critical of religious realism and religious anti-realism (i.e., the two cognitivist positions), the non-cognitivist, non-realist interpretation of religion Scott recommends, by virtue of its not being realist, still faces the irrealist horn of the dilemma and is thus an interpretation of religion that is revisionary in character. So Scott's interpretation of Wittgenstein on religion suffers from two defects: 1) he overlooks the distinction I have noted between what I am calling anti-realism and non-realism, 2) the interpretation of Wittgenstein on religion Scott recommends does not address that non-cognitivist interpretations of religion are revisionary in character. These oversights in themselves do not necessarily reflect badly on Scott's work.[38] However, these issues are raised by his work and need to be addressed nonetheless. Specifically, the concern I need to address is that even if we more aptly understand Wittgenstein's interpretation of religion in the non-realist manner I recommend, we still need to face the idea that such an interpretation of religion will be revisionary by virtue of its not being realist. The following discussion of another recent commentator on Wittgenstein serves in that capacity.

To contextualize this discussion, let's summarize the morals to be drawn from the preceding analysis of Scott's work: a) Wittgensteinian interpretations of religion are neither realist nor anti-realist, b) conflating religious anti-realism with religious non-realism gives rise to confusion and error, c) since Wittgensteinian interpretations of religion are neither realist nor anti-realist, they cast religion in a non-cognitivist light. To consider these matters in more depth, I must give a hearing to Brian Clack's challenge to the idea that Wittgenstein's thought fits the non-realist description I give it. To this end I offer the following analysis of Clack's argument that Wittgenstein's interpretation of religious language cannot be neatly classified as non-cognitivist. By showing that Clack's defense of Wittgenstein from the charge of non-cognitivism misfires because of the inescapably non-cognitivist implications of Wittgenstein's thoughts on religion, I will have reinforced my claim that Wittgensteinian religious non-realism is properly situated within the dilemma by which I have organized this project. More specifically, in having shown that my classification of Wittgenstein's thought as it bears on religion is appropriately situated within the dilemma I have formulated, I will have buttressed my claim that Wittgensteinian religious non-realism offers a revisionary interpretation of religion. Before setting out on that task, though, it will behoove us to consider the context in which Clack makes his argument.

Inspired by Wittgenstein, D. Z. Phillips expresses this non-realist attitude toward "God exists" when he writes, "God is not a 'something' but not a 'nothing' either."[39] Wittgenstein teaches us that realists and anti-realists alike are confused. The debate over realism versus anti-realism, Phillips continues, takes "for granted that there is a genuine philosophical question whether there are or are not metaphysical features of reality underlying structural or logical characteristics of language."[40] Wittgenstein himself expresses the idea that there is no genuine question to be asked in such cases. He eschews the notion that there are metaphysical features underlying language in *Culture and Value* when he indicates that language, religious or otherwise, neither corresponds nor fails to correspond to reality.[41]

We see this attitude as it relates to religious language specifically in the *Lectures and Conversations: On Aesthetics, Psychology and Religious Belief.* Here we can see the connection between the idea that religious language does not conform to the law of the excluded middle and Wittgenstein's theological non-realism. According to the law of the excluded middle, whether there will be, e.g., a Last Judgment, is either true or false. However, Wittgenstein clearly would disagree. "Suppose that someone believed in the Last Judgement, and I don't, does this mean that I believe the opposite to him, just that there won't be such a thing? I would say: 'not at all, or not always.'" Again, "If someone said: 'Wittgenstein, do you believe in this [the Resurrection]?' I'd say: 'No.' 'Do you contradict the man [who does believe in the Resurrection]?' I'd say: 'No.'"[42]

For Wittgenstein, religious questions, e.g., "Will there be a Last Judgment?" or "Does God exist?" apparently do not admit of being true or false with regard to whether they correspond to states of affairs, reality, what have you. It has been fairly customary to interpret this Wittgensteinian attitude, that religious language neither conforms nor does not conform to reality, along non-cognitivist lines. That is, following this standard interpretation, since Wittgenstein maintains that religious language does not make factual claims, religious language is most properly understood as non-cognitive. However, in a detailed analysis of Wittgenstein's works, especially the *Remarks on Frazer's "Golden Bough,"* Clack challenges this approach. That is, Clack challenges the idea that Wittgenstein's thought on religion can be neatly classified as non-cognitivist. If Clack's challenge were successful, this would constitute a significant blow to how I have classified Wittgenstein's work within the context of my dilemma. Accordingly, Clack's argument must be countenanced.

Now, to appreciate the thrust of Clack's argument, we need to see the connection between two of the standard ways of interpreting Wittgenstein's thought on religion. One way, as we saw in our discussion of Scott, is to construe it as non-cognitivist. Another standard way to interpret Wittgenstein's thought on religion is to construe it as expressivist. As we will see, these ways are certainly related.

I will show the connection between non-cognitivist and expressivist interpretations of Wittgenstein by situating them within the context of the dilemma by which I have organized this project. My way of framing Wittgenstein's thought on religion has been to show that it is neither realist nor anti-realist. Though Scott recommended a non-cognitivist interpretation of Wittgenstein, he did so in such a way as to conflate what I am calling religious anti-realism with religious non-realism. This conflation has the effect of allowing Wittgenstein's thought to be interpreted in an anti-realist manner, which is plainly incorrect. Though I argue that it is a mistake to cast Wittgenstein as an anti-realist, I do maintain that an important feature of Wittgenstein's thought on religion is that it is not realist either. It is for these two reasons that I characterize Wittgenstein's thought as non-realist. Although, I argue, Wittgenstein does not promote non-cognitivist interpretations of religion, non-cognitivist interpretations of religion are a consequence of his eschewing religious realism. Clack argues that non-cognitivist construals of Wittgenstein's thought on religion misrepresent it. While I agree with Clack that Wittgenstein does not promote non-cognitivism, refuting Clack's defense of Wittgenstein from the charge of non-cognitivism supports my interpretation of Wittgenstein as follows. Even though I agree that Wittgenstein does not promote non-cognitivism, a consequence of characterizing Wittgensteinian interpretations of religions as non-realist is that this will result in non-cognitivist (and therefore revisionary) interpretations of religion. I will argue that Clack fails in his attempt to defend Wittgenstein from the charge of non-cognitivism. Doing so supports my argument that Wittgenstein's non-realism will have non-cognitivist implications. This discussion of Clack's work also serves to support my larger claim: that Wittgensteinian religion non-realism is subject to the terms of the dilemma by which I have framed these issues and by which this book is organized in that it offers revisionary interpretations of religion.

We begin our analysis of Clack's argument by considering the idea that Wittgenstein's approach to religious language is standardly construed as being expressivist in character. That is, rather than seeing religious language as denoting facts about the world, Wittgenstein is typically seen as interpreting religious language and behavior as expressing attitudes. John Churchill's interpretation is representative of this approach that treats Wittgenstein's religious thought as expressivist and thus, ultimately, as non-cognitivist. Churchill states that, for Wittgenstein, beliefs are "concomitant phenomena" with practices; belief does not give rise to practice.[43] In other words, it is not the case that practices are undertaken on the grounds that they are based on true beliefs. He continues,

> Wittgenstein's response (to Frazer's theory that the religious rituals of preliterate peoples are based on mistaken beliefs) is to assert an expressivist view of ritual. Ritual practitioners are not making *mistakes*, on his view, because they are not acting out of theories. [44]

Not based on theories, ritual activities are *expressions*, and thus seeing them as mistaken (or veridical) is just confused, wrongheaded. Churchill adds, "People do not undertake rituals because of what they think they know about how the world works."[45] D.Z. Phillips also interprets Wittgenstein along what I am calling the standard, non-cognitivist line. Recall that Phillips opposes those who assume "that the dispute between the believer and the unbeliever is over *a matter of fact...*it *makes no sense* to say that God might not exist," since, following this line, God's existence is not a matter of fact.[46]

Having seen some examples of a non-cognitivist interpretation of Wittgenstein, we now have some context so that we can see what it is that Clack is challenging. Clack's argument challenges this standard, non-cognitivist approach. Instead, Clack maintains that Wittgenstein's thoughts on ritual, which I am extending to religion generally, are wrongly categorized as expressivist, non-cognitivist. He writes,

> I will contend that it is unsatisfactory to ascribe such a view (that it was not mistaken beliefs which gave rise to rites but rather 'the need to express something') to Wittgenstein. This will be achieved by uncovering the philosophical roots of the expressivist approach to ritual; such roots as are, it will be shown, so fundamentally at odds with the direction of Wittgenstein's philosophy that his reflections on ritual cannot be straightforwardly expressivist as most commentators insist.[47]

On the matter of whether ritual should be interpreted in an expressivist or instrumentalist manner, Clack offers the following. "Looked upon in this way, the difference between Frazer and Wittgenstein is over whether religious thought is *cognitive* or *non-cognitive* in character..."[48]

Such distinctions, expressive/instrumental and attitude/belief, as we shall see, give rise to the non-cognitive/cognitive distinction of which, according to Clack, the later Wittgenstein will have no part. We will see the development of this idea by considering some examples from the history of these distinctions. According to Clack, R. B. Braithwaite exhibits the notion that religious beliefs are more accurately understood as expressing attitudes, dispositions to act. Here Clack quotes Braithwaite, "'a religious belief is an intention to behave in a certain way (a moral belief)...'"[49] Next Clack cites R. G. Collingwood's interpretation which emphasizes the attitude side of the attitude/belief duality: "Magic used to avert an earthquake or to stop flooding might, by instilling in folk a Job-like acceptance, produce an attitude" whereby such hardships are acceptable.[50] Then we have ritual as expressive-cathartic. Here Clack cites Radcliffe-Brown and Santayana as examples. "Radcliffe-Brown contends that magical and religious rites are 'the regulated symbolic expressions of certain sentiments.'" For Santayana, a religious rite "'will bring about an emotional catharsis', and 'therefore calms the passions in expressing them.'"[51]

We begin to see the problem. Clack argues that expressivist interpretations of religion run counter to Wittgenstein's later work. As Clack puts it,

90

Wittgenstein's relation to the kind of linguistic theories which give birth to the cognitive/non-cognitive distinction is thus quite paradoxical: he is both father-creator and enemy. Consequently, one can use the later work of Wittgenstein in order to criticise those trends in philosophy from which the idea of non-cognitivism springs.[52]

In calling Wittgenstein the "father-creator and enemy" of non-cognitive interpretations of religious language, Clack is referring to the philosophical trends, e.g., logical positivism, which arise from Wittgenstein's earlier, Tractarian doctrines. Such doctrines supposedly stress that expressions of value, including religious language, cannot be said but only shown, and are thus non-propositional in character.[53] And, as Clack is arguing, Wittgenstein's later work indicates that he is the "enemy" of such distinctions. Clack thus poses a crucial question: "Where, then, do the *Remarks on Frazer* stand?" If they belong to the later period (as Clack argues they do), then they should not be interpreted as recommending an expressivist construal of religion. The difficulty is that the *Remarks on Frazer* were written in 1931, right in the middle "(from 1929 until about 1934) which constitutes his 'transitional phase', that period of his writing which, whilst conspicuously unlike the position of the *Tractatus*, had yet to resemble his mature view."[54]

Irrespective of this more or less biographical point, Clack contends that the distinction between cognitive and non-cognitive interpretations of religion is not exhaustive in any case. If it were, this would presume "that 'the descriptive' (i.e., cognitive language) has a general form, and, as we shall now see, this is firmly repudiated by Wittgenstein." For example, Clack writes, "Whereas in the *Tractatus* Wittgenstein had searched for the underlying form of a proposition, in the later work such a form is held to be a philosophical illusion."[55] This point is made by Clack's interpretation of PI #114:

[R]ather than being a 'super-concept', the proposition is a family-resemblance concept, with no essence and no 'general form'. To say 'This is how things stand' is not to express the essence of the proposition, but just to stipulate what we are going to call 'a proposition': 'One thinks that one is tracing the outline of the thing's nature over and over again, and one is merely tracing round the frame through which we look at it'.[56]

Furthermore, like "proposition," "description" is "a family-resemblance concept [that] has no general form."[57] And, as we have already seen, Wittgenstein objects to the possibility of anything like a theory of such notions discussed above, including truth. Here Clack cites one of Wittgenstein's lectures directly: "'it is nonsense to try to find a theory of truth, because we can see that in everyday life we use the word quite clearly and definitely in their different senses (*sic*).'" Clack reminds us: "Instead…of appealing to fixed and unvarying notions, Wittgenstein's suggestion is that whether a sentence is 'true', or 'descriptive', is dependent on the circumstances in which it is uttered."[58]

One element of Clack's argument that the cognitive/non-cognitive distinction does not apply to Wittgenstein's later work is to note the descriptive approach that Wittgenstein takes when interpreting religious language. If such description implies factual content, then Clack has shown the impropriety of applying the expressivist label to Wittgenstein's approach to religion. Clack cites the following passage from *Culture and Value* to support his case. Wittgenstein writes, "Christianity is not a doctrine, not, I mean, a theory about what has happened and will happen to the human soul, but a description of something that actually takes place in human life."[59] Since Wittgenstein refers to Christianity as "a description of something that actually takes place in human life," Clack argues as follows. "It is in such a manner (as described above) that Wittgenstein's philosophy breaks down the neat contrast which is so fundamental to the attributing of an expressivist label to the *Remarks on Frazer*."[60] Moreover, since the belief/attitude distinction cannot be applied to Wittgenstein either, according to Clack, neither can it be used as a way of applying the expressivist (and thus non-cognitivist) label. He writes, "As with the descriptive/non-descriptive distinction, then, the belief/attitude dichotomy can not be the basis for 'Wittgenstein's expressivism.'" And this is the case since there is no essence of description or belief; rather, they are family-resemblance concepts.[61] The upshot is that, according to Clack, the standard move of applying the non-cognitivist label to Wittgenstein's thought on religious language is without solid basis.

Are we to accept Clack's argument? I offer some comments on his recent book, *Wittgenstein, Frazer and Religion*, in which he takes a more comprehensive approach to the same general argument. As we have seen, Clack's argument consists of showing the anti-theoretical bent of Wittgenstein's thought by showing that it does not fit into the usual theories of how religious language must be interpreted. Clack characterizes Wittgenstein's thought as not being susceptible to the following dichotomies: expressive/instrumental, belief/attitude, and I would add realist/anti-realist. As such his ultimate goal is to make a case that Wittgenstein's thought is also wrongly cast as non-cognitive. By commenting on his recent book, my aim is to give a basis for my dispute with Clack's thesis that Wittgenstein's later writings should not be given a non-cognitive interpretation. My dispute with Clack's thesis is that, despite his explicit goal of casting Wittgenstein's later thought as not being susceptible to the cognitive/non-cognitive distinction, the tenacity of Wittgenstein's non-cognitivism concerning religion cannot be suppressed.

Consider the passage just cited that Clack draws from *Culture and Value*. "Christianity is not a doctrine, not, I mean, a theory about what has happened and will happen to the human soul, but a description of something that actually takes place in human life." I do not see how this passage is immune from falling under the expressivist/non-expressivisist dichotomy (and thus, it follows, from the cognitive/non-cognitive dichotomy as well) as Clack contends. Change "a description" to "an expression" above, and I do not see how the meaning of the above passage would change. In saying that "Christianity is not a theory about the human soul, but a description of something that actually takes place in human life," Wittgenstein seems already to be straightforwardly eschewing a theoretical, cognitive understanding of Christianity. If I am right about the implicitly non-cognitive tone of this passage, changing it to "Christianity is an expression of something that actually takes place in human life" does not substantially alter its meaning at all.

Before offering an argument in support of what I think is Wittgenstein's non-cognitivist interpretation of religion, I want to clarify that I am not suggesting that Wittgenstein promotes non-cognitivism. Rather, what I am saying is that a non-cognitivist interpretation of religion is an inescapable result of Wittgenstein's quietism, his shunning of realism, anti-realism, or any philosophical theories. My view that, although Wittgenstein does not promote non-cognitivism, non-cognitivist interpretations result from Wittgensteinian teaching on religion is supported when we consider the options available to us. Given Wittgenstein's reluctance to indicate that religious language is either true or false, how else are we to understand the statement "Christianity is not a theory of what will happen to the human soul."? By Wittgenstein's lights, we certainly seem to be left with the conclusion that it is neither true nor false.

Perhaps we can consider this issue in a more nuanced manner. On the one hand, we have those who promote non-cognitivist interpretations of religion. We saw this in Scott's use of Carnap earlier in this chapter. On the other hand, we have Wittgenstein who does NOT promote a non-cognitivist interpretation of religion. This is in keeping with his generally eschewing of any philosophical theory. There is certainly a difference regarding these two cases with respect to their philosophical "stances." I place "stance" in quotes since Carnap has a stance and Wittgenstein does not. That is, Carnap's stance, according to Scott, would be that religious language is neither true nor false and Wittgenstein's "stance" would be that he has no stance regarding the truth or falsity of religious language. My point is that when interpreting an e claim, e.g., Acts 4:12, Carnap's as it were "stanceful" non-cognitivism and Wittgenstein's "stanceless" non-cognitivism amount to the same. For Carnap, as well as Wittgenstein, Acts 4:12, though not true, is not false either. It seems that Carnap's reaction to Acts 4:12's being neither true nor false would be "so much the worse for Acts 4:12's being a proposition." It seems that Wittgenstein's response would be "so much the worse for non-cognitivism," in that religious language is made to look non-sensical in light of such non-cognitivist theorizing. This difference between Carnap and Wittgenstein, though, does not vitiate the fact that both interpretations amount to being revisionist characterizations of religion. Imagine trying to gain entrance to the Pearly Gates and being posed with the question: "Do you affirm that Acts 4:12 is true?" Carnap's aggressive shrug of the shoulders, indicating his affirmation of a non-cognitivist interpretation of Acts 4:12, and Wittgenstein's quietistic shrug of the shoulders, indicating his refusal to consider religious language in terms of being either true or false, would presumably meet with the same end. That is, if affirming the truth of Acts 4:12 is a requirement for getting through the Pearly Gates, i.e., obtaining the ultimate reward, neither Carnap nor Wittgenstein will be entering.[62]

We see still further the non-cognitivist effect of Wittgenstein's quietism. Clack offers the following as a Wittgensteinian interpretation of language concerning "A creator's purpose": "to view the world as crafted is neither reasoned nor reasonable."[63] First, there is the characterization of purposive as "crafted," perhaps implying a crafter, or similarly, the notion of design might imply a designer. This calls to mind teleological arguments for the existence of God. Such arguments are, of course, theoretical, epistemic, cognitivist undertakings. However, Clack is quick to eschew the notion that a creator's purpose suggests that craftedness implies a cognitivist interpretation. That is, such an understanding of a creator's purpose is not "reasoned." I take this to mean that understanding a creator as having a purpose is not properly thought of as the conclusion of an argument. Such a conclusion would not be "reasonable," either. That is, such a conclusion is not one that makes an appeal to epistemic reasons in some more generic way. As we have seen already, Wittgenstein himself refuses to regard religious language as being true or false. Moreover, even when trying overtly to cast Wittgenstein's teaching as dissolving the cognitive/non-cognitive dichotomy, Clack's interpretation of Wittgenstein has non-cognitivist effects which seem hard to avoid.

Even if I have not succeeded in pointing out the non-cognitive tone of Wittgenstein's later thoughts on religion (despite Clack's argument otherwise) this much is still certain. It is not the case that Wittgenstein's later thoughts on religion should be interpreted as taking a cognitive approach, either. Rather, my point is that Clack has failed to show that Wittgenstein's later philosophy undermines the cognitive/non-cognitive distinction as it pertains to religious language. In addition, even if Clack had persuasively made the case that the non-cognitive label does not apply to Wittgenstein, it would not affect my case. According to the dilemma by which this book is organized, religious irrealism, including Wittgensteinian non-realism, offers revisionary interpretations of religion. As we saw in the overview of religious irrealism, in terms of Hilberg's wager, the revisionary consequences of irrealist interpretations of religions applies to *all* forms of irrealism. This includes Feuerbach's anti-realism and Scott's aggressive non-cognitivism derived from Carnap. This revisionary result also applies to Wittgenstein's quietistic, theory-eschewing interpretation of religion in that Wittgenstein refuses to allow that religious language is true. If only an affirmation of the truth of Acts 4:12 gains one entrance through the Pearly Gates, those who follow a Wittgensteinian interpretation of religion don't get in due to their revisionary interpretation of this Christian *e* claim. A non-revisionary interpretation of Acts 4:12 consists in the following: for "Neither is there salvation in any other: for there is none other name under heaven given among men, whereby we must be saved" to be true, the objective conditions described by *Neither is there salvation in any other: for there is none other name under heaven given among men, whereby we must be saved* must obtain. It is clear that a Wittgensteinian interpretation of Acts 4:12 does not fit this description by virtue of his refusal to allow that religious language is true (or false). As such, Wittgensteinian interpretations of religion are revisionary.

A possibility that Clack does not explore has to do with the idea that Wittgenstein could allow that "I affirm the exclusivist doctrine described in Acts 4:12" is a move in a language-game. However, this has two consequences that seem to be unfavorable for Wittgensteinian interpretations of religious language. First, even if the Wittgensteinian resolutely affirms what I call the salvific formula (only and all those who do or believe *e* get the ultimate reward) as a move in a language-game, the Wittgensteinian is denied realist expectations of the ultimate reward if her manner of affirming an *e* claim is irrealist in nature. Since none of us, including the Wittgensteinian, know whether the ultimate reward exists in a realist sense or whether realist belief is a prerequisite for getting the ultimate reward, if the ultimate reward does exist in a realist sense, then it seems that having realist belief in *e* is the more attractive option. Second, why couldn't the Wittgensteinian allow that "I affirm the correct *e* claim" is a move in a religious language-game? The practice of affirming an *e* claim entails the denial of not-*e*, an anti-realist treatment of religious language that I, among others, have shown that Wittgenstein resists.

Having discussed the work of two recent commentators on Wittgenstein, let's summarize their relevance to this project. The moral to be gleaned from the discussion of the article by Michael Scott is that we need to acknowledge at least three different approaches with regard to the matter of the truth or falsity of religious language. We know that we need at least three in this case since the two approaches countenanced by Scott, what I call realism and anti-realism, do not adequately describe Wittgenstein's response to the matter of God's existence. The moral to be gleaned from the discussion of Brian Clack is that we do not need to acknowledge more than three approaches to the question of God's existence; three will suffice. Clack argues strenuously for the idea that none of the three options I describe 1) realism 2) anti-realism – these are the two cognitivist options – nor non-cognitivism, what I call 3) non-realism, adequately describe Wittgenstein's teachings about God's existence. Clack's efforts fail; i.e., Wittgenstein's interpretation of religion is non-realist. I make this argument, though, with a caveat. While I agree with Clack that Wittgenstein does not promote non-cognitivist interpretations of religious language (as is the case with Scott's Carnap), Wittgenstein's eschewing of religious realism (and religious anti-realism) still amounts to a non-realist and thus, in keeping with the dilemma, revisionary interpretation of religion.

What are we to make of Wittgensteinian interpretations of religious language? We have learned, via our examination of Wittgenstein's remarks regarding God's existence, that Wittgenstein does not accept the comprehensive applicability of the law of the excluded middle; this moral sets the stage for what I have called Wittgenstein's theological non-realism. We have learned, via our examination of Scott's article, that theological non-realism is different from theological anti-realism and that it is a mistake to treat Wittgenstein's thought concerning the interpretation of religious language as being anti-realist in character. We have learned, via our examination of Clack's argument, that even when more appropriately cast as non-realist in character, applying a Wittgensteinian interpretation to religious language still has revisionary consequences. These same revisionary consequences face Carnap's aggressively non-cognitivist interpretation of religious language and Wittgenstein's quietistic non-cognitivist interpretation of religious language. Whatever it is that Wittgenstein might have meant by the remark concerning God's "half-existence," I am confident that we can conclude at least this much, especially given the textual support provided thus far. By appealing to the idea of God's half-existence, Wittgenstein intimates that "God exists" does not admit of truth or falsity, that is, the law of the excluded middle is not applicable to "God exists." Not that the law of the excluded middle is Wittgenstein's criterion for intelligibility,[64] however, I believe that it is safe to conclude this much. We have seen no reason to believe that, by Wittgensteinian lights, a given instance of religious language could be considered to be true in the realist sense required by a non-revisionary interpretation of religion.

What religious and philosophical implications can be drawn from the idea of God's half-existence? The following passage from even the avowed Wittgensteinian D.Z. Phillips shows the practical (ironically, given Wittgenstein's emphasis on looking to practice for the meaning of language) implausibility of such a notion, even if one tries to take it in a light-hearted vein. Phillips writes, "differences between atheism and belief are *real* differences."[65] More precisely, even the Wittgensteinian Phillips seems to acknowledge that the differences between atheism and theism, and perhaps religious realism and non-realism, are, as he indicated, *real* differences and not "*half*"-differences. Wittgensteinian treatments of religious language, and theological language in particular, do seem to have revisionary consequences. This is seen most acutely in the difficulties such treatments have when trying to provide an understanding of exclusivist claims. In the case of *e* claims we seem to have further reason to believe that the difference between religious realism and irrealism is not merely that of a battle cry. I suggest that the revisionary character of Wittgensteinian, non-realist interpretations of religion is what makes the difference between realist and Wittgensteinian interpretations of religion not mere battle cries. That is, if realist beliefs are a requirement for attaining the ultimate reward, the difference between realist and irrealist beliefs does not seem to be merely a battle cry. Stated in terms of the dilemma by which the issues have been framed and by which this book is organized, we face a genuine problem when interpreting religious language. If we try to avoid the problem of interpreting religion in a revisionary manner by having realist belief, as we saw from the first portion of this project, we are left with the philosophical problem of religious diversity. Irrealist interpretations of religion, including Wittgensteinian, non-realist interpretations, are revisionary. Our scenario at the Pearly Gates provides insight as to why revisionary interpretations are problematic. The next chapter, which includes discussions of prominent Wittgensteinian, non-realist interpretations of religion, reinforces the idea that such interpretations are revisionary.

Chapter 7

Religious Non-realism Pushed Beyond Its Limits

As the previous discussion has highlighted, the thought of Wittgenstein as it bears on the interpretation of religious language is enigmatic. The following discussion of the thought of D.Z. Phillips, Norman Malcolm and Peter Winch, examples of prominent critics of religious realism who have been much influenced by Wittgenstein's later philosophy, is an effort to demystify Wittgenstein's later teaching. In the effort to demystify Wittgenstein, it must be acknowledged that there is the risk of misrepresenting his teaching; in other words, by saying that Wittgenstein maintained that such and such was the case, the risk of falling into the philosophical theorizing he admonished us to avoid is present. That said, one must take care not to attribute the thoughts of Wittgenstein's disciples to the teacher himself. Nevertheless it is useful to see how a Wittgensteinian interpretation of religious language plays out when pushed beyond the limits that Wittgenstein himself refused to transgress.[1] This is the main purpose of this chapter. Examining this topic will sharpen the understanding of Wittgenstein's later thought and will help show that non-realist interpretations of religion are revisionary. The subsequent discussion will accomplish this task by clarifying what Wittgenstein's teachings regarding religion do *not* entail.

We see an example of this in the works of D.Z. Phillips. Whereas Wittgenstein's thought resists theoretical pronouncements, Phillips's thought goes further and as such can be more accurately described by the labels that we tend to give to philosophical theories. For example, whereas in the preceding chapter it was argued that it is a mistake to cast Wittgenstein's thought as relativist in character, it can be seen that Phillips's writings are more accurately described by that particular label. The more explicitly relativist character of Phillips's thought is of much significance for the topic of this book; it has the consequence of rendering Phillips's interpretation of religious language outrightly revisionary due its inability to countenance what seem to be the inherently absolute truth claims involved in religious expressions of *e* claims.

One of the ways in which Phillips exhibits the Wittgensteinian character of his thought can be seen in his emphasis on the idea that religious belief gets its sense in practice and thus is misunderstood when considered in terms other than those of the practices in which such belief occurs. For example, for Phillips, assessing religious beliefs by the standards of scientific reasoning is a misguided undertaking.[2] To say that religious belief does not conform to scientific standards of rationality would thus not, in Phillips's view, bear negatively on religious belief; indeed, doing so would simply be misguided. Religious beliefs get their sense from the practice in which they occur; scientific beliefs get their sense from the practice in which they occur. Assessing one kind of belief in terms of another just invites confusion. Of course, Phillips is not alone in asserting the impropriety of judging religion in terms of science. One need not be a critic of theological realism to oppose evaluating religious belief in terms of scientific rationality.[3] Still, this example is illustrative in that it shows one of the typical ways in which religious belief has been assessed historically. The more the advancements of science have been able to explain, the more science encroaches on what has historically been within the domain of religion. Phillips, true to Wittgensteinian form, holds that viewing such as "encroachments" is a misunderstanding, since, according to him, the fruits of scientific life have no bearing on, and therefore cannot encroach on, religious life.

Assessing religion in terms of science is mistaken, according to Phillips, not only because doing so involves understanding one language-game in terms of another, but also because scientific interpretations of religion are reductive. An aspect of Phillips's opposition to religious realism is found in what he considers to be its reductive tendencies. As a critic, one of the problems Phillips has with religious realism is that by "reducing," as he puts it, religious belief to a mental state, "realism cannot take seriously the central religious conviction that God is at work in people's lives."[4] Phillips addresses this matter in some detail; his criticism gives rise to two issues. First, Phillips accuses religious realists of reducing belief to a mental state. Second, since, according to Phillips, they overlook the ways in which religious belief is "at work in people's lives," he claims that religious realists discount the role practice plays in the lives of religious believers. The first charge derives from Phillips's contention that, for the religious realist, belief is logically prior to practice: we act in certain ways because we hold certain religious beliefs, on Phillips's account of realism. Since logical priority is given to belief the realist, according to Phillips, "reduces" religious belief to a mental state. The second charge arises from the realist requirement that a belief must be distinct from what the belief is about. While Phillips is right about this observation, he is mistaken concerning its significance. For example, with regard to religious realism, it would indeed be correct to observe that the presence of socially well-established religious practices does not suffice for verifying that the conditions described by an *e* claim actually obtain. Only that the conditions described by a particular *e* claim, e.g., Acts 4:12, would verify Acts 4:12 by realist standards.

Since each of these charges stem from Phillips's view that beliefs get their sense only from the practice in which they occur, a single realist response can address these matters. To begin, there is no reason why one could not have "religious conviction," to use Phillips's terminology, in the sense of commitedly living a life devoted to religious practice, *and* have realist belief. It is hardly clear why believing in God in a realist way would inhibit one from passionately committing oneself to living a religious life. Just because the realist maintains that the truth of, e.g., "God exists" is contingent upon whether it is the case that God exists, it does not follow that religious practice is omitted from the realist conception of religious life. Indeed, it is entirely possible that the religious realist and her detractor could live identical lives in the sense that they each conduct the same religious practices. The difference would be that that for the realist, the truth of "God exists" still depends on whether it is the case that God exists. Phillips's point seems to be that such an attitude is irreligious: the genuinely faithful do not question God's existence. The realist need not be committed to that; she is not doubting God's existence. She is merely holding that the truth of "God exists" is verified only if God exists. None of this changes the fact that she can live her life in a very religiously committed way while maintaining her realist sensibilities concerning God's existence. Thus, Phillips's contention that religious realism discounts religious conviction and the role of religious practice seems to be without basis. Related to this concept is the idea that, according to Phillips, religious realism reduces belief to a mental state and thus diminishes the role of faith and practice in religious life, is his charge that the realist cannot connect belief to its object. Phillips writes, "what is involved in believing something to be true? The realist can give no intelligible answer to this question."[5] Even if we take Phillips's claim at face value, the realist can address this question. The realist need only point out that there is no incompatibility between living a committed religious life, which is what Phillips advocates, and, in addition to living one's life in such a way, having realist beliefs about, e.g., God.

So even at face value, Phillips's claim about the unintelligibility of the realist's version of what it would mean to hold a religious belief falls short. However, this surface shortcoming in Phillips still does not address the concern religious realists want to raise, namely that even if the they were unable to give an intelligible account of what believing x consists in, this is irrelevant to the realist's concern: *whether x is true.* Phillips's charge that it "is the realist who severs belief from its object"[6] misconstrues the realist concern about religious belief. Whether belief can be connected to its object is not the issue. The religious realist is concerned whether x is the case independent of our experience of x. This realist concern does not imply that, as Phillips must take it, there can be NO relation between a belief and its object. For religious realism, the concern is that the conditions described by a given instance of religious language actually obtain independent of what we do, say or believe. The concern is not what the relation between belief and object consists in. In charging religious realism with the inability to offer an account for how a belief relates to its object, Phillips misses this particular point.[7]

A further indication that the case Phillips makes against religious realism is made of straw is seen in the following description of finding God. Indeed, these are words that a religious realist would utter. Phillips, reporting on his own sensibilities, writes, "To find God is to enter into some kind of affective relationship with the divine."[8] To this it must be asked: What does it mean to enter into a "relationship with the divine" if the divine does not exist independently of what we do, say or believe (that is, in a realist sense)? Put in terms of more ordinary language, we might say entering into a relationship with the divine makes sense only if God really exists. There is nothing in Wittgenstein's writings to indicate that he would oppose this idea as stated; in other words, there is nothing in Wittgenstein's teachings that would debar a religious person from believing that God really exists. Indeed, there are passages that suggest that Wittgenstein would support it. For example, Wittgenstein writes, "It strikes me that a religious belief could only be something like a passionate commitment to a system of reference. Hence, although it's a *belief*, it's really a way of living, or a way of assessing life. It's passionately seizing hold of *this* interpretation."[9] While this passage is indicative of Wittgenstein's penchant for avoiding any sort of metaphysical pronouncement whether it be realist or anti-realist, it certainly expresses no indifference to the matter of whether it is the case that God exists. If anything, this passage reflects an acknowledgment on Wittgenstein's part that one of the moves to be made within the religious language-game will be to commit to a system of reference. Within the context of a theistic language-game, God would certainly be one of the referents. What this shows is not that a metaphysical commitment is to be attributed to Wittgenstein but rather that Phillips goes too far in his rejection of religious realism. To deny that "God exists" has objective truth conditions is akin to the metaphysical commitment associated with religious *anti*-realism. Insofar as Phillips makes this denial he is no longer in keeping with the quietism associated with Wittgenstein's *non*-realism.

It is Phillips, not Wittgenstein, who expresses indifference with regard to assessing the truthfulness of belief in God's existence. We begin to see this when Phillips writes, "An inferred God is no more satisfactory than an inferred world or inferred friends, but it is the result of being at the mercy of the methods of evidentialism."[10] The comment about "an inferred God" is in reference, inter alia, to the theological realist concern that if God's objective existence is intelligible, then we must have some reasons (e.g., "inferences") that we can cite for thinking of God's existence objectively. Phillips offers a supposed corrective to this way of thinking by indicating that being concerned with God's objective existence is no better than being concerned with a friend's objective existence. In either case, it seems that for Phillips what is important is our relationship with God or a friend. Good enough, but that is not the point. Religious realism allows that the believer's relationship with God is important; indeed, it holds that a relationship with God is possible only if God exists in a realist sense. Phillips's treatment of this issue gets off track in the following way. From 1): mere inference is an unsatisfactory basis for a relationship, it does not follow that 2): a basis for knowing that that to which we relate exists is undesirable/unimportant.

Whether one has realist inclinations about God's existence or not, this just seems plainly true. That is, whether one is an irrealist or realist about "my friend exists," this (one's ir/realist inclinations) would have no bearing on whether one would accept the idea that, e.g., trust, is an important basis for friendship. Trust, by its very nature, cannot be entirely based on "inference" (to use Phillips's terminology). If we invite a friend to lunch, we trust that our friend will not miss the lunch date without a legitimate reason. However, one of the conditions of our friend showing up for lunch *is that our friend exists.* The italicized portion is what Phillips dismisses as putting our relationship with our friend "at the mercy of method." The method in this case, analogizing it to God, would be the realist approach to assessing the truth of "God exists." Adopting a realist conception of truth here: "God exists" is true if and only if it is the case that God exists. One could grant Phillips that having a relationship with God is of the utmost importance. However, it also seems plainly obvious that one of the conditions of having a relationship with God is that it is the case that God exists. Phillips discounts the importance of this condition when he dismisses it as putting God at the mercy of method.

One of the realist concerns regarding a Wittgensteinian interpretation of religion is that it entails relativist conclusions concerning truth claims. We can recall the concern expressed earlier by Patrick Sherry that a language-game approach results in a Protagorean relativism. At this point, it is necessary to explore the matter of whether it is necessary to make a metaphysical commitment to dispel relativist interpretations of seemingly absolute claims such as *e* claims. That is, it seems that one of the issues facing Phillips would be to offer an interpretation of *e* claims that acknowledges the religious significance of their seemingly absolute claim while remaining true to his Wittgensteinian aversion to metaphysics. When we consider some passages from Phillips below, it is apparent that his way of dealing with this tension is to offer solutions that suggest a relativist interpretation. It seems that one can interpret *e* claims in such a way that maintains their absolute character without making a metaphysical commitment. That is, one need *not* resort to Phillips's apparent relativism in order to avoid making metaphysical pronouncements. In fact, as was argued earlier, it seems that relativism itself entails a metaphysical commitment.

Phillips suggests that "treating 'God' as a substantive" involves importing "an alien grammar into our language concerning God."[11] Why is this? It seems that here Phillips is insulating religious language-games, that is, making language about God relative to its own standards. If one "grammar" can be alien to another "grammar," it is hard to see how a relativist conclusion can be avoided. A condition of one language-game being alien to another is that a language-game has its own distinctive characteristics by virtue of which the grammars of other language-games would be seen as alien. That a grammar could be alien implies that judgments made according to it could be inappropriate when made of the practices of another language-game. That a language-game could be immune from judgment from another language-game by simply dismissing them as alien does indeed seem subject to the concerns about relativism expressed by Sherry in the preceding chapter. According to the grammar of the, as it were, "alternate arithmetic language-game," acting on the basis of "2+2=5" could be a legitimate move. This notion of grammars being alien to each other seems to run afoul of Wittgenstein's teachings on at least two counts. First, the "alternate arithmetic language-game," in which "2+2=5," contradicts our everyday practices, in which we see the fruits of 2 and 2 making 4 in perfectly ordinary ways. Second, the idea of an alien grammar implies the presence of a home grammar.

The idea of a home grammar, a privileged context which is the arbiter of which claims are true or false, meaningful or not meaningful, implies the metaphysical notions of which Wittgenstein was wary. By invoking this idea of "alien grammars," and by implication "home grammars," Phillips seems to be operating as though Wittgenstein has offered, as it were, a "theory of language-games." It is as though Phillips suggests that the way to settle philosophical questions is to turn to Wittgenstein's, as it were, "theory of language-games" by making sure to stay attuned to "home" instead of "alien" grammars. Wittgenstein, of course, eschews all efforts at trying to settle philosophical questions. It follows, then, that, according to Wittgenstein, it is mistaken to try to settle such questions by referring to a "home grammar." This error made by Phillips can lead to the mistaken conclusion that Wittgensteinian language-games breed relativism. That is, if we allow that there is a home grammar by which we can adjudicate the truth or falsity of the claims made within that language-game, we are left with the idea that truth-claims are relativized to that language-game. Such relativism, though suggested by Phillips's work, will not find textual support in the works of Wittgenstein.

Extending Phillips's logic to our concern about *e* claims, in maintaining that *e* claims are absolutely true across the many religious language-games of the world, what alien grammar has been imported? If, for example, Acts 4:12 were to be applied to, say, Buddhism, it could be said that an alien, Christian grammar is being applied to Buddhism. The point is that the absoluteness expressed within Acts 4:12 is an essential feature of Acts 4:12. To deny this about Acts 4:12, by challenging the legitimacy of applying it to Buddhists, seems to be a revisionary way of interpreting Christianity.

By implying that the application of Acts 4:12 to Buddhists would involve the importation of an alien grammar, the charge of revisionism seems to fit Phillips. The core issue here concerns Phillips's insulating religious language-games from external assessments. Why can't religious claims be evaluated on terms other than their own? A putative messiah who predicts the end of the world has made an historical *and* religious claim. It would certainly be compatible with Wittgensteinian sensibilities to maintain that various language-games are inter-connected in an irreducible plurality such that isolating the claims of one language-game from those of another would be entirely artificial. For example, how would one go about distinguishing historical language-games from religious language-games? Religion and history are inextricably inter-connected and to maintain that religious language-games are utterly distinct ("alien") from historical language-games is artificial. One cannot understand, say, the spread of emergent Islam, a putatively religious phenomenon, without also understanding its historical significance. The spread of Islam changed the economic and political face of the Arabian peninsula (among other places). That Muhammad was both a spiritual and temporal leader illustrates that these factors cannot be understood apart from each other.

When speaking of religious language-games we obviously must be cognizant of their diverse characters. When Phillips writes, "it is only in the context of [religious] language-games that belief in God has any meaning,"[12] we must ask how the sensibility expressed here applies to attitudes within different religions toward e claims? Does a Christian assertion of an e claim apply to a Buddhist (or vice versa)? Is meaningful talk of Christ restricted to practitioners of the Christian language-game? If so, how does a non-Christian even recognize talk of Christ as religious? Perhaps there are paradigmatic uses of religious language (e.g., language about that which is ultimate) and thus we can recognize particular instances of religious language as having this ultimate character. However, at this point Phillips asks, "Why should we think…that different uses of language are all variations of one paradigmatic use?" He continues, "Religious uses of language are often distinctive and will be misunderstood if this distinctive character is not recognized."[13] Taken on their own, these two thoughts from Phillips seem reasonable enough, however, taken together, they seem to reflect a tension within Phillips's thought. Phillips seems correct in suggesting that Acts 4:12 will be misunderstood if its distinctive Christian character is overlooked. However when Acts 4:12 is considered from a non-Christian, e.g., Jewish, perspective, Acts 4:12, it would seem, can only be understood as either 1) irrelevant because it is non-sensical, non-religious, non-applicable within a Jewish context, what have you, or 2) as indeed an instance of religious language but a false one.

If we take Acts 4:12 as an instance of Christ speaking as God, we can apply the following passage from Phillips to the issue being raised. "The possibility of the unreality of God does not occur within any religion, but it might well arise in disputes between religions."[14] With this statement, Phillips could be read as allowing the exclusivity of Acts 4:12 (as an instance of an *e* claim); indeed, with what follows it seems that Phillips would hold that an exclusivist reading of Acts 4:12 or any *e* claim would be the only intelligible reading. He continues, "It follows from my argument that the criteria of meaningfulness cannot be found outside religion, since they are given by religious discourse itself."[15] Given Phillips's emphasis that particular beliefs make sense only within the context of the practice in which they occur, it seems that the proper way to interpret the above, as to the matter of *e* claims, would be that the criteria of meaningfulness of a given *e* claim cannot be found outside of its particular context. The following passages from Phillips support this interpretation.

On the topic of theology and/as grammar he writes, "theology is the grammar of religious discourse." That is, "theology decides what it makes sense to say to God and about God."[16] It should be made clear that Phillips does not mean theology in a typical sense, say, as the deliverances of reason as they bear on matters of religious doctrine. He makes it clear that he means something quite apart from that. Contrasting the thought of, e.g., Thomas Aquinas, with that of Phillips on theological doctrine concerning the existence of God will illustrate this point. Whereas one of Aquinas's contributions to Christian theology was the Five Ways, arguments meant to provide rigorous intellectual support for belief in the existence of God, Phillips's sense of theology is that it describes what it makes sense to say about God (e.g., assenting to "God exists" is what one does when participating in the Christian language-game). Thus, for Phillips, grammar is the arbiter of sense within a given language-game and theology is the grammar of a theistic (e.g., Christian) language-game.

When speaking of grammar in a Wittgensteinian context, it is important to bear in mind that it is not the case that all aspects of language-games are dictated by grammatical rules. That is, whereas grammar is the arbiter of sense within a given language-game, it is not the case that grammar rules in some totalizing sense. Consider the analogy Wittgenstein offered regarding the game of tennis.[17] Clearly, tennis is a well-ordered game with rules describing and prescribing its orderly proceedings. However, there is no rule dictating how high one can toss the ball when serving. This does not bear unfavorably on the fact that tennis is an orderly game. While it is certainly the case that rules do not cover every eventuality within the game of tennis, the rules of tennis still hold within the game of tennis and hold within the game of tennis only. Similarly, within language-games, though the criteria for meaningfulness are provided by grammar, grammar might not provide rules for every eventuality within a particular language-game; however, this does not change the fact that within a particular language-game, the rules for what makes sense within that language-game are what we mean by grammar in a Wittgensteinian context. By noting that grammatical rules hold only within the particular language-game in which they occur, one might be tempted to ask whether the Wittgensteinian notion of grammar bespeaks a relativist tendency within Wittgensteinian thought. Is relativism the proper term to describe the phenomenon whereby the rules of tennis hold within the game of tennis? It does not seem so; even though they might not be exhaustive, they certainly hold absolutely over all cases which they can adjudicate and are irrelevant outside of the game of tennis.

The above is still another example of the reservations one should have concerning casting Wittgenstein as a relativist. That said, it still seems that Phillips is indeed a relativist about e claims in that his thought does not countenance the religious significance of e claims. This can be seen in the following analogy. For Phillips, theology is to religious language as logic is to language generally. Furthermore, for Phillips, "logical principles can have no meaning apart from the language in which they are found."[18] We should be able to conclude from his analogy that theological principles can have no meaning apart from the language in which they are found. So if Acts 4:12 is an example of a theological principle, what consequences can be drawn from the contention that it has no meaning apart from a Christian language-game? That Acts 4:12 "can have no meaning" to the, e.g., Buddhist, is not the issue. What matters within religious life is whether only and all those who uphold the correct e claim get the ultimate reward. If, e.g., Acts 4:12, is true the, e.g., Buddhist, isn't concerned with her inability to derive meaning from Acts 4:12; the Buddhist, one would think, would be concerned with whether she still would receive the ultimate reward in the absence of her not having upheld the correct e claim!

One of the issues Phillips would raise concerning my formulation of e claims would involve the matter of how one would go about assessing the truth of the articulation of an e claim in one religion over against such an articulation in another religion. It might seem that one would need to postulate an adjudicatory meta-language whereby one could make such assessments.[19] Such a scenario entails the notion that each articulation of an e claim makes a truth claim and insofar as these claims conflict, at most one could be correct. In this respect, then, differing articulations of e claims entail factual information, that is, in the case of Acts 4:12, the world is so constituted such that only adherents of Acts 4:12 will gain the ultimate reward. Thus, we would have those who assent and those who do not assent with regard to a particular instance of an *e* claim. However, considering this matter in broader terms, Phillips opposes those who assume "that the dispute between the believer and the unbeliever is over a matter of fact." This is the case, according to Phillips, since "it makes no sense to say that God might not exist" since God's existence is not a matter of fact. After all, what "is to count in deciding whether something is a fact or not is agreed upon in most cases."[20] Perhaps Phillips is right: it makes no sense to postulate a meta-language whereby we could agree about the meaning of "God exists," or more specific to our issue, about the meaning of a particular instance of an *e* claim, across religious traditions. However, it seems that in principle it is possible to adjudicate whether an *e* claim is *true*: an *e* claim is true if its believers and/or practitioners gain the ultimate reward. In other words, if, for example, the Christian articulation of an *e* claim (e.g., Acts 4:12) is true in a realist sense, those who are not adherents of Christian articulations of *e* claims are denied realist expectations of a Christian ultimate reward.

To what in this scenario described above might Phillips object? Perhaps he would object that, with regard to my contention that any and all religions insofar as they have exclusivist tendencies contain some version of an *e* claim, the "sameness of the language does not consist of anything like the formality of a system."[21] The point to be made is that the religious significance of *e* claims is not their intelligibility across religious contexts but is rather the prospect of their being true. In response to this, Phillips might ask dismissively, intending to show the meaninglessness of the idea that there could be a meta-language by which conflicting truth claims from different language-games might be adjudicated: From what language-game would such an undertaking (assessing the truth of conflicting *e* claims) proceed? In response to my charge that such a move on his part insulates religious language from interaction and assessment from without, Phillips might respond, again indicating the impossibility of an adjudicatory meta-language, that "it is only in practice…that concepts have their life and meaning."[22] It should be clear by now that religious realists have no qualms per se regarding the issues raised in the question attributed to Phillips above. Alston, for one, acknowledges the significance of practice in determining the rational justifiability of (religious) beliefs. However, in doing so, he also acknowledges that the religious significance of, e.g., an *e* claim, is to be found in its claim to truth, not meaningfulness. We could, in principle, assess the truth of an *e* claim described above. For example, if it is the case that only the adherents of Acts 4:12 gain the ultimate reward then we may justifiably infer that only Acts 4:12 is true among competing *e* claims. It is not at all clear that I have invoked an adjudicatory meta-language; moreover, if I have not invoked an adjudicatory meta-language, it follows that I am not committed to the meaninglessness Wittgensteinians associate with such a meta-language. It seems that the claim entailed in, e.g., Acts 4:12, is either true as per the realist account, false as per the anti-realist account, or neither true nor false (e.g., not making a prediction about some future event) as per the non-realist account. To offer a prescriptive answer regarding which of these three accounts is correct *would* require an adjudicatory meta-language. That is not what I am doing. My point is not that a particular *e* claim *is* true; rather, my point is that it is conceivable that an *e* claim *could be* true. Furthermore, if it is true, those who are not adherents of that particular *e* claim should not expect the ultimate reward. This is what the religious significance of an *e* claim consists in. Such a conclusion does not invoke an adjudicatory meta-language.

If, as Phillips would have it, there is no meta-language against which claims can be checked with regard to their (absolute) truth or falsity, it would seem that the putatively absolute truth claims which occur within religious language are then somehow deflated or relativized with regard to whatever their sphere of applicability might be. For example, following this line, Christian truth claims are true for Christians and Buddhist truth claims are true for Buddhists, and so on. However, this seems to be a reductive (and thus revisionist) account of religious belief. It would be odd to maintain that, e.g., Acts 4:12, is true for Christians only. To wit, Christian exclusivists will maintain that the Christian version of the ultimate reward is the *only* version of the ultimate reward thus making adherence to Christian *e* claims the *only* means by which this reward can be attained. It is easy to see why, then, some would view the relativist character of Phillips's thought as reductive and revisionary.

At this point it is useful to note that the discussion above uncovers a possible source of the confusion within the literature dealing with religious realism and religious irrealism. A prevailing tone among critics of Wittgensteinian interpretations of religion is that the supposedly relativist character of such interpretations does violence to the seemingly absolute nature of religious doctrine. As I argued in the preceding chapter, though, it is mistaken to construe Wittgenstein's work as promoting relativism. However, as we have just seen, there *is* reason to regard the Wittgensteinian Phillips's work as promoting relativist interpretations of religion. This subtlety within Wittgensteinian interpretations of religion has gone too long overlooked.

Though Phillips does not acknowledge this relativist thread in his thought, he does acknowledge concerns about reductionist, and thus revisionary, interpretations of religion. His acknowledgment of this concern makes the tenaciously revisionist character of his work all the more noteworthy. That Phillips's interpretation of religion is revisionary is significant to the overall argument of this book, to recall, in that the horn of the dilemma facing religious irrealists such as Phillips is that their interpretations of religion are revisionary.

Phillips grants that religious irrealism is reductionist and cites reductionism as the root of religious realists' fears. More specifically, theological realists fear that irrealist accounts of God's existence render God's existence as being dependent on human experience. For example, for Feuerbach, God is entirely a human construction or projection. In this extreme case of theological anti-realism, God's existence is completely dependent on and reduced to human experience. This dependence changes in degree with less extreme cases of irrealism.

With regard to theological realism, the reductionism issue centers on the question: Is it the case that God exists? Using Feuerbach again as our example of a reductionist account, the answer to this question would be: "No, all that really exists would be the human ideals Love, Will, and Reason." Thus in this account "God" is "reduced" to human experience. Another way to address this question concerning reductionism is to take an entirely emic approach, which, as we see, is the approach Phillips recommends.

We see Phillips's emic tendencies in the following passage: "for a psychoanalytic analysis to be the correct analysis, the person undergoing the analysis must assent to it."[23] That is, an emic approach maintains that the correct interpretation of a particular phenomenon is one with which the person being interpreted would agree. For example, if one were to offer a Feuerbachian interpretation of theistic belief (that belief in God really amounts to affirming the human ideals of Love, Will, and Reason), by the emicist's lights, such an interpretation would be correct only if the theist whose belief is being interpreted agrees to it.

Why should we accept this emicist account of what counts for a valid interpretation? Can I not be mistaken about my own understanding of something? Surely Phillips would allow that there is a difference between my being correct about something and thinking that I am correct about it. This, after all, is the moral of PI #202:

> And hence also 'obeying a rule' is a practice. And to *think* one is obeying a rule is not to obey a rule. Hence it is not possible to obey a rule 'privately': otherwise thinking one was obeying a rule would be the same thing as obeying it.[24]

From this passage we see that Wittgenstein allows that one can be mistaken about one's own understanding of something. So the emicist standard that, e.g., the theist must agree with the interpretation of her theism for that interpretation to be correct, will not find support in the writings of Wittgenstein himself.

Here we see another example of Phillips insulating a social institution, e.g., religion, from any non-religious assessment. "Durkheim said, rightly, that a psychological explanation of a social institution is invariably the wrong one."[25] This proscription is indicative of Phillips's relativist and insulating treatment of (religious) language-games. Using the example above, why can't a partial (e.g., psychological) explanation of a social institution still be correct to the degree that it explains a part of that particular social institution? That Phillips disallows such an obvious scenario bespeaks the insular view he has of language-games. In this case, it would be the language-game of a social institution. The applicability of this point to religious language-games is obvious. According to Phillips, religious language-games can be understood in their own terms, period. Such relativism concerning religious language-games is revisionary in that it is obviously at odds with religious conceptions of the absoluteness of e claims.

Discussing these disparities between the thought of Wittgenstein himself and that of those who purport to offer Wittgensteinian interpretations of religion is useful in that, as mentioned above, by doing so we can reveal some of the sources of confusion in the literature. Additionally, comparing Wittgenstein's thought to that of those who purport to offer Wittgensteinian interpretations of religion can help to sharpen our understanding of what can accurately be attributed to Wittgenstein. Moreover, analysis of these purveyors of Wittgensteinian interpretations of religion will reinforce further the claim that irrealist interpretations of religion are revisionary.

Moving from Phillips's thought as it bears on our topic, we will find that Norman Malcolm's relevant work faces similar issues though in a more subtle form. Accordingly, addressing this subtlety will further sharpen our understanding of Wittgensteinian interpretations of religion. According to Malcolm, "there are four analogies between Wittgenstein's conception of the grammar of language, and his view of what is paramount in a religious life." These analogies, according to Malcolm, are: first, "in both there is an end to explanation"; second, "in both there is an inclination to be amazed at the existence of something"; third, "into both there enters the notion of an 'illness'"; fourth, "in both, doing, acting, takes priority over intellectual understanding and reasoning."[26]

The following discussion of Malcolm's interpretation of Wittgenstein's thought as it pertains to religion will be an assessment of these four analogies, critically evaluating their aptness in capturing a Wittgensteinian interpretation of religion. Throughout the course of this discussion, the following themes: emphases on practice over doctrine, religious feeling over belief, and faith over having intellectual grounds for belief, will reveal themselves in Malcolm's Wittgensteinian interpretation of religion. This analysis will reveal the revisionary character of such an interpretation.

Fundamental to Malcolm's interpretation of Wittgenstein on religion is the idea that religious life is analogous to a language-game. Though the following is about the story of Job, we can still draw from this passage the general point that religious life is analogous to a language-game.

> The significance of this ancient biblical drama (Job), as I understand it, is that it displays something of the sense of the *concept* of God – or rather, of *a* concept of God…[T]here is an analogy between this conception of God, and Wittgenstein's view of the human 'language-games' and 'forms of life.'[27]

From this it follows that, according to Malcolm's Wittgensteinian interpretation of religion, aspects of religious life (e.g., a concern for the meaning of life, how to live one's life, humility), having a particular conception of God or having an understanding of that which is holy or religious generally (i.e., those ideas expressed in the story of Job), are analogous to a language-game.

What is it that Malcolm has in mind when he invokes Wittgenstein's conception of language-games? As Malcolm sees it, possibly the most important feature of language-games is that they contain the rationale we seek for the practices we undertake. While seeking comprehensive explanations might be something of which Wittgenstein is wary, this idea needs to be refined. Malcolm attempts to do so in the following:

> Wittgenstein's emphasized theme – that reasons, justifications, explanations come to an end – does not mean that there are no reasons, justifications, explanations, for anything. For these concepts do have a place with the boundaries of many of our language-games. Nor does it mean that we do not have the time or energy to go on giving reasons and explanations. What it means is that these come to an end *somewhere*. Where is that? It is at *the existence* of the language-games and the associated form of life. There is where explanation has reached its limit. There reasons stop.[28]

Explanations are fine. What we need to acknowledge, according to this understanding of Wittgenstein, is that explanations are always contextual; they make sense only within the appropriate language-game.

Why, according to Malcolm, can religious life and Wittgenstein's conception of philosophy be seen analogously? The first analogy Malcolm sees is that "in both there is an end to explanation."[29] As we will see later in Winch's discussion of Malcolm and Wittgenstein, wrong-headed accounts of language, and religious language specifically, tend to "ask too many questions." At some point questions must stop and we must just accept that this (a given human endeavor) is what we do. In religious life such acceptance takes the form that the certainty associated with religion is better described as being visceral as opposed to intellectual. The certainty by which people live religious lives is not founded on intellectual proof. It is a felt commitment, not the product of ratiocination. For example, according to Malcolm's Wittgensteinian interpretation, faith is non-rational. Malcolm writes, "Many…people would have no understanding of what it would *mean* to provide a 'rational justification' for their religious belief – nor do they feel a need for it. Many would regard their faith as itself an undeserved *gift* from God."[30] There is no explanation for an undeserved gift; if the gift were deserved, its explanation would consist in the nature of the desert. Even if we could imagine that some form of explanation is appropriate, explanation comes to an end within the context of religious life itself.

Similar to religious language-games, for language-games generally, once we reach a certain point we do not seek further explanations. For example, it would be odd for someone familiar with the English language and its use to ask, "Why do we call that a chair?" The answer, plausibly (unless this occurs in a course on etymology, perhaps), would be that "this is just what we do." Analogously, in religious language-games, it would seem odd for someone familiar with the appropriate religious idiom to ask, "What is faith?" On Malcolm's Wittgensteinian view, a reply to such a question might plausibly be: "We regard faith as an undeserved gift." This reply, not an explanation, reflects an acknowledgment that explanation goes only so far; that is, there is an end to explanation.

The next analogy Malcolm sees between Wittgensteinian conceptions of language-games and religious life is that "in both there is an inclination to be amazed at the existence of something."[31] In this case, the analogy is less apparent. With regard to Wittgenstein's view of language-games, perhaps Malcolm has in mind that one might be amazed that we have organically formed linguistic communities. With regard to religious life, one is amazed at the meaningfulness of life itself. As such, religious life, understood along Wittgensteinian lines, involves a commitment to the meaningfulness of life. Malcolm draws textual support for this point from the *Tractatus* Notebooks, in which Wittgenstein indicates that "to pray is to think about the meaning of life" and "to believe in God means to see that life has a meaning."[32]

In a more apparent analogy, Malcolm sees a similarity between Wittgenstein's conceptions of religious life and of philosophy since "into both there enters the notion of an 'illness.'"[33] That is, according to Malcolm's interpretation of Wittgenstein, religion and philosophy both serve as therapy for illness. For Wittgenstein's language-game approach to philosophy, the illness to be treated consists of our tendencies to impose metaphysical confusions on ourselves, e.g., "in order for x to be true, y must be the case." Wittgenstein's approach to philosophy recommends that we look at x first. Philosophical therapy involves disentangling ourselves from the following kinds of notions: having the requirements imposed by y obscure our view of x.

With regard to the idea of religion as therapy, as can be seen in the following, a Wittgensteinian interpretation includes the idea that religion is a treatment for illness as well. Malcolm writes, "There is a kind of moral and spiritual illness that possesses us, even when we think we are healthy. That is how a genuinely religious person thinks and feels about *himself*."[34] Wittgenstein himself puts it: "People are religious in the degree that they believe themselves to be not so much *imperfect*, as *ill*."[35] Religion, on this view, consists in doing certain things and having certain attitudes regarding the way one conducts one's life. When healing is what one seeks, orthodoxy is not the answer. When healing is what one needs, one does not seek the right beliefs; rather, one seeks treatment, therapy. Religion so conceived would consist in conducting and orienting oneself in ways that, as it were, treat the illness. For example, if one found herself with the feeling that life is devoid of meaning, the treatment for such an "illness" would be to situate herself in a context that conduces to encounters with meaningfulness. Religion, by Wittgensteinian lights, is such a context. At least one will be inclined more so to living her life in a way that is regarded as meaningful. We see this emphasis on practice (over orthodoxy) in the next and final analogy Malcolm sees between Wittgenstein's conceptions of religion and philosophy.

In "both, doing, acting, takes priority over intellectual understanding and reasoning."[36] A possible reflection of this priority is seen in the fact that Malcolm regards ethics as a necessary condition of a Wittgensteinian understanding of religious life. However, this must be ethics construed in a certain way since ethics is typically treated as a subdiscipline of philosophy traditionally conceived, that is, inter alia, a rational exercise. Seen in this way, the notion of prioritizing ethics over intellectual endeavors seems somewhat odd. Perhaps this can be reconciled by emphasizing the idea that ethics is an element of *practical* reason. Be that as it may, considering ethics as an instance of prioritizing action over intellection should be done advisedly since ethics inherently involves acting according to an understanding of right/wrong, good/bad. Typically, this is considered an intellectual undertaking.

The foregoing discussion is necessary since one of the issues raised by Malcolm concerns whether Wittgenstein reduces religion to ethics. Regardless of whether he reduces religion to ethics, one of the chief points expressed in Wittgenstein's "Lecture on Ethics" is the idea that he sees important similarities between ethics and religion. In the "Lecture on Ethics," Wittgenstein discusses the affinities he sees between religion and ethics; additionally, he makes his view on the non-cognitive character of ethical language apparent. He writes, "What [ethics] says does not add to our knowledge in any sense. But it is a document of a tendency in the human mind which I personally cannot help respecting deeply and I would not for my life ridicule it."[37] If we understand ethics in this non-cognitive sense, we can see why Malcolm would consider Wittgenstein's emphasis on ethics as constituting an instance of doing and acting as taking priority over intellectual understanding. Thus, it can be seen how Malcolm might posit an analogy between Wittgenstein's understanding of religion and philosophy.

Whether or not Wittgenstein reduces religion to ethics, Malcolm cites an instance where Wittgenstein makes it clear that ethics is central to his conception of religious life; it also seems clear that, for Wittgenstein, an ethically well-lived life is a necessary condition of religious life. He writes, "only if you try to be helpful to other people will you in the end find your way to God."[38] Malcolm affirms the Wittgensteinian emphasis on orthopraxy over orthodoxy when he states that "what is most fundamental in a religious life is not the affirming of creeds, not even prayer and worship – but rather, doing *good deeds...*"[39]

This theme, emphasizing right practice versus orthodox belief, comes through when considered in the context of Wittgenstein's aversion to metaphysical treatments of religion. In the following passage we see that, in the works of the Apostle Paul, Wittgenstein gets, as it were, a whiff of the metaphysical spirit. Wittgenstein writes,

> In the Gospels – so it seems to me – everything is *less* pretentious, humbler, simpler. *There* are huts; with Paul a church. There all men are equal and God himself is a man; with Paul there is already something like a hierarchy; honours and offices. – That is, as it were, what my *nose* tells me.[40]

While this response to Paul is not itself naturalistic, clearly Wittgenstein's response *is* visceral. Not only does Wittgenstein invoke an olfactory metaphor, it is fairly clear that his response to Paul's teachings is not favorable.

In the course of making his case that in philosophy as well as in religion Wittgenstein emphasizes doing and acting over reason and speculative intelligence, Malcolm appeals to the same passage that Clack did earlier when the latter was emphasizing Wittgenstein's descriptive approach in religion and philosophy. In this passage, "Christianity is not a doctrine; I mean, not a theory about what has happened and will happen with the human soul, but a description of an actual occurrence in human life,"[41] we also see a more straightforwardly naturalistic account of religion. This is a more straightforwardly naturalistic account of religion since Wittgenstein emphasizes that Christianity is "a description of an actual occurrence in human life." Wittgenstein makes it clear that there is nothing *supernatural* about his conception of Christianity; and while "natural" and "supernatural" are not necessarily antonyms, I do not know how else to characterize a description of religious phenomena that is explicitly *not* supernatural. Given the terminology we have available to us, characterizing the description of Christianity provided to us by Wittgenstein above as naturalistic seems apt.

Further indication that, for Wittgenstein, the certainty associated with religion is visceral and not intellectual is seen in the following: "But if I am to be *really* saved – then I need *certainty* – not wisdom, dreams, speculation – and this certainty is faith. And faith is faith in what my heart, my *soul* needs, not my speculative intelligence."[42] Regardless of the question of whether Wittgenstein favors a naturalistic interpretation of, e.g., the soul, this much is clear from the passage above: the certainty that Wittgenstein describes in reference to being saved is a felt, gut, visceral kind of certainty – not the kind of certainty one might experience after having completed a mathematical proof. Thus it seems safe to conclude that religious certainty, on a Wittgensteinian interpretation of religion, is not to be associated with orthodox belief. According to the following passage from Wittgenstein, doctrines do not reflect the true nature of Christianity: "One of the things Christianity says, I think, is that all sound doctrines are of no avail."[43] What moral can we glean from these passages? These statements from Wittgenstein give us an indication of the way in which his understanding of religion, Christianity specifically, would be inclined. Even if we cannot settle questions concerning whether Wittgenstein's conception of religion is properly characterized as non-cognitivist, naturalistic, what have you, this much seems clear. Doing (versus believing) is what Wittgenstein sees as being central to religious life. Additionally, Wittgenstein seems to be concerned with what happens in this life, not in the hereafter, whatever one might mean by that. In sum, orthopraxy takes precedence over orthodoxy.

Having seen some statements by and about Wittgenstein concerning the place of doctrine in religion, we must ask, how might the attitudes expressed above bear on *e* claims, that is, doctrinal statements such as Acts 4:12, which, we will recall, reads as follows: "And there is salvation in no one else, for there is no other name under heaven given among men by which we must be saved." It is safe to presume that Wittgenstein would have two objections to *e* claims such as Acts 4:12. First, Wittgenstein expresses an ecumenical attitude toward religion. Second, Wittgenstein opposes religious doctrine. That is, Wittgenstein indicates that interpreting religious language as asserting absolute, doctrinal pronouncements is mistaken.

The ecumenical attitude expressed in the following reflects his opposition to the exclusivism enunciated in Acts 4:12. Wittgenstein writes, "All religions are wonderful, even those of the most primitive tribes. The ways in which people express their religious feelings differ enormously."[44] "All religions are wonderful" is certainly indicative of an ecumenical attitude. Combining this with what I anticipated would be Wittgenstein's second objection to Acts 4:12 (or any *e* claim) provides us with a sense of how he might weigh in on the philosophical problem of religious diversity. We have seen enough textual evidence to state that Wittgenstein would object to interpreting Acts 4:12 (or any *e* claim) as stating a doctrine. His admiration for the intensity of Pascal's religious exclusivism indicated in the following passage shows that though

Wittgenstein himself had ecumenical inclinations it is not exclusivism per se that he opposed. Peter Winch writes,

> Wittgenstein would have respected [Pascal's Christian exclusivism] for its very intensity, [but] such exclusiveness was foreign to his way of thinking. He was early influenced by [the pluralistic spirit of] William James' *Varieties of Religious Experience.*[45]

It has been made clear that Wittgenstein admires sincerely held religious convictions and exclusivism is certainly one such conviction. His objection to exclusivism would be in regarding it as a doctrine, a metaphysical requirement to which religious belief must adhere.

Although we have seen ample textual support for the claim that Wittgenstein considers it a mistake to interpret religious language as expressing doctrine, this is where we encounter a problem. There seems to be no religious way of interpreting an *e* claim except as an absolute, doctrinal statement. For example, when giving a Christian interpretation to Acts 4:12, it seems that such a reading inevitably will be doctrinal in nature, i.e., teaching us what to do (in this case, follow the way of Christ). Moreover, this teaching is absolute; there is *no* other way except through Christ that salvation may be attained.

When considering some plausible Wittgensteinian interpretations of an *e* claim, e.g., Acts 4:12, one should also consider how they might square with typical, ordinary interpretations of Acts 4:12. The following are examples of plausible Wittgensteinian responses to Acts 4:12. Whereas a typical Christian response to Acts 4:12 might plausibly be that "Acts 4:12 is true," a typical, say, Muslim response to Acts 4:12 might plausibly be that "Acts 4:12 is false." In contrast to these responses, the discussion of Wittgenstein's thoughts on the idea of "God exists" in Chapter 6 gives reason to believe that Wittgensteinian teaching would indicate that Acts 4:12 is neither true nor false. Affirming Acts 4:12 is a move in the Christian language-game. Doing so expresses, evinces, and evokes an attitude reflecting commitment to Christian life. However, one of the consequences of expressing such a commitment is that it seems to entail a commitment to the falsity of any claims that oppose Acts 4:12. Sticking with the comparison with Islam (although the comparison could be made with any religion), imagine an equivalent Muslim *e* claim: "only through following the teachings of Muhammad can one attain salvation." If one were to embrace Acts 4:12 employing a Wittgensteinian interpretation of it, a Wittgensteinian way of articulating the falsity of the Islamic *e* claim stated above is inconceivable. For one, proclaiming the falsity of the Muslim *e* claim runs counter to Wittgenstein's ecumenical spirit. Additionally, to be false (or true) the Muslim *e* claim must be regarded as expressing the kind of proposition that admits of truth or falsity. That Wittgenstein would agree with such a notion is, to say the least, suspect. There is no textual support for the idea that

Wittgenstein regards religious language as being true or false. Moreover, as was made evident in Chapter 6, there is much textual support for the claim that Wittgenstein holds that religious language is neither true nor false.

Another possibility for reconciling the supposed conflict between Christian and Muslim *e* claims would be that, as articulated above, the teachings of Jesus and the teachings of Muhammad do not actually conflict. That is, they contain the same core message: Live a good life. However, one of the entailments of an *e* claim is that to live a good life one must disavow other *e* claims. Following Acts 4:12 excludes the possibility of living a good Muslim life. The proper way to put this is that, from a Christian frame of reference, one might be able to live a good Muslim life: help the poor, refrain from vice (however construed), praise God/Allah (keeping in mind, of course, that these two words are supposed to translate to one another), etc., except that by so living a good Muslim life one would not have lived in accordance with Acts 4:12 and thus would be denied the rewards promised by Acts 4:12. Ultimately, then, competing *e* claims cannot be reduced to having the same core meaning, just expressed in the terminology of different religions. Embracing an *e* claim from one religion *means* denying the *e* claims of other religions.

Having considered some plausible Wittgensteinian responses to Acts 4:12, that it expresses a claim that is neither true nor false and that affirming it is a move in the Christian language-game, let us consider how these might compare with what could be regarded as a plausible, typical or ordinary interpretation of the message of Acts 4:12. One, obvious Christian interpretation of Acts 4:12 is that if you are not Christian, then damnation is your fate. A premise of such an interpretation is that Acts 4:12 expresses a true proposition. While Wittgenstein might acknowledge that many people interpret Acts 4:12 in this way, clearly, there is nothing in his corpus to indicate that he would agree with such an interpretation. This is not necessarily a strike against a Wittgensteinian interpretation; however, it is noteworthy that here we have a case of what could plausibly be considered an instance of ordinary usage running counter to a Wittgensteinian interpretation of that same instance of language. This is noteworthy indeed since Wittgensteinian teaching is associated with the dictum, "the meaning of a word is its use."

Moving our discussion from Malcolm to Winch, addressing these matters ever more subtly, it can be seen that the issue of whether Wittgensteinian interpretations of religion are properly regarded as reductionist is a common theme. In fact, that Malcolm's interpretation leaves open the charge that Wittgenstein reduces religion to ethics is one of Winch's criticisms of the essay by Malcolm just discussed. While it is clear that Wittgensteinian interpretations of religion focus on good works, Winch takes issue with Malcolm's account, an account which leaves open the interpretation that Wittgenstein reduces religion to ethics. Winch aims to refine Malcolm's treatment of Wittgenstein on this matter by showing that, for Wittgenstein, ethics is a necessary, but not necessarily sufficient, condition of religious life. For Winch, whether Wittgenstein reduces religion to ethics is an open question. Winch points out that for Wittgenstein, "good works" is only a necessary (and not sufficient) condition for "finding God" (thus interpretations of Wittgenstein's work which indicate that he reduces religion to ethics are too hasty).[46] Winch's point is well taken in that it is more in line with the subtlety one typically associates with Wittgenstein's later work. The idea that Wittgenstein reduces religion to ethics is too dogmatic and rigid to attribute to a thinker whose thought resists such programmatic formulations. Moreover, one will not find textual support for such a reduction in Wittgenstein's corpus, especially in his later work. Having noted this nuance, it is clear that an emphasis on good works still occupies a central place in a Wittgensteinian understanding of religion.

In a theistic context, clearly, one's understanding of "God" will bear on one's understanding of religion. Also, though we have acknowledged the subtlety usually associated with Wittgenstein's thought, it should be noted that the following Wittgensteinian conception of God is certainly open to a reductionist interpretation. We see what Wittgenstein might mean by "God" in this excerpt from the foreword to *Philosophical Remarks*, "I would like to say 'this book is written to the glory of God'…It means that the book was written in good will…[as opposed to] written from vanity…"[47] Similar to the question regarding whether Wittgenstein reduces religion to ethics, we could ask whether Wittgenstein regards good will and absence of vanity as necessary or necessary *and* sufficient conditions of expressing the "glory of God." If he means that they are necessary and sufficient conditions, clearly, this is a reductive interpretation of "the glory of God." If he means that they are necessary conditions, the question of whether Wittgenstein reduces "the glory of God" to human experience (good will and absence of vanity) is still open. Trying to answer the question of whether Wittgenstein is a reductionist regarding the interpretation of religious language is a matter unlikely to be settled given the resistance of his thought to having theoretical labels applied to it. That is my reason for having considered what is at stake concerning particular interpretations of religious language instead of trying to determine definitively and comprehensively which labels best describe Wittgenstein's thought. So while we can see how the preceding Wittgensteinian conceptions of ethics and God might be construed as being reductionist in nature, my point is that we should exercise caution before we ascribe such labels to a thinker as subtle as Wittgenstein. Nevertheless, sharpening our understanding of whether Wittgensteinian interpretations of religion may or may not be regarded as revisionary is crucial to this book since an implication of the dilemma I have posed is that irrealist interpretations of religion (including Wittgensteinian non-realism) are revisionary.

One reason we are unlikely to find labels that describe Wittgenstein's thought definitively and comprehensively, Winch reminds us, is that Wittgenstein considers the meaning of words and concepts within the context of a given language-game; this is a method which resists being labeled as having some comprehensive theoretical orientation. For example, according to Winch, a Wittgensteinian understanding of God can be derived only within the context of a religious language-game. This context-sensitivity is seen in the idea that employing the grammar from one language-game in another language-game invites confusion. For example, Winch suggests that looking for God to intervene in the natural order leads to looking for God in all the wrong places.[48] That is, our experience of the natural order involves one language-game, we might call it the natural science language-game. Looking for God in causal chains (in that seeking causes is part of customary scientific practice), according to Winch's interpretation of Wittgenstein, is misguided. Religion, the proper context in which our experiences regarding God would be understood, is not concerned with, e.g., causal chains. This view might seem odd given the presence of biblical creation stories in which God is the first in a causal chain which results in the world as we know it. Nevertheless, the Wittgensteinian point here is that we would not (and should not) expect one's religious commitment to rise and fall based on the ability to find God at the beginning of the causal chain which resulted in creation. As such, applying the grammar from the natural science language-game, one in which seeking causal chains makes sense, will only lead to confusion when conceiving of God.

Winch provides the following to illustrate how employing the norms from one context in another context can be improper. In this vein, seeking naturalistic explanations for putatively religious phenomenon is by definition irreligious. For example, in the story of Moses and the burning bush, the kinds of questions that seek causal explanations, according to Winch, "are *forbidden*; it is a condition of Moses' properly understanding what is happening that he should *not* ask them."[49] A causal account along naturalist lines of why the bush is burning is, by definition, an irreligious account. A religious account involves, e.g., that the story of the burning bush orients one's life somehow, involves a commitment to live one's life a certain way.

Pertinent to the idea of understanding miracles which, on this view, is the appropriate way to understand the story of Moses and the burning bush, is the idea of language-game autonomy. For Winch, language-games exhibit autonomy in that explanations come to an end within the context of the relevant language-game. If language-games are autonomous, that the rules dictated by their grammars would be relative to themselves seems apparent. On the matter of language-game autonomy, Winch writes, "To regard a certain event as a miracle...is rather to react to the event in a way which requires us to desist from asking, or at least pressing, those questions."[50] The kinds of questions to which Winch refers here are scientific questions, those which seek, e.g., causal explanations along the lines of "what causal account might we give for why that bush is burning?" Winch suggests that it is hard for us to keep from asking these kinds of questions because, to use Winch's adaptation of a phrase from Wittgenstein, of the (scientific) "pictures that force themselves upon us."[51]

One must ask, though, if naturalistic, causal language is inappropriate to an understanding of God, what non-revisionary sense could be made of the following? "Wittgenstein speaks of miracle as 'a gesture that God makes' and this strikes me as a splendidly apt characterization...[Furthermore], witnessing a miracle" amounts to "gratitude and perhaps praise of God for his beneficence and wondrous *deeds*" (my emphasis).[52] If a deed is something one *does*, then the causal implication of the word "deed" is clear. If it is improper to interpret "God's deeds" causally, then significant elements of religious language are seemingly undermined. Genesis 1:1 reads "In the beginning God created the heavens and the earth." That is, according to the scripture for major religious tradition(s), God *caused* the heavens and the earth to come into being. Is it religiously improper to interpret scripture as having causal connotations when the connotations seem so clear? The Wittgensteinian ban on interpreting religious language as having causal implications seems to be at odds with the religious doctrine expressed in Genesis 1:1.

This ban seems congruous with Wittgenstein's philosophical teachings generally. That is, Wittgenstein's writings indicate an aversion to comprehensive, theoretical pronouncements. For example, there is the idea that context is a necessary condition in determining sense. As Winch puts it, language, "when used in such a contextless way, is drained of the kinds of sense it bears in its normal uses."[53] For example, seeking causal explanations in the story of Moses and the burning bush is bound to lead one astray, by this Wittgensteinian line, when one considers that the context of the story indicates that its message concerns Moses faithfully accepting Yahweh's authority.

Naturally, the idea that (religious) language is to be understood in its proper context bears on the matter of religious diversity. This is the case since each religion would presumably provide the context within which its own language would be interpreted. In this connection, Winch writes, "[To think of life as a 'gift' and hence as something for which one can be grateful] are...attitudes which, in different religions, are set in specific doctrinal contexts."[54] The point here is the idea that to understand particular religious attitudes, they must be understood in their own contexts. For example, one could expect that "to think of life as a gift" would be understood differently in, say, a theistic context, one in which life might be viewed as being literally a gift from God, as compared to a nontheistic, e.g., Theravadan Buddhist, context, one in which thinking of life as a gift would clearly take on a different meaning.

Similarly, according to Winch, religious works cannot be fully comprehended outside of the particular faith in which they occur. About religious works, he indicates that they cannot be "understood independently of the ways in which they are or are not connected with a particular faith on the part of the doer..."[55] A consequence of the requirement that religious attitudes and religious works must be understood within their proper context is that this requirement gives rise to the prospect of a relativist interpretation of religious phenomena. This must be said advisedly since, as I argued in chapter 6, it is a mistake to treat Wittgenstein as a relativist. However, as was argued at the beginning of this chapter, a case can be made that Wittgenstein's followers take his ideas further than he might have. Winch's insistence on the context sensitivity of particular religious phenomena is a case in point. The following from Winch evinces such religious language-game relativism. He writes, "[The words of a saint invoke] a concept which has its sense only in a context of religious belief."[56] If a concept means m in one context but does not mean m in another, relativism is the term typically employed to describe this notion. I am not arguing that a relativist reading of religious language is necessarily an incorrect one; but, such a reading certainly seems to offer a revisionary account of the absolutism inherent in e claims.

With this, we need to face the prospect that Wittgensteinian interpretations of religious language are inherently revisionary, at least in the context of religious diversity, a context which includes the possibility (if not fact) that each religion has its own claims which are to be regarded as being uniquely and absolutely true. Winch's use of this passage from Wittgenstein brings this issue into view:

> "God has commanded it, therefore it must be possible to do it" (*Culture and Value*, p. 77e). That means nothing. There is no 'therefore' about it. At most the two expressions might mean the *same*. In this context 'He has commanded it' means roughly: 'He will punish anybody who doesn't do it.' And nothing follows from that about what anybody can or cannot do. And *that* is what 'predestination' means.[57]

What non-revisionary sense can be made of this? Winch is telling us what predestination means, and it does not resemble standard religious understandings of predestination. While predestination might not bear directly on our topic, the relevance of this Wittgensteinian interpretation of a religious idea, predestination, certainly has application to our topic. For one, this matter could be construed such that one's religious associations (Hindu, Buddhist, Jewish, Christian, Muslim, none of the above) could be understood as being predestined. What are the implications of applying the ideas expressed in the above passage from Winch to Acts 4:12? God has commanded us to obey Acts 4:12 means that is possible to follow Acts 4:12. Following Acts 4:12, or any Christian *e* claim, is possible for a Christian; however, it simply is not possible for, e.g., a Muslim, to follow Acts 4:12. A Wittgensteinian counter to this claim could be that I have confused matters by applying the grammar of the Christian language-game to the Muslim language-game. But is predestination language-game specific? If it is true that predestination obtains, its effects seemingly would apply to everyone, not only to adherents of the "predestination language-game." Maintaining that predestination is applicable only to adherents of the relevant language-game overlooks the absolutism inherent in religious language. This idea can also be applied to the topic of religious diversity. Within a religious context, *e* claims are absolute; not acknowledging that is a revision of ordinary understandings of religious language.

On the matter of revising ordinary understandings of religious language, these conclusions follow regarding Wittgensteinian interpretations of religious language. Phillips's insistence that comparing claims from different language-games requires an adjudicatory meta-language, the prospects of which he regards as quite dubious, amounts to insulating language-games from any kind of external assessment. The relativism engendered by such insistence certainly revises the absolute character of *e* claims. The emphasis Malcolm places on orthopraxy over orthodoxy, insofar as it involves reducing religions to ethics, not only offers a revisionary account of religion, it also is in danger of infidelity regarding the interpretation of Wittgenstein's teaching in that reducing religion to ethics is much too formulaic to resonate with the subtle spirit of Wittgenstein's thought. The emphasis Winch places on context-sensitivity with regard to understanding (religious) language encounters difficulties similar to those facing Phillips. Interpretations of religious language that do not acknowledge the absolute character of *e* claims is bound to misrepresent the ostensibly religious character of the language under consideration.

Chapter 8

Conclusion

The first portion of the book dealt with authors whose work most explicitly exemplifies the problems facing religious realism. Alston's thought was utilized as an exemplar of religious realism showing that realism entails the philosophical problem of religious diversity. Hick interprets the world's religious landscape in such a way that religious exclusivism, which is entailed by religious realism, is made to look arbitrary. Though Plantinga and van Inwagen address the charge of being arbitrary, their accounts still do nothing by way of convincing us why any one form of religious exclusivism is epistemically superior to any other. The second portion of the book dealt with the thought of authors whose work poses the most penetrating challenge to religious realism. These authors, though they avoid the problems facing religious realism, face problems of their own. As much as the later work of Wittgenstein avoids the confusions that arise from the metaphysical commitments religious realists (and anti-realists) make, Wittgensteinian religious non-realism still faces the problem of revisionism in that non-realist interpretations of religion drop essential features of religious doctrine, e.g., the idea that e claims are absolutely true. Thus we are left with the conclusion that the dilemma by which this book has been organized is genuine. Both horns of the dilemma face problems that seriously call into question their viability as interpretations of religion. In short, religious realism and religious irrealism both come with significant costs; religious realism faces the philosophical problem of religious diversity and irrealist interpretations of religion are revisionary.

As discussed in chapters 1 and 2, religious realism entails the law of non-contradiction and thus results in the philosophical problem of religious diversity since, according to the law of non-contradiction, at most one of the conflicting e claims of the world's religions can be true. That is, one religion maintains that there is one correct path to the ultimate reward and other religions maintain that the correct path to the ultimate reward involves something else. Given that we cannot tell which if any of these claims to truth are correct, this presents a problem: the philosophical problem of religious diversity. While a bit more about Hick and much more about Alston will be said below, it is useful at this point to note how the works discussed in the chapter devoted to Plantinga and van Inwagen exemplify important features of the religious realists' response to the philosophical problem of religious diversity. Given this situation wherein there are conflicting e claims, the idea that we could settle on the correctness of one, such as is the case with religious exclusivism, is considered by some (notably Hick) to be arbitrary. Religious exclusivism is considered to be arbitrary given the epistemic parity of the e claims of the religions of the world. Though

Plantinga's and van Inwagen's exclusivist treatments of this matter have their merits, neither alters the fact that the presence of conflicting e claims calls into question the notion of the unique claim to truth of any one e claim, a uniqueness that is characteristic of religious exclusivism.

Religious irrealism comes with significant costs, too. Religious anti-realism, like religious realism, still entails a metaphysical commitment to what must be the case and thus also bears the burden of indicating what the nature of the match between language and the world consists in. We saw this in Feuerbach's assertion that theological language is not actually about what it purports to describe but is rather about something else. At least as significant, religious anti-realism offers a revisionary account of religion. This is a problem in that revisionary accounts of religion drop essential features of religious doctrine. As we have seen this is most notable with regard to e claims, e.g. Acts 4:12. An account that indicates that anything other than what Acts 4:12 describes obtains exemplifies revisionism in that it drops essential features of religious doctrine since such a revisionary account will be about something other than the absolute claim to truth entailed by an e claim. This description also applies to religious non-realism since neither religious anti-realism nor religious non-realism regard what e claims describe as actually obtaining. Accordingly, both are subject to the problem facing the irrealist horn of the dilemma: that of revisionism.

The conclusion is to recommend an Alstonian exclusivism as the most attractive response to the issues raised by the dilemma. As such, we need to reinforce our understanding of how his religious realism fits into the overall context of this project. Central to the conception of realism I have employed throughout this book is what Alston has called the T-schema: "p" is true if and only if p. As we have seen, realism so formulated entails the law of non-contradiction in that only p can make "p" true; if anything other than p obtains then "p" is not true. Applied to the world's religious landscape with its conflicting e claims, again, we are left with the philosophical problem of religious diversity. The different religious realists considered throughout this book have attempted to address these concerns. Each of them, *qua* religious realist, faces the critiques leveled against realism by its detractors. The teachings from the later works of Wittgenstein have especially been a focus of attention due to how penetrating their criticisms of realism can be. For example, although the problems facing Hick's professedly religious realist position are numerous and have already been discussed at length, to the extent that Hick is a religious realist he is also subject to Wittgensteinian criticism. Not only does Hick's pluralist hypothesis involve a metaphysical commitment to what must be the case regarding religious life, the revisionary character of Hick's thought *redefines* what Wittgenstein would admonish us not to define in the first place: what a religious conception of the world *must* look like.

One can imagine a variety of responses to the philosophical problem of religious diversity. Indifference could be a response. One could respond with the idea that the conflicting *e* claims of the world's religions are in some ways true and in some ways false. However, if we seek clarity regarding the nature of this conflict both of these responses are unsatisfactory. The first response ignores the conflict and the second response muddles the terms by which there is a conflict. There is a response to the philosophical problem of religious diversity, though, that acknowledges the *e* claims of one's religious counterparts, even if these *e* claims conflict with one's own convictions. The book thus concludes with an account of what an attractive response to the philosophical problem of religious diversity should include. Such a position should include a non-revisionary realism of an Alstonian sort, an understanding of realism that is theologically robust and that can address the penetrating criticisms of Wittgenstein. Religious exclusivism is an inevitable result of this conclusion. Incorporating religious realism to avoid undesirably revisionary accounts of religion is not merely a necessary evil. Rather, it is something to embrace. A tolerant exclusivism is an essential feature of an attractive response to the philosophical problem of religious diversity. Part of taking one's religious counterpart seriously is acknowledging that he or she takes herself to be exclusively right about religious matters; that is, an attractive response to the philosophical problem of religious diversity should include that others embrace their own *e* claim, a truth claim that quite possibly conflicts with one's own convictions.

Again, as religious realists, all those discussed within this book who fit that description face the same issues. Since Alston is the one who responds most explicitly and arguably most adequately to Wittgensteinian critique, his response will be discussed in more detail. Furthermore, although it still faces difficulties, Alston's is recommended as the most attractive response to the issues raised by the dilemma explored throughout the book. Thus, Alston also provides an attractive response to the problem facing the realist horn of the dilemma: that of religious diversity.

Despite the costs that the religious realist must pay, a form of religious realism is nevertheless suggested to provide the most attractive option with respect to the dilemma. Although Alston in large part addresses Wittgensteinian concerns regarding realism, it is not as though Alston's thought on this matter is without problems. After all, his interpretation of religion is subject to the dilemma, too. With respect to ordinary religious realism, Alston must contend with the philosophical problem of religious diversity. Part of what makes his response to the problem of religious diversity attractive is that he invokes

Wittgensteinian concepts without losing sight of his realism, enabling Alston to avoid revisionism. In some ways, then, Alston's response to religious diversity draws from the strengths of religious realism and Wittgensteinian non-realism. With respect to theoretical realism, Alston's work also constitutes an attempt to provide an account of what the match between language and what it describes would consist of. The discussion of his work on this topic appears in the Appendix.

Following the logic of the dilemma by which this book has been organized, the cost of irrealism is that it results in revisionism. While Alston's religious realism enables him to avoid revisionism, as he acknowledges, the cost of (what I have called his ordinary) religious realism is that he faces the problem of religious diversity. As he puts it, a difficulty he has not been able to address by grounding his realism within the context of doxastic practices is "the one posed by the diversity of religions."[1] The difficulty arises from the similar epistemic credentials of the religions of the world.

The world's diverse religious landscape lends credence to the idea that one can be certain regarding the truth of neither one's own religious convictions nor those of one's religious counterparts. Alston thus recommends that religious practitioners concerned by the epistemic challenges posed by other religions stay with their own religious DP if it has already shown itself to be reliable. He writes, "In the absence of any external reason for supposing that one of the competing practices is more accurate than my own, the only rational course for me to take is to sit tight with the practice of which I am a master and which serves me so well in guiding my activity in the world."[2] Despite the problems posed by the epistemic challenges from other religions, Alston insists that "sitting tight" does not amount to staying with one's own religion arbitrarily. One can remain within the bounds of rationality and "sit tight." When Alston writes "religious pluralism does not show any irrationality in the use of CP," he means that practitioners of Christian DP are prima facie rationally justified in continuing to partake of that practice. People are prima facie justified in maintaining their beliefs if there are no defeaters; such defeaters would include "any external reason," where external means outside any given DP. This allowance for external considerations is what permits Alston's DP approach to maintain its realist character. By continuing to participate in a practice that has proven itself to be reliable, practitioners of that DP violate no epistemic duties. By conceding that "it is right and proper for one to be worried and perplexed by religious pluralism, epistemically as well as theologically," Alston acknowledges that the philosophical problem of religious diversity is worthy of our concern. However, as he sees it, one need not be so vexed "to the extent of denying the rationality of CP."[3]

Christian exclusivism, for Alston, is rationally justifiable since CP is epistemically on a par with SP (the DP based on sense experience) in that there is no non-circular justification for either. Critics of Alston's account of the rational justifiability of CP, e.g., Richard Gale, point out the disanalogies between CP and SP with the overall point that CP loses whatever rational justification it might have gained by virtue of its putative parallels with SP. Alston, aware of these criticisms, attempts to defend his position by explaining why these disanalogies occur. Gale describes this interplay between Alston and his critics by articulating what he calls the "Alston fallacy." Gale writes,

> we find Alston committing the fallacy of thinking that if he can give a categoreally based explanation for a disanalogy between the religious- and sense-experience doxastic practices, it renders the disanalogy harmless. This should be called the 'Alston fallacy.'[4]

All the details of Gale's critique need not concern us as they take us too far afield from our topic. However, Gale does offer a more specific version of this criticism that is central to our considerations. On the whole, Gale argues that the disanalogies between SP and MP (DPs of those claiming to have perceptions of divine manifestations) are too damaging to maintain the comparison. Expressing this concern, Gale suggests that

> Probably the most damaging disanalogy between the tests for sense and M-experience results from religious diversity. Whereas there is a multiplicity of established rival M-experience doxastic practices having incompatible tests and creeds that are epistemically on all fours, there is a single sense experience doxastic practice in which everyone participates.[5]

What, according to Gale, makes religious diversity a problem for Alston is precisely its *dis*analogies with sense experience. Whereas practitioners of differing religions would, Gale suggests, have significantly similar sense experiences, they have significantly dissimilar experiences within the context of their religious lives. Furthermore, whereas the tests for the validity of sense experience can be regarded as significantly similar across religions,[6] the tests for the validity of religious experience vary from one religious context to another. For Gale, this disanalogy between SP and MP is sufficiently damaging as to render any hopes of justifying MP rationally based on its putatively analogous nature to SP futile.

Gale is prepared for Alston's response to this criticism. Gale writes,

> Alston has tried to lessen the force of this disanalogy by arguing that since they do not share a common method for warranting or overriding claims based on M-experience the discreditation is far less than it would be if they shared the same method but differed in their output beliefs.[7]

Alston's reply to Gale thus amounts to the idea that we should not be surprised that different DPs result in different beliefs. I tend to agree with Gale that the problem of religious diversity damages Alston's claim to have given MP rational justification by having argued for its seeming analogies to SP. In other words, Gale's argument that explaining the disanalogies between MP and SP does not make MP and SP any the less disanalogous is not successfully countered by Alston. However, whether MP is rationally justifiable is of no consequence to the overall argument of this project. If anything, Gale's criticism of Alston reinforces one of my main arguments: the problem posed by the realist horn of the dilemma, that of religious diversity, is a genuine problem. Nevertheless, the problems facing the realist horn of the dilemma seem less imposing than those facing the irrealist horn.

While Gale's criticisms are apt, the recommendation of Alston's religious realism based on his idea of doxastic practices and the attendant religious exclusivism to which his realism gives rise does not depend on the analogy between CP and SP. After all, that any one particular religion is rationally justifiable is not the position being advanced here. The thesis of this chapter is that acknowledging religious exclusivism is the only way to take the philosophical problem of religious diversity seriously. If no religions contain true *e* claims, then there is no *problem* of religious diversity. In this scenario there is no problem because none of the religions provides true *e* claims. If all of the great historical religions of the world are regarded as maintaining true *e* claims (the scenario depicted by Hick's pluralistic hypothesis), again, there is no *problem* of religious diversity. In this scenario there is no problem because all of these religions provide true *e* claims. The problem arises only when one *e* claim is regarded to be true and all others are regarded to be false. Thus it is only when religious exclusivism comes to the fore that the philosophical *problem* of religious diversity even presents itself.

The costs and benefits of religious realism and religious irrealism have a symmetry to them. Religious realism avoids revisionism but must contend with the philosophical problem of religious diversity and irrealist critiques of metaphysics. While irrealist interpretations of religion are revisionary, at least religious non-realism does not have to defend itself from charges of having lapsed into metaphysical confusion. Upon analyzing the costs and benefits, Alston's realist conception of truth, with the support of DPs, emerges as the most satisfactory option given the issues raised by the dilemma.

In his articulation of DPs, Alston shows the value of the affinities his conceptions of DPs has with Wittgensteinian language-games without compromising his insistence on realism. Alston shows the compatibility of DPs (and thus, to a significant extent, language-games) with granting the relevance of external factors, which Wittgenstein's insistence on language-game autonomy

128

would seem to disallow. In doing so, Alston addresses a Wittgensteinian charge against him. The Wittgensteinian non-realist argues that by making the truth of religious language accountable to external factors, e.g., states of affairs beyond language, Alston has divorced the meaning of language from its use and has thus made language idle. Such language is "on holiday," to use the terminology from *PI* #38.

However, these charges against Alston lose much of their sting when viewed against Alston's grounding of the meaning of language in DPs, given their significant similarities with language-games. The added benefit of Alstonian DPs is that, in addition to their compatibilities with language-games, thus keeping the Wittgensteinian emphasis on use and practice as the basis of the meaning of language, they allow the possibility of evidential appraisal from without. Even if external considerations, such as evidential appraisal from sources outside a given DP, can never settle questions of the viability of beliefs within a given DP "it does not follow that these attempts are irrelevant," since "considerations can be relevant without being decisive…"[8] No epistemic harm is done if one seeks support for one's belief outside a given DP. If within DP x it were held that $2+2=5$ but outside of DP x it were held that $2+2=4$, this would obviously be useful information to an adherent of DP x. While it might very well be the case that such information would not be decisive in revising DP x, or it might not cause any changes in DP x at all, it is hard to see that such information would be any the less relevant. This shows that there is no fundamental incompatibility between allowing evidential appraisal from without and keeping the emphasis on practice and use as the basis for the meaningfulness of language. Therefore, with Alstonian DPs we get the Wittgensteinian benefit of grounding the meaningfulness of language in practice but without the Wittgensteinian cost of language-game insularity, to the extent that Wittgenstein proscribes assessments of one language-game by the rules of another.

That Alstonian DPs allow for external assessments is simply in keeping with Alston's conception of realism about truth, that truth can be determined independent of what we do, say, or believe. With Wittgensteinian concerns at heart, one could rightly ask at this point: How can we go about knowing such a thing, whether an *e* claim is true independent of our linguistic or cognitive undertakings? Alston addresses this concern while maintaining his insistence on realism. Additionally, Alston shows appreciable Wittgensteinian sympathies by acknowledging the significance of practice in determining the use or meaning of our language. While acknowledging that practice influences meaning within a DP, Alston maintains that the degree to which this is so is a question to be explored. We need to examine "the extent to which a practice determines the meaning of what is said within [a DP]." We need to recognize "some such influence but without taking it to be the whole story."[9]   That is, epistemic justification includes practice, but does not stop there. Alston writes, "the question of where, if anywhere, the search for justification comes to an end is one that arises only after we have mapped enough of the relevant support relations…"[10] He says this in the light of his view that beliefs can be supported by a network of DPs. Alston's articulation of DPs not only approximates a Wittgensteinian understanding of how language derives its meaning, but also retains a realism that is vital to non-revisionary interpretations of Christian, and possibly all religious life. Alston's inquiries regarding the veridicality of Christian language are not free-floating, divorced from context. His articulation of DPs makes this clear.

A response to the Wittgensteinian concern raised in the preceding paragraph would be: An Alstonian would look to the same place in assessing the meaningfulness and rational justifiability of an *e* claim as would a Wittgensteinian. They both would look to practice, use, what we actually do, and so on. The difference between Alston and Wittgenstein is that for Alston it is also relevant to look to evidence beyond a given DP. A possible difference between Alston and Wittgenstein on this topic might be that whereas Alston explicitly indicates that the outputs of one DP can bear on the reliability of the outputs of another DP, there is no explicit statement from Wittgenstein expressing the same regarding language-games. If anything, there is textual support for the contrary.[11]

Here we see a point at which a Wittgensteinian interpretation mischaracterizes religious realism. A Wittgensteinian could say, "We can look for evidence beyond a given language-game, too. However, such inquiries, being outside the context of a given language-game, would be nonsense, would have no meaning. Differences of opinion in such matters (How do we conceive of the world beyond language?) do not amount to anything because such thinking is just confused."   I once again cite the relevant passage from *Zettel* since it reflects this attitude so aptly:

> One man is a convinced realist, another a convinced idealist and teaches his children accordingly. In such an important matter as the existence or non-existence of the external world they don't want to teach their children anything wrong. What will the children be taught? To include in what they say 'There are physical objects' or the opposite?…But the idealist will teach his children the word 'chair' after all, for of course he wants to teach them to do this and that, e.g. to fetch a chair. Then where will be the difference between what the idealist educated children say and the realist ones? Won't the difference only be one of a battle cry?[12]

"Won't the difference (in this case between religious realism and religious irrealism) only be one of a battle cry?" No, it won't. For theists, whether "God

130

exists" is true (beyond the undertakings of a DP or a language-game) is not a matter of a mere battle cry. In this case, the truth of "God exists" (again, beyond the undertakings of a DP or a language-game) is a matter of salvation. "God grants salvation" cannot be true unless "God exists" is also true. It could be that our Wittgensteinian would maintain non-realist interpretations of religious beliefs comprehensively. However, as has been shown in Hilberg's Wager, this runs afoul of the idea that even if we are mandated to uphold non-realist interpretations of religious beliefs we are left with at least one belief that we are to uphold in a realist manner: that we are mandated to uphold non-realist interpretations of our religious beliefs. With Alston's religious realism based on his idea of DPs, we can avoid the revisionism entailed by religious irrealism and we get a way of understanding religious truth claims which is also grounded in practice. As such, we can accommodate the realist character of religious language and have a plausible response to Wittgensteinian charges that religious realism lapses into mere nonsense.

Thus the overall argument of the book concludes by recommending a realist interpretation of religious language. Religious exclusivism is a consequence of this recommendation. By endorsing a tolerance for exclusivism, Alston's position of "sitting tight" is not necessarily being endorsed as well. "Sitting tight" involves staying with the DP (in Alston's case, the Christian DP) with which one is already familiar as long as no other competing DP is epistemically superior. Since the DPs of the great historical religions of the world are, as Alston sees it, epistemically on a par with each other, the adherents of each religion are well served and epistemically warranted in continuing to live their religious lives as they are. The argument here deemphasizes the notion that one is warranted in "sitting tight" with regard to one's own religious beliefs. Rather, what is being emphasized here is the warrant one's religious counterpart has to "sit tight." One should acknowledge that the religious counterpart from a DP other than one's own adheres to an *e* claim that is different; furthermore, that other *e* claim might even be *true*. By emphasizing the epistemic rights and possible claim to truth of the religious "Other," perhaps one might be more tolerant with regard to how vigorously one upholds her own *e* claim. Such an increase in tolerance could cause one to adhere to one's own *e* claim in a way that would impinge on the rights of others less. Although this book concludes by advocating religious exclusivism, it seems that tolerance for the claim to truth of one's religious counterpart constitutes the heart of religious tolerance. While religious realism and religious irrealism do indeed form the horns of a dilemma, Alston's DP approach provides an interpretation of religion that is maximally attractive. This is so in that, unlike the revisionary accounts of religious irrealism, religious realism acknowledges the claims to truth that are essential to religious doctrine, e.g., *e* claims, conflicting though these claims may be.

Nevertheless, it is recommended that we hold these truth claims with a degree of epistemic modesty, a modesty that is entirely appropriate given the epistemic credentials of rival claims. Acknowledging the truth claims of others and having appropriate modesty about one's own characterize an attitude that takes the philosophical problem of religious diversity seriously and could decrease the amount of blood that is needlessly spilled over religious conflict.

Appendix

Throughout the body of this book, it has been argued that when interpreting religion we face a dilemma: religious realism is faced with the philosophical problem of religious diversity and religious irrealism is revisionary. In the Introduction, it was stated that two levels of realism would be invoked. Ordinary religious realism entails the law of non-contradiction (not both p and not-p); in addition to the law of non-contradiction theoretical realism employs a correspondence theory of truth. Ordinary religious realism, by entailing the law of non-contradiction, accomplishes two tasks. It gives us the means to see how the matter of the conflicting truth claims of the world's religions does indeed constitute a problem: if one religion maintains p and other religions maintain not-p, we are left with the problem of knowing which, if any, of the e claims of the world's religions are true. Additionally, ordinary religious realism provides the means to show how irrealist interpretations of religion are revisionary; for a non-revisionary interpretation of religion when a given "p" is upheld, it is p that is being upheld. For ordinary religious realism, only that p obtains can make "p" true. This is not the case for religious irrealism which, as we have seen in the portion of the book devoted to religious irrealism, allows that any manner of states of affairs can count as truth-makers for a given religious "p." What ordinary religious realism does not provide is an account of what a match between "p" and p would consist in; nor is such an account needed since ordinary religious realism is not upheld as the correct interpretation of religion. That is, ordinary religious realism includes no attempt to provide an account of what the correct relation between a religious "p" and p must be in order for "p" to be true. Rather, ordinary religious realism is upheld here as the only possible prospect for a non-revisionary interpretation of religion. The task of providing an account of what the match between a religious "p" and p must be for "p" to be true falls within the province of what I have called theoretical religious realism. This discussion is the topic of the appendix.

Before beginning with the main business of the appendix, it should be noted that whether or not theoretical religious realism succeeds in providing an account of what the match between "p" and p should be for "p" to be true has no impact on the success of the overall argument in the main body of the book. This is because the dilemma by which this book is organized is based on what I have called ordinary religious realism. My intent here is simply to show how an account of theoretical realism might proceed even though such an undertaking is fraught with difficulties.

Though removed from the organizing principle of this project, a matter central to theoretical realism needs to be addressed. It has been argued that in order to avoid revisionism religious language must be interpreted in a realist sense. The dilemma by which the book has been organized is committed to ordinary religious realism only. However, the theoretical realist would be committed to the claim that if a particular instance of religious language is true, then what is described within that instance corresponds to an actual state of affairs. Furthermore, by being committed to the latter claim, the theoretical religious realist is responsible for providing an account of what it would mean for what is described within a particular instance of religious language to correspond to an actual state of affairs. It would seem that the obvious response to this concern would be to provide a viable correspondence theory of truth. And, if it were being argued that religious realism offers the only correct interpretation of religion and that religious irrealism offers an incorrect interpretation of religion, such a correspondence theory of truth would be necessary to provide. However, the overall argument of the book is not committed to the correctness of religious realism as "the one true story of the story of the world," as it were; accordingly, providing a compelling account of theoretical realism is not necessary. It has been argued only that ordinary religious realism is required to avoid revisionary interpretations of religion; theoretical religious realist interpretations (which I not only avoid but discourage), are those which are committed to providing an account of what the match between "p" and p must be for "p" to be true. As such, it is the theoretical religious realist that is obligated to give an account of what the match between "p" and p consists in. Despite the fact that theoretical realism has been avoided by the main argument of this book, the debate over the coherence of theoretical realism is an important one and is thus worthy of discussion. This discussion is the task of the appendix.

To give a plausible account of our everyday experiences might not be so difficult for a correspondence theorist of truth. The proposition, "That cup has coffee in it" is true if it corresponds to an actually obtaining state of affairs: that the cup in question has coffee in it. This proposition can be easily verified with the simplest of empirical tests, provided that one can reach the cup and knows what coffee tastes like. Countless times do we successfully operate in this manner. We could think of all of the times we have managed not to hurt ourselves by acting on the belief that our heads are lower than the ceiling: a belief that is true, according to this theory, since it corresponds with what is actually the case. Whether or not one is a proponent of a correspondence theory of truth it seems that we get around fine in our day to day lives in this manner. However, when it is the truth of religious language that is in question, testing the truthfulness of the claims of such language is not nearly so easy. How do we test the truthfulness of the claim that only through Jesus Christ can we be saved?

Since empirically testing the truthfulness of the claim that only through Jesus Christ can we be saved is unavailable to us, something other than the method described above is called for in this case. Additionally, promoting a correspondence theory of truth in this way would go against the philosophical grain of this book. Accordingly, an alternative course is taken here. Since the realist conception of truth articulated within this book has largely been drawn from the works of William Alston, it would seem reasonable to expect that a correspondence theory of truth, or at least something resembling one, could be culled from his thought. Alston's formal contribution to this topic, *A Realist Conception of Truth*, neither endorses nor repudiates a correspondence theory of truth. Within *A Realist Conception of Truth*, Alston argues that his realist conception of truth is compatible with correspondence theories and coherence theories of truth. I make this point out of fairness to Alston and to convey the overall spirit of this book. The general moral here: either be a religious realist and face the philosophical problem of religious diversity or be a religious irrealist and own up to being a revisionist commits one to no global philosophical theories. Accordingly, no global correspondence theory of truth will be forthcoming in this appendix.

However, there are important lessons to be learned from assessing the strengths and weaknesses of a correspondence theory of truth. Considering the classic exchange between J.L. Austin and P. F. Strawson[1] will serve as useful point of entry into the issues as they concern our current question: What would a match between language and what it describes consist in? In order for the match to be compatible with realism, the match must be between language and what it describes. Austin attempts to offer an account of the match between language and non-linguistic objects by providing a refined correspondence theory of truth. We get to the heart of the matter by considering what Strawson denies regarding Austin's correspondence theory of truth. Strawson doubts that we can even articulate what it would mean for language to describe extra-linguistic objects. Strawson writes

> Mr. Austin offers us a purified version of the correspondence theory of truth. On the one hand he disclaims the semanticists' error of supposing that 'true' is a predicate of sentences; on the other, the error of supposing that the relation of correspondence is other than purely conventional, the error which models the word on the world or the world on the word. His own theory is, roughly, that to say that a statement is true is to say that a certain speech-episode is related in a certain conventional way to something in the world exclusive to itself.[2]

Austin's refinement is to concede to the coherence theorist that a more robust correspondence theory is mistaken in "supposing that the relation of correspondence is other than purely conventional, the error which models the word on the world or the world on the word." Austin continues by allowing that we can, though, speak intelligibly of an extra-linguistic world. He writes,

136

"There must be also be something other than the words, this may be called the 'world.'" However, by adding that "[t]here is no reason why the world should not include the words..." Austin allows there to be the following ambiguity: words can be both part of the world and not part of the world.[3] This ambiguity leaves open the question of whether and how Austin will articulate what match there might be between language and what it describes.

Austin expresses this ambiguity further by articulating what he regards as truisms about correspondence theories of truth and coherence theories of truth. Of correspondence theories he writes, "When a statement is true, there is, *of course*, a state of affairs which makes it true and which is *toto mundo* distinct from the true statement about it: but equally of course, we can only *describe* that state of affairs *in words*."[4] While acknowledging this feature of coherentism (that we cannot escape language) Austin suggests the following with regard to relating language to what it describes. Acknowledging that language only replicates what it describes, Austin nevertheless argues that referring, having words represent objects outside of language, is a function of language. He writes, "Yet even when a language does 'mirror' such features very closely (and does it ever?) the truth of statements remains still a matter...of the words used being the ones conventionally appointed for situations of the type to which that referred to belongs." He continues, "There are various *degrees and dimensions* of success in making statements: the statements fit the facts always more or less loosely, in different ways on different occasions for different intents and purposes."[5]

While Austin acknowledges, of course, that we cannot conduct discourse outside of language, he again emphasizes that assertions describe a state of affairs beyond language. "To say that I believe you 'is' on occasion to accept your statement; but it is also to make an assertion, which is not made by the strictly performative utterance 'I accept your statement.'"[6] That is, to say "I believe you" also refers to a state of affairs beyond language showing that "I believe you" matches a state of affairs that is not merely a set of propositions. That is, the state of affairs described "I believe you" is not merely within language. One can observe from events that occur within the world and outside of language that "I believe you" is a true proposition. The overall point is one that is congenial to realism. Such observation does not occur within language, accordingly, we see that language relates to what it describes and not just to other instances of language.

Strawson objects to Austin's argument that a correspondence theory of truth can be purified. He contends that Austin's argument turns on an ambiguity concerning the idea that language refers. Wanting to clarify this ambiguity, Strawson writes,

This is not, of course, to deny that there is that in the world which a statement is about (true or false *of*), which is *referred to* and *described* and which the description fits (if the statement is true) or fails to fit (if the statement is false). This truism is…[indicative of]…a certain general way of using language, a certain type of discourse, viz., the fact-stating type of discourse.[7]

Strawson's point is that, while it is not the case that facts are in the world, the objects we refer to in statements of fact are in the world. He continues, "The only plausible candidate for the position of what (in the world) make the statement true is the fact it states; but the fact it states is not something in the world. It is not an object…Statements are about such objects; but they state facts."[8] Indeed, the notion that there is something about the world that makes factual statements true is, for Strawson, logically impossible:

[I]t is evident that the demand that there should be such a relatum [an extra-linguistic object described within language] is logically absurd: a logically fundamental type-mistake. But the demand for something in the world *which makes the statement true* (Mr. Austin's phrase), or *to which the statement corresponds when it is true*, is just this demand.[9]

The idea underlying correspondence theories of truth is that it is some extra-linguistic feature about the world that makes statements true or false. Strawson's objection to this notion is that for him, as cited above, facts occur entirely within language. He reinforces this idea when he indicates that, "Facts are what statements (when they are true) state; they are not what statements are about."[10] Again, for Strawson, facts occur entirely within language. According to Strawson, Austin employs the idea that a statement states a fact in an ambiguous fashion. According to Strawson, "the fundamental confusion of which Mr. Austin is guilty" is that he conflates "(*a*) the semantic conditions which must be satisfied for the statement that a certain statement is true to be itself true" with "(*b*) what is asserted when a certain statement is stated to be true."[11] He concludes by arguing that Austin's

central mistake is to suppose that in using the word 'true' we are asserting such conditions [the conditions which must obtain if we are correctly to declare a statement true] to obtain. That this is a mistake is shown by the detailed examination of the behaviour of such words as 'statement,' 'fact,' etc., and of 'true' itself, and by the examination of various different types of statement.[12]

Despite Austin's efforts to offer a refined correspondence theory of truth, the mistake Strawson cites above shows why his assessment is that the "correspondence theory requires, not purification, but elimination."[13]

Having acknowledged that for Strawson facts are not in the world and that the objects to which factual statements refer *are*, a question arises. We could ask how Strawson's account, by maintaining that factual statements refer to objects in the world, differs from correspondence theories of truth. For Strawson, as we have seen, facts occur within language, and according to P. F. Snowdon, "Strawson treats talk of states of affairs as equivalent to talk of facts..."[14] If "states of affairs" are indeed properly assimilated to "facts" then we can see that for Strawson what makes a statement true has to do entirely with linguistic considerations, not with considerations about how statements match what they purportedly describe about the world. The following passages shed light on this matter. According to Strawson, "There is no nuance, except of style, between 'That's true' and 'That's a fact.'...although we use the word 'true' when the semantic conditions described by Austin are fulfilled," the word 'true' patently does not state that those conditions are fulfilled."[15] These passages align with the idea that, for Strawson, to say that a statement is true is not to say that that statement matches the world beyond language which it purportedly describes; this shows the fundamental difference between Strawson's account and correspondence theories of truth. In contrast to correspondence theories of truth, which *do* hold that the truth of a statement consists in its matching the world beyond language it purportedly describes, for Strawson, to maintain that a statement is true is rather to confirm that it fulfills the functions of fact-stating language.

In his opposition to Austin's correspondence theory of truth, Strawson articulates what we call a coherence theory of truth. My aversion to such debates as those between coherence theorists and corresponding theorists has to do with a longstanding philosophical frustration. Placing this debate within a broader historical context will illustrate this. The following passage is from Austin, written in connection with the idea that language is an inadequate mirror of reality. "A picture, a copy, a replica, a photograph – these are *never* true in so far as they are reproductions..."[16] Though Austin expresses this idea as a report and Plato expresses the same idea throughout his corpus as a lament, the idea invoked by Austin reminds us that the question of what is most real ("true") and how this can be expressed has been around as long as people have been doing philosophy. Adapting Plato's lesson for the allegory of the cave to our topic, as shadows are less real than the objects of which they are shadows, words are less real than the objects they describe. Words fail to replicate what they describe. That we generally know the difference between the word "dog" and a dog,[17] despite the word's inability to replicate the furry barking animal might provide solace given that despite the efforts of some of the best minds from Plato up to the present we still do not have a compelling account of what such replication would consist in. Or, perhaps the fact that some two millennia plus years later we still have philosophers of the stature of Austin and Strawson debating over what is essentially the same matter should give us pause. Adapting a lesson I learned as an undergraduate in a course on the history of modern philosophy (this adage was told to me in connection with Rationalists and Empiricists): Throw a brick at a correspondence theorist and a coherence theorist; they'll both duck. That for a correspondence theorist "Getting struck with a brick hurts" corresponds with a non-linguistic feature of the world and that for a coherence theorist "Getting struck with a brick hurts" is an instance of language (as is my writing about it now, of course) that coheres with other propositions we know to be true about getting struck with heavy objects seems irrelevant. It's the ducking that matters; stating that the reason for one's ducking is due to being a proponent of a correspondence or coherence theory seems to be appending a mere battle cry in the most trivial sense as expressed in the passage from *Zettel* cited earlier.[18] Regardless of the theoretical positions we may or may not advocate, we all have ways of interacting with the world that are generally successful. If they were not, we would have much greater incidence of people running into things, these collisions the consequence of disconnects between what we hold to be true ("p") and what is the case (p).[19]

Consistent with the entirety of this book, I find the later thought of Wittgenstein to have provided the most penetrating critiques of realism. Thus we could turn to Wittgenstein in assessing the viability of trying to give an account of what the match between language and what it describes would consist in. We could make this challenge to Wittgenstein; wisely, though, he would not bite. For Wittgenstein, if we want to know how language relates to what it is describing…we should look to see how such language is used;[20] we should look at the practice in which this language has its sense. He would not fall prey to the idea by which the debate between correspondence and coherence theories of truth even gets started: that the truthfulness of language has to do with sorting out the nature of how it matches what it describes. Within what linguistic community would an inquiry concerning this match take place? In an article from 1981, returning to our source for conceiving of realism concerning truth, Alston begins to answer just such a question; and, in Alston's answer we see that his realism, that is, his way of addressing the issue of the nature of the match between language and what it describes, has significant affinities with the later work of Wittgenstein.

In addition to outlining his Wittgensteinian affinities, in the context of religious language Alston argues that whatever such a linguistic practice might consist in, it must be able to take into account a non-revisionary interpretation of religion. Alston's attention to Wittgensteinian concerns regarding grounding the meaning of language within practice coupled with his realist concerns regarding avoiding revisionary interpretations of religion make his work a maximally attractive response to the dilemma by which the book has been organized. Alston articulates these two concerns within the context of the idea of a personal God who acts. He develops this argument as follows. The

Christian understanding of God entails that God is a personal being since the kinds of activities attributed to God within Christian doctrine, such as "promising, thanking, and confessing are only suitable for games concerned with 'personal' beings."[21] So, according to Alston, a Christian life includes an understanding of God which involves God doing things, creating the heavens and the earth, say. Even if we maintain such an agential understanding of God, that is, an understanding God that has God doing things, along the lines of a language-game which by its nature is epistemically autonomous, this does not seem to help as far as having a God who *does* things. This is the case since any understanding of God which includes a God who *does* things still seems to require a realist interpretation. That is, for God to *do* things, God must exist independently of what we believe, do, or say. A construct of my cognitive machinations or linguistic practices cannot do anything; i.e., such a construct could not be a personal agent such Christian doctrine holds God to be.[22]

Suppose "God exists" can be construed as being true within a language-game. What does "'God exists' is true" mean within that language-game? Alston offers the following Wittgensteinian interpretation of truth: "If you play the game, you are committed to those standards and their application; if you don't, you are not. And that's all that can be said."[23] The question to be raised at this point, then, is: Does such an understanding of truth, so contextualized within the parameters of a language-game, allow for the possibility that Christian language could be in touch with reality? However, a Wittgensteinian approach will not countenance this question at face value. This is seen in the Wittgensteinian reply anticipated by Alston to the question above: "from within what language-game will you conduct this inquiry?"[24]

Alston, while acknowledging the epistemic significance of language-games, maintains that language-games can be assessed by external measures of truthfulness. He writes, "language-games are only relatively autonomous, claims in one can conflict with claims in another, can support or weaken claims in another..." But how can a seemingly epistemically autonomous language-game be assessed by anything other than its own criteria? To answer this, Alston offers the following three "language-game neutral standards and criteria": consistency, parsimony, and adequacy of explanation.[25] What we have here seems to be a clear case of "language idling," according to Wittgenstein. That is, how can the above three criteria have any sense apart from linguistic practice? In just what sense are they neutral? These are fair questions. However, rather than trying to sort out whether there could be such a thing as an adjudicatory meta-language, which is another important question, Alston considers the implications of asking whether the Christian language-game is in touch with reality. To do so, Alston offers an analysis of how it differs from other language-games, e.g., the physical world language-game. The point of this comparison is to assess whether one can intelligibly ask whether a language-game is in touch with reality.

Alston considers how the following five factors influence whether the Christian language-game is any more or less in touch with reality than, e.g., the language-game about physical world. The first point to consider regarding the Christian language-game is that, as Alston puts it: 1) "Not everyone plays."[26] So the point here is that we seem to have an important dissimilarity in that whereas everyone plays the physical-world language-game, only a portion of people participate in the Christian language-game. Likewise concerning the second factor: 2) "those who play (or many of them) can imagine what it is like not to do so." Whereas we cannot help but play the language-game about the physical world, the Christian language-game does not have that same inevitability attaching to it.[27] Playing the physical world language-game, if one sees an anvil falling from the sky, about to land on her head, she would know, *a propos* to the language-game, that the next move would be, "Get out of the way!" However, and this brings us to 3): within the Christian language-game, even "among the players there is a great deal of uncertainty about various moves…" And this leads into the next, fourth factor for consideration. Given the uncertainty of what moves are to be made within the Christian language-game, we can see why it would be the case that 4): "Mastery of the Christian language-game is unequally distributed among the participants."[28] Another way to put this is that, within the Christian language-game, there is enough uncertainty regarding which moves are to be made, there are people designated to help sort through this uncertainty thus constituting the unequal distribution of mastery. To put it more starkly, while there is an apparent need for a clergy to sort through the uncertainties of life within the Christian language-game, there is no analogous clergy required to sort out moves within the physical world language-game.[29] Finally, the idea that the physical world language-game is more in touch with reality than the Christian language-game, according to Alston, is further buttressed by 5): our "confidence that we are really on to something with physical-object talk is shored up by the fact that the predictions we make within the game are, by and large, borne out."[30] We can be fairly certain that the aforementioned anvil plummeting overhead will continue to fall; meanwhile, countless Christians are still awaiting the parousia. This lack of predictive efficacy contributes to Alston's overall point that these five factors "add up to a rather considerable case against the supposition that the Christian language-game puts us in touch with reality."[31] This point, taken together with Alston's insistence that Christian doctrine be given a realist interpretation adds up to an interesting conclusion. While the five cases that Alston makes against the Christian language-game's being in touch with reality echo positions critical of religion, it is clear that Alston is sympathetic to religious life. So what Alston is criticizing is not Christianity but the language-game approach to it. Its central weakness, as we have begun to see, is that a language-game approach to Christian doctrine cannot accommodate alethic realism.

Having used the five factors above to argue that whereas a strong case can be made that the physical world language-game is in touch with reality but the Christian language-game is not, Alston is quick to add that it is not the case that he has trumped up a weak case of Christianity to be considered as a language-game. Indeed, he offers three criteria for a viable language-game and indicates that the physical world language-game as well as the Christian language-game can satisfy them. They are 1) "it (the language game in question) is an ongoing concern, an established practice…" 2) "We can determine whether it contradicts anything that is firmly established in other language-games we play"; and, 3) "We can see whether it is internally coherent." A typical Wittgensteinian objection at this point would be to argue that language-games cannot be assessed except from within. Alston acknowledges the circularity of his criteria when he states: "we cannot carry out these tests without using the language-game being tested, with 3) being the most important test."[32]

Now we are at the interesting point suggested earlier. The Christian language-game could be a viable one, according to Alston's three criteria above, but, the language-game approach to Christianity seems to have no way to articulate such crucial elements of traditional Christian belief and practice as, e.g., God's bestowal of grace, which requires a realist interpretation. Indeed, Alston asks, "What implications does [the language-game] approach have for the explication of theological concepts?" Furthermore, "how does [the language-game] approach help us to understand what it is for God to forgive, speak, or love?"[33] In short, irrealism, Wittgensteinian non-realism included, seems to have no way to include divine action within Christian life since divine action requires an independence of human experience that a language-game approach cannot accommodate.

How can such seemingly essential aspects of Christian life as divine agency be saved while also taking into account Wittgensteinian criticisms of metaphysics? We can see how Alston begins to take on such a question in his next work for consideration. The first thing to establish in trying to find any relation between Wittgensteinian and realist approaches to God is whether these two very different approaches are even addressing the same matters. For example, a realist might be likely to say, "either God exists or not" versus a Wittgensteinian who, as we have seen, might say, "why must it be either/or?" Alston begins to address the matter of such "talking past" each other on the part of theological realists and non-realists, focusing on the Wittgensteinian, D.Z. Phillips. Alston writes,

> practically everyone who rejects Phillips's position on what is and what is not relevant
> to the assessment of religious beliefs has no use for the language-game framework...if
> [Phillips's detractors] did agree to talk language-game lingo, they would be arguing that
> Phillips has misconstrued the character of religious language-games.[34]

Alston, while retaining his realism, maintains that the language-game framework can be very useful, thus showing that he is not "talking-past" Wittgensteinian issues but addressing them head-on. In "Taking the Curse off Language-Games" Alston does just this with his discussion of how what he calls "doxastic (belief-forming) practices," which have significant similarities to Wittgensteinian language-games, can take into account Wittgensteinian critiques of metaphysics yet retain their compatibility with realism.

For ease of reference I reproduce the features associated with Wittgensteinian language-games so that we can compare and contrast them with DPs construed along Alstonian lines.

a. Like a game, language is rule-governed.

b. Rules determine which moves make sense.

c. The meaning of the word is determined by the rules of the game.

d. There is an irreducible multiplicity of language-games.

e. The idea of a language-game does not have an essential definition but is a family-resemblance concept.

f. Using the rules of one language-game to assess another invites confusion.

g. Language-games are connected with practice.

h. Language-games do not require justification by external sources.

i. Language-games are rooted in our natural activities.[35]

By comparing these ideas associated with Wittgensteinian language-games with features associated with Alstonian DPs, the burden is on Alston to show that his DP approach does not lapse into confusion by virtue of its allowing a realist conception of truth. Alston's realist conception of truth is supported through its relation to doxastic practices; and, insofar as Alston's conception of doxastic practices (DPs) does indeed reflect Wittgenstein's conception of language-games, Alston has a significant response to the Wittgensteinian charge that realism lapses into metaphysical confusion. Alston describes DPs with the four following points, in large part derived from Wittgenstein's conception of language-games.[36] 1) "There is an irreducible plurality of DPs;" 2) DPs have a "pre-reflective genesis;" that is, they "are acquired and engaged in well before one is explicitly aware of them and subjects them to criticism." Also, 3) most "DPs are thoroughly social"; and 4) DPs have "[i]nvolvement in wider spheres of practice" since, and this seems to be a deviation from Wittgenstein, "there can be…external criticism of a DP."[37]

The similarities between language-games and DPs will be discussed; then, the most significant dissimilarity must be noted. Obviously, feature 1) from the list characterizing DPs is identical with feature d), and thus intimates feature e), from the language-game list. This is significant since it indicates a shared attitude of these endeavors (DPs and language-games) as being best described as family-resemblance concepts. There is no essential definition for either; but, there is an irreducible multiplicity of endeavors that we would recognize as DPs or language-games. Feature 2) of DPs resonates with h) and j) from the language-game list. We do not think first and then have a DP or language-game that is an outgrowth of that thought. We have our natural activities and practices which are constituted by rules for what makes sense within that practice. DP feature 3), I suggest, is very rich with regard to its compatibility with many features from the language-game list. In order for a practice to be genuinely (and "thoroughly") social, there must be some *shared* sense of what is proper and improper within that practice. This squares with the Wittgensteinian sensibility that games (including language-games) are rule-governed, even if every detail of a game is not dictated by rules. So while games, and other social activities, might be very loosely structured, there is that backdrop of structure against which moves within that activity are recognized as proper or not.

So while the first three characteristics of DPs echo Wittgenstein's conception of language-games, there is the dissimilarity that Alston allows external criticism in the fourth aspect of a DP cited above. This is a dissimilarity given feature f) suggesting that assessing a language-game from without invites confusion. While acknowledging that practice is at least partially determinative of meaning *within* a DP, Alston argues that a DP can be assessed externally. To wit, "a massive and persistent inconsistency between the outputs of two (DPs) is a good reason for regarding at least one of them as unreliable." Additionally, Alston also emphasizes that the internal incoherence of a DP can be used to assess that DP when he writes, "it counts against a DP if its outputs exhibit massive and persistent mutual inconsistency."[38] Thus, a massive and persistent inconsistency *between* one or more DPs is reason to regard at least one of them as unreliable; moreover, massive and persistent inconsistency *within* a DP is reason to regard it as unreliable.

By emphasizing the epistemic autonomy of a given language-game, contrary to Alston, Wittgensteinians are typically not prepared to indicate how it is that claims within a language-game link up with "the world" or "reality." Thus language-games are regarded as being insulated from evidential appraisal from without. Indeed a Wittgensteinian reply would be that such efforts are mistaken. "What would it mean to 'link up' with reality?" "How would such an inquiry proceed?" Such would be typical Wittgensteinian remarks. But, Alston contends, utilizing the example of religion, this Wittgensteinian demurral regarding the "linkability" of language to external (i.e., non-linguistic) reality

> is incompatible with what also seems obvious – that religion typically involves commitments to certain states of affairs obtaining in the world. In theistic religions there is the commitment to supposing that God is real and active in certain ways, has a certain nature, and makes certain requirements on us. One can acknowledge this without in any way denying the primacy of the practical and affective in the religious life.[39]

As we saw earlier in the passages cited from Wittgenstein, true propositions, construed along the lines of language-games, do *not* refer to extra-linguistic states of affairs. What is true is determined within the language-game. This runs contrary to the realist conception of truth allowed by Alstonian DPs: "p" is true if and only if it is the case that p.

So while Wittgensteinian language-games bear striking resemblances to Alstonian DPs, there is the significant difference that whereas a language-game approach will not allow a realist conception of truth, a DP approach will; as such, we have a means for treating the match between language and what it describes that has significant affinities with the later thought of Wittgenstein and the advantages thereunto appertaining. For example, if we want to understand the truthfulness of a given instance of language, we are recommended to look at the practice in which the language has its sense. The requirement to look beyond language to find what state of affairs would make a given "p" true is thus recognized to be the wild goose chase that it is. However, by grounding his realist conception of truth within the context of DPs, Alston retains the ability to acknowledge religious truth claims in a non-revisionary way. This approach is not without problems. Alston must contend with the philosophical problem of religious diversity; and, we still have no account for what the match between language and what it describes consists in. I close by having thus reinforced the idea that this book was organized according to the dilemma facing the interpretation of religion. Though Alston has provided a maximally attractive account for how we might go about negotiating this dilemma, it is a dilemma nonetheless. Alston's realism is subject to the dilemma, too.

Notes

Chapter 1: Introduction

[1]   The idea that religious realism gives rise to the philosophical problem of religious diversity has been overlooked in the past, causing much of the literature on this topic to suffer from obfuscation. One of the goals of this book is to clarify such confusions. The idea that irrealist interpretations of religion are revisionary is also addressed in this book as is the concept of making realism a condition of a non-revisionary interpretation of religion. Any credit that is due must be shared with two sources, the latter somewhat ironically. I first encountered this idea in William Alston's "Realism and the Christian Faith," *International Journal for Philosophy of Religion* 38 (1995). I became further convinced that realism is a condition of a non-revisionary interpretation of religion upon reading John Hick's "Religious Realism and Non-Realism: Defining the Issue," in *Is God Real?* Joseph Runzo ed. (Houndsmills, *et al*: Macmillan, 1993). Even though Hick argues compellingly for the idea that realism is a condition of a non-revisionary interpretation of religion, as I will argue in the chapter devoted to my analysis of Hick's relevant works, the well known case he makes for religious pluralism is essentially revisionary. Though the focus will be on the problems posed by religious diversity and revisionism, there are other problems facing his interpretation of religion. These involve the metaphysical commitments of religious realism, a topic that will be discussed in the Appendix. This dilemma is most applicable considered within the context of what we might call theoretical reason as opposed to practical considerations, e.g. practical reason and ritual.

[2]   The terminology "instance of religious language" is used here instead of the more standard "religious proposition" to keep open the question of whether religious language is propositional. The issue of whether religious language admits of truth or falsity or is factual in nature will be discussed in the portion of the book devoted to religious non-realism.

[3]   By referencing Acts 4:12 I am not privileging Christianity; *mutatis mutandis*, we can make any religion our reference point. I use Acts 4:12 because of its clear articulation of its being uniquely true among conflicting *e* claims. That is, according to Acts 4:12, salvation cannot be attained by following the teachings of Christ *or* Muhammad (*or* Buddha, *or* Mahavira, *or* Zoraster, and so on). *Only* the teachings of Christ can provide the means to salvation, according to Acts 4:12. It is this presumption of being uniquely true that characterizes an *e* claim.

[4]   This is based on what William Alston calls the "T-schema." Alston's articulation of alethic realism, realism concerning truth, appears throughout his work; however, he explicitly enunciates it as the T-schema in his *A Realist Conception of Truth* (Ithaca, NY: Cornell University Press, 1996), 179. While it is the case that I have drawn my formulation of realism from Alston, our two formulations have a significant dissimilarity. My conception of realism involves the commitment that "p" is true if and only if p obtains. Alston's conception of realism is formulated as p is true if and only if p. For my articulation of realism, the match between a given "p," an instance of language, and p, what that language describes, I am not committed to providing an account of what constitutes the nature of the match between "p" and p. My argument throughout the book is not that realism provides the correct interpretation of religion but that realism provides the only non-revisionary way to interpret religion. Thus my argument does not rise or fall based on the ability to give a realist account of what the match between a given "p" and p would consist in. However, since this issue is central to realism, it will be discussed it in the Appendix.

[5]   The independence condition I describe includes *independent of our personal mental inventories*. This caveat disallows first person incorrigible statements to count as being true in a realist sense. These are the kinds of statements whose truth depends entirely on their author's

holding them to be true. "I say chocolate ice cream is delicious" is an example of such a statement; it can be true only if I assent to it and it cannot be false as long as I do. The kinds of religious propositions on which I am focusing are statements that ostensibly report on that which transcends our personal mental inventories. It might also be noted that my description of realism excludes Kantians, according to whom our cognitive input is essential to our perceiving the external world. Technically, this is correct; Kantians are excluded from realism as I define it, and they probably would have no problem with that. Whenever Kantians do consider themselves realists, e.g., John Hick, they typically qualify this identification by calling themselves "critical realists." In fact, this is precisely what Hick does. Furthermore, as I argue in the chapter devoted to Hick, it is Hick's Kantianism that undermines his claim to religious realism.

6   I define religious pluralism as the belief that more than one of the world's religions contains the path to the ultimate reward. As I will be using the terms, pluralism, ecumenism, inclusivism, and universalism are sufficiently similar for our purposes such that I will use them synonymously unless otherwise noted.

7   This claim needs to be qualified with regard to what I call Wittgensteinian non-realism. Such Wittgensteinian nuance, I argue that Wittgenstein is not a relativist, will be discussed in more detail in chapters 6 and 7.

8   It should be noted that a realist interpretation of religion could still be revisionary. One could be a realist about God, e claims, what have you, but uphold revisionary truth conditions by which the veridicality of these ideas would be assessed. For example, a realist conception of the Christian God that maintains that this deity is a flower would still be revisionary even though upheld to be true in a realist sense. Noting this in no way alters the terms of the dilemma. All religious realist interpretations of religion face the philosophical problem of religious diversity and all irrealist interpretations of religion are revisionary. My point here is simply that being a realist does not preclude the possibility of also being a revisionist.

9   I thank Tony Edwards of the University of Pittsburgh for suggesting this distinction.

10   In "God, Commitment, and Other Faiths: Pluralism vs. Relativism," in *Philosophy of Religion: An Anthology*, ed. Louis P. Pojman, (Belmont, CA: Wadsworth Publishing Company, 4th edition, 2003), Joseph Runzo presents six responses to the issue of the conflicting truth claims of the religions of the world. Runzo's suggestion that there are six such responses is indicative of the confusion that arises when one does not explicitly countenance the matter of religious realism as presented by the dilemma I pose. His six responses split insignificant hairs without addressing the fundamental issue to be faced in terms of the conflicting truth claims that comprise the world's religious landscape: whether one is realist or irrealist about these truth claims. Not acknowledging this matter explicitly leads Runzo into a rather inconsistent position. Though in other contexts (see, for example, Joseph Runzo, "Perceiving God, World-Views, and Faith: Meeting the Problem of Religious Pluralism," in *The Rationality of Belief and the Plurality of Faith,* ed. Thomas D. Senor, [Ithaca, NY: Cornell University Press, 1995]) he recommends religious realism, the stance he recommends in the 2003 article he calls religious relativism. I am arguing that relativism is revisionary, irrealist. To put it in Runzo's words, religious relativism is the position that "at least one, and probably more than one, world religion is correct, and the correctness of a religion is relative to the worldview(s) of its community of adherents" (Runzo, 2003, 536). As I have indicated, this may be a fine position to take; however, we should be clear that a relativist interpretation of an e claim (which Runzo acknowledges that all religions make in some form) is inescapably irrealist and revisionary.

11   The position that no e claims are correct still must contend with the philosophical problem of religious diversity in that it maintains a truth claim, that no e claim is correct, that conflicts with other religious claims to truth.

12   *Faith and Philosophy* 14, no. 3, (1997).

13   Having indicated why I will give more attention to realist exclusivism, I should also offer an explanation for why I will not give any attention to irrealist exclusivism. Applying an irrealist conception of truth to *e* claims will not yield the same precise results due to irrealism's lack of an independence condition. For example, to be an irrealist exclusivist is an incoherent notion. Christian exclusivism can illustrate this point. Christian exclusivism consists in the idea that the conditions described by Acts 4:12 do obtain and that only the obtaining of these conditions *could* make Acts 4:12 true. For irrealism the truth of a given *p*, in this case Acts 4:12, does not depend on its matching the conditions it describes. Thus, there is no precise or systematic connection between irrealist interpretations of *e* claims and options a) b) and c) described above.

14   The following account supports my characterization of philosophical theory. When asked why knowledge is constituted the way that it is, the, e.g., Rationalist, *qua* Rationalist, will give an answer that consists of one organizing principle. The, e.g., Empiricist, *qua* Empiricist, will give a different answer that consists of a different organizing principle. In contrast, the Wittgensteinian would not seek an organizing principle such as we associate with these theories of knowledge. For the Wittgensteinian, the way to avoid the vicious regresses that questions like "What is the nature of knowledge?" bewitch us into embarking upon, is not to ask the question. We employ the concept "knowledge" successfully in our ordinary language and practice; we trip ourselves up when we confusedly ask questions like "What is the nature of knowledge."

15   Consider the following example: Question: "Why do we call that a 'chair'?" Answer: "That's what we call pieces of furniture that have that kind of form and function." Question: "Why do we call a piece of furniture that has that kind of form and function a 'chair'?" Answer: "Because we speak English." Question: "Why do we speak English?" A philosophical theory might offer an a priori answer to end the regress of such questions. A candidate for such an a priori answer could be, "because we are mentally constituted in such and such way…" However, it is such regresses that the later works of Wittgenstein, I think rightly, suggest that we should not even start. The response, "This is what we do," would, in this case, express an appropriate aversion to philosophical theorizing. Such matters get treated more fully in chapter 6.

Chapter 2: Overview of Religious Realism

1   Some works by prominent twentieth-century religious realists include the following: The collection of essays *Is God Real?* ed. Joseph Runzo (Houndsmill: Macmillan, 1993). See Roger Trigg, *Reality at Risk* (Brighton: Harvester Press, 1980), and his entry "Theological Realism and Antirealism," in *A Companion to Philosophy of Religion*, eds. Philip L. Quinn and Charles Taliaferro (Cambridge, Mass.: Blackwell Publishers, 1997). Peter Byrne, *Prolegomena to Religious Pluralism: Reference and Realism in Religion* (Houndsmills et al: Macmillan Press; New York: St. Martin's Press, 1995). For a forceful expression of Alvin Plantinga's realist views on theological matters, see especially his *Warranted Christian Belief* (Oxford: Oxford University Press, 2000). John Hick's expression of realism is of special interest within this project.

2   It should be noted that "alethic realism" is not being used in identical ways in William P. Alston, *A Realist Conception of Truth* (Ithaca: Cornell University Press, 1996) and William P. Alston, "Realism and the Christian Faith," *International Journal for Philosophy of Religion* 38 (1995). In *A Realist Conception of Truth*, Alston maintains that alethic realism is compatible with various kinds of metaphysical anti-realism, in particular Hilary Putnam's "conceptual relativity," as well as its

Kantian antecedents. I thank Professor Alston for pointing this out to me. For our purposes here, I will adhere to the criteria set out above in "Realism and the Christian Faith."

3   Alston, "Realism and the Christian Faith," 39.

4   Alston, "Realism and the Christian Faith," 39.

5   Alston, *A Realist Conception of Truth* , p. 74.

6   Alston, *A Realist Conception of Truth*, 74.

7   William Alston. *A Realist Conception of Truth A Realist Conception of Truth*, 75.

8   William Wainwright does discuss the matter of truth claims based on mystical experience within cross-cultural context in his *Mysticism: A Study of Its Nature, Cognitive Value, and Moral Implications* (Madison: University of Wisconsin Press, 1981). For one, Wainwright argues that cross-cultural mystical experiences are sufficiently similar to categorize them together. For example, Hindu, Buddhist, Jewish, Christian and Islamic instances of mystical experience are sufficiently similar to be properly thought of as all being mystical experiences. Arguments that tradition-specific instances are too culturally determined to count as being instances of a generic concept "mystical experience" (e.g., that of Steven Katz) are not compelling, according to Wainwright. He offers the following analogy to discredit such arguments. "The gastronomic experiences of Eskimos, Parisians, and Vietnamese are quite different. There is a strong correlation between these experiences and their cultures. Nevertheless, it would be absurd to suppose that the connection was anything but contingent, and that a person from a different culture could not have the gastronomic experience of an Eskimo" (pp. 20-21). What we can glean from this regarding the matter of religious diversity is that although mystical experiences may indeed be (to some extent) culturally determined, this in itself does not rule out the possibility that mystical experiences could be experiences of a similar nature. Of course, the case made by Wainwright does not prove that cross-cultural mystical experiences *are* similar in nature (nor is such proof his stated goal).

9   Alston, *A Realist Conception of Truth*, 73.

10   Alston, "Realism and the Christian Faith," 37. Theological irrealism is subversive in that irrealist interpretations of religion drop essential features of standard, traditional, classical religious doctrine. To make this claim, though, we need to stipulate what we mean by such doctrine. Obviously this topic is vast and a thorough treatment of this matter is beyond the scope of this project. Nevertheless, the words of Alvin Plantinga will suffice for our purposes here. "When I speak here of Christian belief, I mean what is common to the great creeds of the main branches of the Christian church, what unites Calvin and Aquinas, Luther and Augustine, Menno Simons and Karl Barth, Mother Theresa and St. Maximus the Confessor, Billy Graham and St. Gregory Palamas – classical Christian belief, as we might call it" (Plantinga, *Warranted Christian Belief*, vii).

11   Alston, "Realism and the Christian Faith," 49.

12   Whether or not Hick believes himself to have demonstrated that God exists in a realist sense (his Kantian inclinations would preclude such a conclusion), his conception of divinity indicates that he wants to reap the benefits of a realist conception of divinity.

13   Alston, "Realism and the Christian Faith," 45.

14   Alston, "Realism and the Christian Faith," 47.

15   There is an unfortunate coincidence of terminology within the literature. Therefore, I want to make it clear that I am employing a different usage of *epistemic* here. Whereas I have been using "epistemic status" in contrast to "truth status," here I am using the term *epistemic* somewhat differently. Here I am using epistemic arguments (or reasons) in contrast to prudentialist arguments (or reasons); that is, the cosmological, teleological, and ontological arguments are all epistemic arguments for the existence of God. Such arguments contrast with prudentialist

arguments for the existence of God (e.g., Pascal's Wager). The former are attempts to show that there are good reasons for believing in God; the latter employ the benefits that come with believing in God.

[16]   John Hick, "The Epistemological Challenge of Religious Pluralism," *Faith and Philosophy* 14 (1997): 277.

[17]   William P. Alston, "Religious Diversity and Perceptual Knowledge of God," in *The Philosophical Challenge of Religious Diversity*, eds. Philip L. Quinn and Kevin Meeker (Oxford: Oxford University Press, 2000), 193.

[18]   Alston, "Religious Diversity," 201. A "doxastic practice" (DP) is a belief-forming practice. This is a term used by Alston to represent the idea that while our beliefs are formed by our practices, our beliefs can still be true or false in a realist sense. DPs will be discussed in greater detail in chapter 8.

Chapter 3: A Realist Interpretation of Religious Diversity

[1]   The first edition was published in 1989; the second in 2005, both by Yale University Press.

[2]   I am not concerned with all authors who have written in response to Hick; the following list is limited to authors who focus on Hick's pluralism. These treatments include the anthologies *The Rationality of Faith, the Plurality of Belief* (Ithaca, NY: Cornell University Press, 1995) Thomas D. Senor, ed.; *The Philosophical Challenge of Religious Diversity* (Oxford: Oxford University Press, 2000) Philip L. Quinn and Kevin Meeker, eds.; the issue of *Faith and Philosophy*, vol. 14, no. 3, 1997 devoted to John Hick's pluralistic hypothesis; Jerome Gellman, "In Defense of Contented Religious Exclusivism," *Religious Studies* 36 (2000), 401-17; Robert McKim, *Religious Ambiguity and Religious Diversity* (Oxford: Oxford University Press, 2001); Paul J. Griffiths *Problems of Religious Diversity* (Oxford: Blackwell, 2001); David Basinger, *Religious Diversity: A Philosophical Assessment* (Burlington, VT: Ashgate, 2002). Kevin Schilbrack's recent review article also provides an informative overview, "Religious Diversity and the Closed Mind," *Journal of Religion*, 83 (2003), 100-7. I make special note of Harold Netland's *Dissonant Voices* (Grand Rapids, MI: Eerdmans, 1991). I make special note of his work since the criticisms I level against Hick's pluralistic hypothesis are congenial to Netland's. However, my criticisms are the result of addressing fundamental issues concerning the interpretation of religion. I am not offering a proposed solution to the problem of religious diversity; I am trying to shed light so that we may better understand the problem. Netland's work differs from mine in that his criticisms of Hick occur within the context of his defense of Christianity in the face of religious diversity; i.e., I include Netland's work in the category of proposed solutions to the problem of religious diversity.

[3]   John Hick, *An Interpretation of Religion* 2nd ed. (New Haven: Yale University Press, 2005), 177.

[4]   For our purposes we can gloss this as meaning that he holds that more than one religion offers true e claims.

[5]   This thread is woven throughout Hick's body of work. He is chiefly concerned that irrealism gives rise to reductionist (naturalist, specifically) interpretations of religion. He states this explicitly in John Hick, "Religious Pluralism and Salvation," in *The Philosophical Challenge of Religious Diversity*, eds. Philip L. Quinn and Kevin Meeker (Oxford: Oxford University Press, 2000), 61.

[6]   The same reasoning could be applied to non-theistic religions, giving rise to the awkward neologism "poly-religionism."

[7]   Hick, *An Interpretation of Religion*, 248. To be true to Hick's terminology, instead of employing the terminology of deity, he describes various forms of Personae and Impersonae of the Real. Even so, Hick consistently describes "the Real" as singular.

[8]   Hick, "Religious Pluralism and Salvation," 59

[9]   Hick, *An Interpretation of Religion*, 56.

[10]   Immanuel Kant, *Critique of Pure Reason* trans. Norman Kemp Smith (New York: Random House, Inc., 1958), A 51 = B 75. Hereafter, Kant's first *Critique* will be cited by referring to the first (A) edition and/or second (B) edition.

[11]   David Hume, *An Enquiry Concerning Human Understanding*, The Nelson Philosophical Texts series (Austin: University of Texas Press, 1953), 172.

[12]   Donald Palmer, *Looking at Philosophy* (London: Mayfield Publishing Company, 1994), 191.

[13]   Kant, *Critique of Pure Reason*, B 306.

[14]   Paul Guyer, "Introduction," in *The Cambridge Companion to Kant*, ed. Paul Guyer, (Cambridge: Cambridge University Press, 1992), 17, hereafter to be cited as CCK.

[15]   Frederick Beiser, "Kant's Intellectual Development: 1746-1781," in CCK, 47.

[16]   Beiser, in CCK, 48.

[17]   Albert W. J. Harper, *Discussion and Commentary on Kant's Critiques* (Lewiston, NY: The Edwin Mellen Press, Ltd., 1996), 29.

[18]   Harper, *Discussion and Commentary on Kant's Critiques*, 29.

[19]   Kant, 1958, B 315, in Harper, *Discussion and Commentary on Kant's Critiques* 1996, 39, note 75.

[20]   Harper, *Discussion and Commentary on Kant's Critiques*, 29.

[21]   Beiser, in CCK, 49.

[22]   Kant, *Critique of Pure Reason*, B 310.

[23]   *Critique of Pure Reason*, A 255.

[24]   *Critique of Pure Reason*, B 307.

[25]   *Critique of Pure Reason*, B 309.

[26]   *Critique of Pure Reason*, A 255 = B 310, emphases in original.

[27]   *Critique of Pure Reason*, B 312-315.

[28]   Philip J. Rossi, "The Final End of All Things," in *Kant's Philosophy of Religion Reconsidered*, eds. Philip J. Rossi and Michael Wreen (Bloomington and Indianapolis: Indiana University Press, 1991), 140.

[29]   Godlove goes even further in forwarding the nonsubjectivist (and nonrelativist) import of Kant's epistemology. He does so by highlighting Kant's transcendental strategy when he writes, "In fact, for Kant, the necessity attaching to the categories and forms of receptivity is (somehow) independent of *me* altogether, insofar as I am a psychological subject capable of entertaining thoughts. Since the categories make objectivity possible, they are rather a condition for my having thoughts about anything, including about the epistemic status of my own categories and forms of receptivity" (Godlove, *Religion, Interpretation, and Diversity of Belief*, 16, original emphasis in original).

[30]   Kant, *Critique of Pure Reason*, A 591 = B 619.

[31]   Alston, "Realism and the Christian Faith," 46-47.

[32]   Hick, *An Interpretation of Religion*, 174.

[33]   John Hick, "The Epistemological Challenge of Religious Pluralism," *Faith and Philosophy*, 1997, vol. 14, 279.

[34]   Hick, "The Epistemological Challenge of Religious Pluralism," 279.

[35]   Hick, *An Interpretation of Religion*, 291.

[36]   John Hick, "Religious Realism and Non-Realism: Defining the Issue," in *Is God Real?* ed. Joseph Runzo (Houndsmills: Macmillan, 1993), 12.

[37]   Hick, "Religious Pluralism and Salvation," 55, 58.

[38]   Alston, "Realism and the Christian Faith," 39-40.

[39]   Alston, "Realism and the Christian Faith," 42.

[40]   Alston, "Realism and the Christian Faith," 43.

[41]   As already noted, whether or not Hick believes himself to have demonstrated that God exists in a realist sense, the conception of divinity he employs throughout his work indicates that he wants to reap the benefits of a realist conception of divinity, namely, to avoid the charge of giving a revisionary interpretation of religion.

[42]   George Mavrodes describes Hick as "probably the most important philosophical defender of polytheism in the history of Western philosophy"; see (George I. Mavrodes, "Polytheism," in *The Philosophical Challenge of Religious Diversity*, eds. Philip L. Quinn and Kevin Meeker (Oxford: Oxford University Press, 2000), 139. While Hick rejects this description, Mavrodes's paper is still very useful. For example, he makes the helpful distinction between descriptive polytheism and cultic polytheism. The former consists in acknowledging the effects of more than one deity. The latter consists in worshipping more than one deity. While Hick is probably correct in denying that he is a cultic polytheist, he would face more difficulty in denying that he is a descriptive polytheist.

[43]   Paul J. Griffiths argues against this trend, which he calls "an underlying scholarly orthodoxy" which he characterizes as the idea "that an active defense of the truth of [exclusivist religious] beliefs and practices to which one's community appears committed is always to be shunned"; see his (*An Apology for Apologetics: A Study in the Logic of Interreligious Dialogue* (Maryknoll, New York: Orbis Books, 1991), xi. Hick's work on this topic is not only representative of this orthodoxy, but at its forefront. My purpose here is to provide reasons why I regard Hick's version of this ecumenicalist othodoxy problematic. Given Hick's place within this orthodoxy, the likelihood that other ecumenicalists face the same problems is high.

[44]   Hick, *An Interpretation of Religion*, 367, 369.

[45]   Hick, *An Interpretation of Religion*, 363.

[46]   Hick, *An Interpretation of Religion*, 370-71.

[47]   Hick, *An Interpretation of Religion*, 371.

[48]   Though this theme permeates Hick's work, he makes it explicitly on page one of *An Interpretation of Religion*.

[49]   Hick, *An Interpretation of Religion*, 373.

[50]   Hick, *An Interpretation of Religion*, 374-75.

[51]   Hick, "Religious Pluralism and Salvation," 55, 58-59.

[52]   Hick, "Is God Real?" 15. See also, Hick, *An Interpretation of Religion*, 175-77.

[53]   Hick, "Religious Pluralism and Salvation," 61.

[54]   Hick, "Religious Pluralism and Salvation," 64.

[55]   Hick, "Religious Pluralism and Salvation," 64.

[56]   As already noted, Hick disavows a polytheistic reading of his work.

Chapter 4: Religious Exclusivism: The Problem of Being Arbitrary

[1]   Alvin Plantinga, "Ad Hick," *Faith and Philosophy* 14 (1997), 297.

[2]   Plantinga, "Ad Hick," *Faith and Philosophy* 14 (1997), 297.

[3]   Plantinga, "Ad Hick," *Faith and Philosophy* 14 (1997), 297.

154

4   Alvin Plantinga, *Warranted Christian Belief* (New York and Oxford: Oxford University Press, 1999), xii.

5   Plantinga, *Warranted Christian Belief,* 31.

6   Walter Kaufman, *The Theological Imagination: Constructing the Concept of God* (Philadelphia: The Westminster Press, 1981), 41, 50, 48.

7   Plantinga, *Warranted Christian Belief,* 42.

8   This is not to say that Plantinga does not appreciate the symbolic character of religious language. My point is that, in addition to whatever symbolic features a particular instance of religious language might have, Plantinga is open to the possibility that it might also be true or false.

9   Plantinga, *Warranted Christian Belief,* 47.

10   Hick, *An Interpretation of Religion,* 239.

11   Plantinga, *Warranted Christian Belief,* 63.

12   Plantinga, *Warranted Christian Belief,* 63.

13   Alvin Plantinga, "Pluralism," in *The Philosophical Challenge of Religious Diversity,* ed. Philip L. Quinn and Kevin Meeker (Oxford: Oxford University Press, 2000) 173.

14   Plantinga, "Pluralism," 176.

15   Plantinga, "Pluralism," 177.

16   Plantinga, "Pluralism," 177.

17   Plantinga, "Pluralism," 179.

18   Plantinga, "Pluralism," 180.

19   Plantinga, "Pluralism," 180.

20   In *Warranted Christian Belief* Plantinga attributes our evidentialist tradition to Locke. It is from Locke, Plantinga argues, that we the idea that we have an epistemic duty to proportion degree of belief to the available evidence (see especially chapter 3, 67-107).

21   Plantinga, "Pluralism," 180.

22   For a systematic account of evidentialism and alternative approaches to epistemology, the more recent works of Plantinga, of which *Warranted Christian Belief* is the third in a trilogy, are masterful. See also *Warrant: The Current Debate* (New York: Oxford University Press, 1993) and *Warrant and Proper Function* (New York: Oxford University Press, 1993). An example of an alternative epistemological approach to evidentialism which is relevant to this book is provided by Alston. In *Perceiving God,* Alston argues, to give a brief summary, that since there is no non-circular justification for either sense experience or mystical experience (i.e., when seeking to justify the beliefs formed by sense experience we will turn to instances of sense experience and when seeking to justify the beliefs formed by mystical experience we will look to instances of mystical experience), mystical experience is no epistemically worse off than sense experience.

23   Plantinga, "Pluralism," 180.

24   Plantinga, "Pluralism," 181.

25   Plantinga, "Pluralism," 181.

26   Plantinga, "Pluralism," 181.

27   Richard Gale, *The Existence of God* (International Research Library of Philosophy: Dartmouth Publishing Co.,2003), Introduction, 56. Pagination is from the original typescript.

28   Gale, *The Existence of God,* 56.

29   Gale, *The Existence of God,* 58.

30   Plantinga, "Pluralism," 182.

31   Plantinga, "Pluralism," 183.

32   Plantinga, "Pluralism," 183.

33   Plantinga, "Pluralism," 183-84.

[34]   Plantinga, "Pluralism," 184.

[35]   Plantinga, "Pluralism," 184.

[36]   Plantinga, "Pluralism," 184-85.

[37]   Plantinga, "Pluralism," 185-86.

[38]   Plantinga, "Pluralism," 186.

[39]   Plantinga, "Pluralism," 186.

[40]   To recall, these two statements are (1) "The world was created by God, an almighty, all-knowing, and perfectly good personal being (one that holds beliefs; has aims, plans, and intentions; and can act to accomplish these aims)" and (2) "Human beings require salvation, and God has provided a unique way of salvation through the incarnation, life, sacrificial death, and resurrection of his divine son" (Plantinga, "Pluralism," 173).

[41]   Plantinga, "Pluralism," 187.

[42]   Plantinga, "Pluralism," 187.

[43]   Plantinga, "Pluralism," 187-88.

[44]   Plantinga, "Pluralism," 188.

[45]   Plantinga, "Pluralism," 189.

[46]   Peter van Inwagen, "Non Est Hick," in *The Rationality of Belief and the Plurality of Faith*, ed. Thomas D. Senor, (Ithaca and London: Cornell University Press, 1995), 219.

[47]   *Bible, The Holy*. King James Version, Acts 4:12.

[48]   Note that this description of Christianity generally does not fit the Roman Catholic Church specifically; that is, the Roman Catholic Church is not one of the "religions of the world." In a not too terribly strained analogy, neither is the mosque down the street. That is, in both cases, the Roman Catholic Church and the local mosque refer to discrete communities of worshippers. Such communities are not humanly constructed abstractions in the same way that Christianity and Islam are. "Christianity" and "Islam" refer to ideas; "Christians" and "Muslims" refer to the people who, *inter alia*, instantiate (aspects of) these ideas and who populate, e.g., cathedrals and mosques.

[49]   van Inwagen, "Non Est Hick," 239.

[50]   Peter van Inwagen, "A Reply to Professor Hick," *Faith and Philosophy* 14 (1997), 300.

[51]   van Inwagen, "Non Est Hick," 239.

[52]   van Inwagen, "Non Est Hick," 235.

[53]   van Inwagen, "Non Est Hick," 235.

[54]   van Inwagen, "Non Est Hick," 235.

[55]   van Inwagen, "A Reply to Professor Hick," 300.

[56]   van Inwagen, "A Reply to Professor Hick," 300.

[57]   van Inwagen, "Non Est Hick," 225.

[58]   van Inwagen, "Non Est Hick," 236.

[59]   van Inwagen, "Non Est Hick," 227.

[60]   van Inwagen, "Non Est Hick," 226.

Chapter 5: Overview of Religious Irrealism

[1]   Other prominent, twentieth-century, religious irrealists include Henry Nelson Wieman; see, for example, *Is There a God?* With D.C. Macintosh and M. C. Otto (Chicago: Willet, Clark & Co., 1932); Gordon Kaufman; see, for example, *God the Problem* (Cambridge, MA: Harvard

University Press, 1972); Donald Cupitt; see, for example, *After God* (New York: Basic Books, 1997).

2   Hick, "Religious Realism and Non-Realism: Defining the Issue," 3.

3   Ludwig Feuerbach, *The Essence of Christianity*, trans. George Eliot (New York: Harper & Row, Publishers, 1957), 2.

4   Feuerbach, *The Essence of Christianity*, 36, 72.

5   Byrne, *Prolegomena to Religious Pluralism*, 167-68. In *God and Realism* (Burlington, VT: Ashgate, 2003); Byrne offers an account of these matters that provides a useful updated overview of the literature on these matters pertaining to theological realism and theological anti-realism. However, there is nothing in this more recent book that would affect our disagreement concerning Feuerbach.

6   Byrne, *Prolegomena to Religious Pluralism*, 168.

7   Alston, "Realism and the Christian Faith," 40.

Chapter 6: Religious Non-realism: Neither Realist nor Anti-realist

1   Ludwig Wittgenstein, *Philosophical Investigations,* trans. G. E. M. Anscombe (New York: MacMillan Publishing Co., Inc., 1968), #352, henceforth PI.

2   Jeffrey Price, *Language and Being in Wittgenstein's "Philosophical Investigations"* (The Hague: Mouton, 1973), 96.

3   PI #523.

4   PI #352 as cited in Price, *Language and Being in Wittgenstein's "Philosophical Investigations,"* 36.

5   James Conant, in his editor's introduction to Hilary Putnam's *Words and Life* (Cambridge, Mass.: Harvard University Press, 1994), lvii.

6   PI ## 348, 350, 351.

7   Ludwig Wittgenstein, *On Certainty* eds. G. E. M. Anscombe and G. H. von Wright, trans. Denis Paul and G. E. M. Anscombe (New York: Harper & Row, Publishers, 1969), #199.

8   Garth Hallett, *A Companion to Wittgenstein's "Philosophical Investigations"* (Ithaca &London: Cornell University Press, 1977), 409.

9   P. M. S. Hacker, *Insight and Illusion* (Oxford: Clarendon Press 1986), 333.

10   PI #500.

11   Robert L. Arrington, "'Theology as Grammar': Wittgenstein and Some Critics," in *Wittgenstein and Philosophy of Religion*, eds. Robert L. Arrington and Mark Addis (London and New York: Routledge, 2001), 172.

12   For example, Gordon Kaufman writes, "The central problem of theological discourse, not shared with any other 'language-game' is the meaning of the term 'God.' 'God' raises special problems of meaning because it is a noun which by definition refers to a reality transcendent of, and thus not locatable within, experience." Gordon Kaufman, *God the Problem* (Cambridge, MA: Harvard University Press, 1972), 8.

13   Purely formal statements have been offered as exceptions. For example, John Hick suggests that the following can legitimately be predicated of God: "logically generated properties such as 'being a referent of a term' and 'being such that our substantial concepts do not apply'" (Hick, 2005, 239).

14   Such construals of Wittgenstein's thought as it bears on religion persist, though, as my discussion of Michael Scott later in this chapter indicates.

15   Ludwig Wittgenstein, *Zettel*, eds. G. E. M. Anscombe, G. H. von Wright, trans. G.E.M. Anscombe, (Oxford: Blackwell, 1981), #717.

16   Hacker, *Insight and Illusion*, 189.

17   Hans-Johann Glock, *A Wittgenstein Dictionary* (Cambridge, Mass.: Blackwell Reference, 1996), 196.

18   Glock, *A Wittgenstein Dictionary*, 193-98.

19   Patrick Sherry, *Religion, Truth and Language-Games* (New York: Barnes and Noble Books, 1977), 40.

20   Michael Scott, "Framing the Realism Question," *Religious Studies*, 36 (2000): 470, 456. It must be noted that, given my distinction between theological anti- and non-realism (which Scott lumps together as "non-realism"), what Scott means by "non-realism" is not entirely clear. Robin Le Poidevin also makes a distinction within what I call theological irrealism that should be noted. However, his distinction between theological instrumentalism and theological positivism both fall within my classification of theological anti-realism since they both entail that the objective conditions described by a given religious "*p*" do not obtain (Robin Le Poidevin, "Internal and External Questions about God," *Religious Sudies*, 31 (1995): 489-90. I do not mention this as a criticism of Le Poidevin, since distinguishing between what I call theological anti-realism and theological non-realism was not the point of his work. I cite this by way of documenting my claim that the distinction I suggest between theological anti-realism and theological non-realism is both needed and novel.

21   Wittgenstein, *Zettel*, # 413-414, as it appears in, Scott, "Framing the Realism Question," 458.

22   Scott, "Framing the Realism Question," 458.

23   Scott, "Framing the Realism Question," 459.

24   Scott, "Framing the Realism Question," 459.

25   David Hume, *An Enquiry Concerning Human Understanding* (Austin: University of Texas Press, The Nelson Philosophical Texts series, 1953), 172.

26   William P. Alston, *Perceiving God* (Ithaca: Cornell University Press, 1991), *passim*.

27   Stathis Psillos, *Scientific Realism: How Science Tracks Truth* (London and New York: Routledge, 1999), xvii-xix.

28   Psillos, *Scientific Realism*, xxiii.

29   Scott, "Framing the Realism Question," 460.

30   In Michael Scott "Wittgenstein and Realism," *Faith and Philosophy* 17 (2000), 170-190, he does make many fine-grained distinctions within realism and what he calls irrealism. However, none of these distinctions is particularly relevant to the case I make since in the above article Scott still does not acknowledge the distinction I draw between anti- and non-realism.

31   Scott, "Framing the Realism Question," 461.

32   Scott, "Framing the Realism Question," 466.

33   A previous article by Michael Scott, co-written with Andrew Moore "Can Theological Realism Be Refuted," *Religious Studies* 33 (1997), 401-417, reflects the interpretation of Phillips's thought I recommend. That is, the article above acknowledges Phillips's Wittgensteinian non-cognitivism and thus does not cast him inaccurately as an anti-realist. I can only speculate as to the reason for this change.

34   Scott, "Framing the Realism Question," 467.

35   Dewi Zephaniah Phillips "On Really Believing" in *Is God Real?* ed. Joseph Runzo, (Houndsmills, *et al*: Macmillan, 1993), 100.

36   Dewi Zephaniah Phillips, *Wittgenstein and Religion* (New York: St. Martin's Press, 1993), 1.

37   Dewi Zephaniah Phillips, "At the Mercy of Method" in *Philosophy and the Grammar of Religious Belief*, eds. Timothy Tessin and Mario von der Ruhr, (New York: St. Martin's Press, 1995), 3.

38   After all Scott was certainly writing with interests besides those of meeting the concerns I am raising some time later!

39   Phillips, "At the Mercy of Method," 5.

40   Phillips, "At the Mercy of Method," 18.

41   Ludwig Wittgenstein, *Culture and Value*, ed. G.H. von Wright in collaboration with H. Nyman, tr. P. Winch (Oxford: Blackwell, 1980), 5 (hereafter CV).

42   Ludwig Wittgenstein, *Lectures and Conversations: On Aesthetics, Psychology and Religious Belief*, compiled from notes taken by eds. Yorick Smythies, Rush Rhees, James Taylor, Cyril Barret, (Berkeley: University of California Press, 1967), 53.

43   John Churchill, "The Squirrel Does Not Infer by Induction: Wittgenstein and the Natural History of Religion" in *Philosophy and the Grammar of Religious Belief*, eds. Timothy Tessin and Mario von der Ruhr, (New York: St. Martin's Press, 1995), 59.

44   Churchill, "The Squirrel Does Not Infer by Induction," 59.

45   Churchill, "The Squirrel Does Not Infer by Induction," 60.

46   Dewi Zephaniah Phillips, *Wittgenstein and Religion* (New York: St. Martin's Press, 1993), 1.

47   Brian Clack, "Wittgenstein and Expressive Theories of Religion," *International Journal for Philosophy of Religion* 40 (1996): 47.

48   Clack, "Wittgenstein and Expressive Theories of Religion," 48.

49   Clack, "Wittgenstein and Expressive Theories of Religion," 51.

50   Clack, "Wittgenstein and Expressive Theories of Religion," 51.

51   Clack, "Wittgenstein and Expressive Theories of Religion," 52.

52   Clack, "Wittgenstein and Expressive Theories of Religion," 54.

53   "The distinction between what can be said by meaningful propositions and what can only be shown pervades the *Tractatus* from the Preface to the famous final admonition 'Whereof one cannot speak, thereof one must remain silent.'" See Hans-Johann Glock, *A Wittgenstein Dictionary*. (New York: Blackwell, 1996), 330.

54   Clack, "Wittgenstein and Expressive Theories of Religion," 54.

55   Clack, "Wittgenstein and Expressive Theories of Religion," 55.

56   Clack, "Wittgenstein and Expressive Theories of Religion," 55-56.

57   Clack, "Wittgenstein and Expressive Theories of Religion," 56.

58   Clack, "Wittgenstein and Expressive Theories of Religion," 57.

59   CV, 28.

60   Clack, "Wittgenstein and Expressive Theories of Religion," 57.

61   Clack, "Wittgenstein and Expressive Theories of Religion," 58.

62   Again, invoking the same caveat I have throughout the project, none of this is meant to privilege Christian notions of "heaven." Mutatis mutandis this same line of reasoning could be applied to any religion's construal of the ultimate reward.

63   Brian Clack, *Wittgenstein, Frazer and Religion* (NewYork: St. Martin's Press, 1999), 116.

64   However, Hacker argues to this effect and then goes on to cite an instance where Wittgenstein did so as well. The following passage is drawn from one of Wittgenstein's lectures. "If a logic is made up in which the law of excluded middle does not hold, there is no reason for calling the substituted expressions propositions." One who offers such phrases, ones to which the law of the excluded middle does not apply, "has actually discovered something which…is misleading to call a proposition. He has not discovered a proposition, but something that has the

appearance of a proposition"; see *Wittgenstein's Lectures, Cambridge 1932-5, from the Notes of Alice Ambrose and Margaret McDonald*, ed. Alice Ambrose (Oxford: Blackwell's, 1979), 140, as it appears in Hacker, 1986, 331-32. Sorting out what Wittgenstein might mean by nonsense is, of course, an enormous topic in its own right and beyond my present scope. See Hacker, 1986, especially, "Wittgenstein's Later Conception of Philosophy," and Cora Diamond, *The Realistic Spirit* (Cambridge, Mass: MIT Press, 1991), especially "What Nonsense might Be".

[65]   Phillips, "At the Mercy of Method," 14.

Chapter 7: Religious Non-realism Pushed Beyond Its Limits

[1]   There will be instances where the meaning of "Wittgensteinian" is ambiguous; and the context will not make it entirely clear whether by "Wittgensteinian" I mean a proper adjective, referring to the thought of Ludwig Wittgenstein himself or I am referring to the thought of a disciple of Wittgenstein, in this case, D. Z. Phillips, Norman Malcolm, or Peter Winch. This ambiguity is intentional. In the first case, ambiguously attributing a thought to Wittgenstein seems to be the only way to go, given the resistance of his thought to having theoretical labels, e.g., anti-realist, irrealist, non-cognitivist, describe it. The second case is related to the first. Wittgenstein does not come out and make theoretical pronouncements, even if his thought invites being interpreted as offering, say, a non-cognitivist account of religion. In some cases, people who see themselves as faithful expositors of Wittgenstein's philosophical approach will take a more straightforward, again, say, non-cognitivist approach. The question arises, which merits the description, e.g., "non-cognitivist," the thought of the teacher or that of the student trying to articulate the thought of the teacher? The ambiguity involved in calling such interpretations "Wittgensteinian" seems entirely appropriate. Perhaps, insofar as we could make the distinction between the thought of Wittgenstein and that of his followers, we could call the former Wittgensteinian and we could call those who promote it "Wittgensteinianists." Cora Diamond calls attention to a similar idea and refers to it as "chickening out" (Diamond, 1991, 194). One who "chickens out" is one who relies dogmatically on Wittgenstein's teachings, as though Wittgenstein were promoting a theoretical philosophical agenda that was to be followed as though it were a recipe. Those who chicken out are standing squarely on the ladder that Wittgenstein admonished us to pull up at the conclusion of the *Tractatus*.

[2]   This idea is a theme of Phillips's, "On Really Believing" in *Is God Real?*, ed. Joseph Runzo, (Houndsmills, *et al*: Macmillan, 1993).

[3]   Even a professed realist like Alston makes such an objection. See Alston, "Realism and the Christian Faith," 48.

[4]   Phillips, "On Really Believing," 99.

[5]   Phillips, "On Really Believing," 92.

[6]   Phillips, "On Really Believing," 107.

[7]   It is important to note that these concerns do not come up in the context of Wittgenstein's thought itself since, for Wittgenstein, the relation of belief and its object is not an issue. For Wittgenstein, this relation is seen in practice so the (pseudo-)matter of articulating the connection between belief and its object does not arise. In fact, Wittgenstein recommends that seeking an explanation for the nature of such a connection is to be avoided. See John McDowell, *Mind, Value, and Reality* (Cambridge: Harvard University Press, 1998), 276.

[8]   Phillips, "At the Mercy of Method," 5.

[9]   CV, 64e.

160

10 Phillips, "At the Mercy of Method," 5.

11 Phillips, "On Really Believing," 103.

12 Phillips, *Wittgenstein and Religion*, xi

13 Phillips, *Wittgenstein and Religion*, xii.

14 Phillips, *Wittgenstein and Religion*, 3.

15 Phillips, *Wittgenstein and Religion*, 3.

16 Phillips, *Wittgenstein and Religion*, 4.

17 Bryan Magee, *The Great Philosophers* (London: BBC Books, 1987), 337.

18 Phillips, *Wittgenstein and Religion*, 4.

19 For Phillips, language is meaningless beyond the circumscriptions of the appropriate language-game. A standard criticism of this sort of relativism, attributed to Wittgenstein, originates from the works of Kai Nielsen and Michael Martin. In a representative passage Nielsen writes, "It is not that there is such a thing as religious language, for there is not, but there are religious uses of language…" *Contemporary Critiques of Religion* (New York: Herder and Herder, 1971), 103. Michael Martin approvingly references Nielsen on this topic: "[I]t does not follow that just because an expression has a use in our language it has factual meaning. Nielsen vigorously attacks the view he calls Wittgensteinian fideism – the notion that every so-called form of life has its own language game with its own rules and logic and that one cannot critically evaluate a language game from the outside" *Atheism* (Philadelphia: Temple University Press, 1990), 46.

20 Phillips, *Wittgenstein and Religion*, 1.

21 Phillips, *Wittgenstein and Religion*, xii.

22 Phillips, *Wittgenstein and Religion*, xiii.

23 Phillips, "At the Mercy of Method," 11.

24 PI, # 202.

25 Phillips, "At the Mercy of Method," 11.

26 Norman Malcolm, *Wittgenstein: A Religious Point of View?* ed. Peter Winch (Ithaca: Cornell University Press, 1994), 92.

27 Malcolm, *Wittgenstein: A Religious Point of View?* 3.

28 Malcolm, *Wittgenstein: A Religious Point of View?* 82.

29 Malcolm, *Wittgenstein: A Religious Point of View?* 92.

30 Malcolm, *Wittgenstein: A Religious Point of View?* 84.

31 Malcolm, *Wittgenstein: A Religious Point of View?* 92.

32 As it appears in Malcolm, *Wittgenstein: A Religious Point of View?*10.

33 Malcolm, *Wittgenstein: A Religious Point of View?* 92.

34 Malcolm, *Wittgenstein: A Religious Point of View?* 87.

35 Ludwig Wittgenstein, *Vermischte Bermerkungen*, 45 in Malcolm, *Wittgenstein: A Religious Point of View?* 87.

36 Malcolm, *Wittgenstein: A Religious Point of View?* 92.

37 Ludwig Wittgenstein, "Lecture on Ethics," 14.

38 Ludwig Wittgenstein, *Personal Recollections*, ed. Rush Rhees, 129 in Norman Malcolm, 1994, 11.

39 Malcolm, 1994, 92.

40 Wittgenstein. *Vermischte Bermerkungen*, 30, in Malcolm, *Wittgenstein: A Religious Point of View?* 16.

41 Wittgenstein, *Vermischte Bermerkungen*, 28, in Malcolm, *Wittgenstein: A Religious Point of View?* 16.

[42]   Wittgenstein, *Vermischte Bermerkungen*, 33, in Malcolm, *Wittgenstein: A Religious Point of View?* 17.

[43]   Wittgenstein, *Vermischte Bermerkungen*, 53, in Malcolm, *Wittgenstein: A Religious Point of View?* 18.

[44]   This statement is attributed to Wittgenstein in *Ludwig Wittgenstein, Personal Recollections*, ed. Rush Rhees, 123, in Malcolm, *Wittgenstein: A Religious Point of View?* 11.

[45] Peter Winch, "Discussion of Malcolm's Essay," in Malcolm, *Wittgenstein: A Religious Point of View?* 108.

[46]   Winch, "Discussion of Malcolm's Essay," 121.

[47]   Ludwig Wittgenstein, as cited in Winch, "Discussion of Malcolm's Essay," 96.

[48]   Peter Winch, "Asking Too Many Questions" in *Philosophy and the Grammar of Religious Belief*, eds. Timothy Tessin and Mario von der Ruhr, (New York: St. Martin's Press, 1995), 202-3.

[49]   Winch, "Asking Too Many Questions," 206.

[50]   Winch, "Asking Too Many Questions," 210.

[51]   Winch, "Asking Too Many Questions," 210.

[52]   Winch, "Asking Too Many Questions," 211.

[53]   Winch, "Asking Too Many Questions," 200.

[54]   Winch, "Discussion of Malcolm's Essay," 109.

[55]   Winch, "Discussion of Malcolm's Essay," 124.

[56]   Winch, "Discussion of Malcolm's Essay," 117.

[57]   Winch, "Discussion of Malcolm's Essay," 119.

Chapter 8: Conclusion

[1]   Alston, "Religious Diversity and Perceptual Knowledge of God," 199.

[2]   Alston, "Religious Diversity and Perceptual Knowledge of God," 203-04. Jerome Gellman discusses a similar idea in "In Defence of a Contented Exclusivism," *Religious Studies* 36 (2000). He writes, "An exclusivist need not necessarily reflect on the rival claims of religions other than her own…The defense of my position rests on the claim that religious beliefs may stay rationally unreflective for the religious believer in the face of other religions…[A] person cannot subject all his beliefs to critical scrutiny. In order to begin to engage in reflective scrutiny a person must leave some beliefs as unreflective" (403). He continues, "My point is that *tmimut*" ("trust," roughly, in this context) "can be an epistemic virtue in that it affords an insight into the truth of the matter lacking to those devoid of *tmimut*. So, an exclusivist can be rationally justified in her contentment if she perceives that her *tmimut* in her relationship to God affords her an epistemic advantage over others" (406). Perhaps it is this attitude that David Basinger intends to address with what he calls "Basinger's Rule": "once a religious exclusivist acknowledges epistemic peer conflict, for her to choose to retain a purely defensive posture – to claim she is under no obligation to consider the matter further – is for her to forfeit her right to claim justifiably that her perspective is superior" *International Journal for Philosophy of Religion* 47 (2000), 48. Thus Basinger's rule would require Alston, when confronted with epistemic peer conflict, to do more than "sit tight" if Alston were to maintain the truth of Christianity.

[3]   Alston, "Religious Diversity and Perceptual Knowledge of God," 205.

[4]   Richard Gale, *On the Nature and Existence of God* (Cambridge: Cambridge University Press, 1991), 322.

[5]   Gale, *The Existence of God*, 55.

162

6   According to Gale, "The primary tests for the veridicality of a sense experience are agreement among observers", "predictive success", "the normality of the perceiver", "the standardness of the circumstances", "the experience being caused in the right way by its apparent object" (Gale, *The Existence of God*, 53).

7   Gale, *The Existence of God*, 55.

8   William P. Alston "Taking the Curse off Language-Games," in *Philosophy and the Grammar of Religious Belief*, eds. Timothy Tessin and Maria von der Ruhr, (New York: St. Martin's Press, 1995), 20-21.

9   Alston "Taking the Curse off Language-Games," 37.

10   Alston "Taking the Curse off Language-Games," 16-17.

11   For example, in the lectures on religious belief, Wittgenstein indicates that belief in a Last Judgment that is based on its being an historical event is no longer really a religious belief. Similarly, he indicates that he thinks that it was absurd that consecrated bread was kept in chromium steel. In the first case we have the idea that beliefs from the history language-game cannot be applied to the religion language-game. In the second case we have what we might consider the idea that beliefs from the causality language-game (I call it this since presumably the chromium steel would protect the bread from something *causing* harm to it) cannot be applied to the religion language-game. See Ludwig Wittgenstein, *Lectures and Conversations on Aesthetics, Psychology and Religious Belief*, 53.

12   Wittgenstein, *Zettel*, # 413-414.

Appendix

1   As it appears in *Theories of Truth*, ed. Paul Horwich, (Aldershot: Dartmouth Publishing Co. Ltd., 1994). The exchange originally took place in the *Proceedings of the Aristotelian Society*, Supplement 24, 111- 56.

2   P. F. Strawson, "Truth" in *Theories of Truth*, ed. Paul Horwich, (Aldershot: Dartmouth Publishing Co. Ltd., 1994), 185.

3   J.L. Austin, "Truth" in *Theories of Truth*, ed. Paul Horwich, (Aldershot *et al*: Dartmouth Publishing Co. Ltd., 1994), 171.

4   Austin, "Truth," 173.

5   Austin, "Truth," 176, 180.

6   Austin, "Truth," 183.

7   Strawson, "Truth," 191, note 4.

8   Strawson, "Truth," 191.

9   Strawson, "Truth," 190.

10   Strawson, "Truth," 192.

11   Strawson, "Truth," 199.

12   Strawson, "Truth," 212.

13   Strawson, "Truth," 185.

14   P. F. Snowdon, "P. F. Strawson" in *A Companion to Analytic Philosophy*, eds. A.P. Martinich and David Sosa, (Oxford: Blackwell Publishers, 2001), 338.

15   As cited by Snowdon, "P. F. Strawson," 338.

16   Austin, "Truth," 176.

17   Bernard Williams aims to put to rest the concern about the ability of language to refer to objects outside of language pithily. He indicates that if *dog* is merely a "sign for a dog, it is at

any rate a sign for a dog, and that must mean that it can refer to a dog: and a dog is a dog, not a word." Bernard Williams, *Truth and Truthfulness* (Princeton, NJ: Princeton University Press, 2002) 6. Now, of course, it must be conceded that "dog" is a word and thus occurs within language and that the furry barking animal to which it refers is not a word and thus does not occur within language. Alvin Plantinga characterizes such a distinction as "boring" (*Warranted Christian Belief*, 425).

[18]   Wittgenstein, *Zettel*, # 413-414.

[19]   Anticipating what I think would be legitimate concern, my reader could wonder, "How does the author address the potential for subjectivism, a theoretical orientation disavowed by the realist since the subjectivist is not concerned with what is the case but rather is concerned with what is the case *for her*." For example, our subjectivist could operate by avoiding trees that only she perceives; by doing so she could be successfully operating within the parameters of her practical ontology even though her practical ontology, with its imaginary trees, does not match what is the case. As such, one could argue that the idea of practical ontologies I describe above can accommodate subjectivism, a position a realist should oppose. I do oppose subjectivism; I disallow it by invoking the moral of #202 of Wittgenstein's *Philosophical Investigations*. There is a difference between following a rule and merely thinking that one is following a rule. Our subjectivist, by acting on her belief in imaginary trees merely thinks she is following a rule: "avoid running into trees." But since her trees our only imaginary, she is not actually following the rule.

[20]   At least, this is what Wittgenstein recommends "For a large class of cases – though not for all…" staying true to the language and tone of PI #43; I do not wish to appear to be propounding a Wittgensteinian theory of truth or of meaning or of anything. Doing so would clearly violate the quietistic spirit of his later work.

[21]   William P. Alston, *The Autonomy of Religious Belief* (Notre Dame, IN: University of Notre Dame Press, 1981), 130.

[22]   Plantinga presents a very similar argument in the context of assessing the compatibility between postmodern thought and Christian doctrine, 1999, 425.

[23]   Alston, *The Autonomy of Religious Belief*, 147.

[24]   Alston, *The Autonomy of Religious Belief*, 148, 149.

[25]   Alston, *The Autonomy of Religious Belief*, 149.

[26]   Alston, *The Autonomy of Religious Belief*, 149.

[27]   Alston, *The Autonomy of Religious Belief*, 149-50.

[28]   Alston, *The Autonomy of Religious Belief*, 150-51.

[29]   While it could be said that physicists are the analogue of clergy within the physical world language-game, it should be clear that physicists and clerics perform vastly different social functions. While both physicists and clergy are regarded as having expert knowledge of the rules governing their respective language-games, the apodictic nature of, e.g., Christian law ("Thou shalt…"), indicates the difference with respect to how Christian law is *enforced*. Even for the likes of Isaac Newton, a virtual Pope among physicists, it makes no sense to say that he enforces the law of gravity. The point is that Christian laws are enforced by its clergy in ways in which physical laws are not enforced by physicists. Martin Luther was excommunicated because Pope Leo X enforced church law; gravity occurs whether or not the law describing it is enunciated by a physicist.

[30]   Alston, *The Autonomy of Religious Belief*, 152.

[31]   Alston, *The Autonomy of Religious Belief*, 152.

[32]   Alston, *The Autonomy of Religious Belief*, 158-59.

[33]   Alston, *The Autonomy of Religious Belief*, 162.

[34]   Alston, "Taking the Curse off Language-Games," 19.

[35] Glock, *A Wittgenstein Dictionary*, 193-98.
[36] Alston, "Taking the Curse off Language-Games," 35.
[37] Alston, "Taking the Curse off Language-Games," 35-37.
[38] Alston, "Taking the Curse off Language-Games," 41.
[39] Alston, "Taking the Curse off Language-Games," 26.

Bibliography

Alston, William P. "The Christian Language-Game." In *The Autonomy of Religious Belief*. Frederick J. Crosson, ed. Notre Dame: University of Notre Dame Press, 1981.

————. *Divine Nature and Human Language*. Ithaca: Cornell University Press, 1989.

————. "The Elucidation of Religious Statements." In *Process and Divinity* William A. Reese and Eugene Freeman, eds. LaSalle, IL: Open Court Publishing Company, 1964.

————. *Faith, Reason, and Skepticism*. Marcus Hester, ed., Philadelphia: Temple University Press, 1992.

————. *Perceiving God*. Ithaca: Cornell University Press, 1991.

————. *Philosophy of Language*. Englewood Cliffs, NJ: Prentice Hall, Inc., 1964.

————. "Realism and the Christian Faith." *International Journal for Philosophy of Religion* 38 (1995): 37–60.

————. *A Realist Conception of Truth*. Ithaca and London: Cornell University Press, 1996.

————. *Religious Belief and Philosophical Thought*. New York: Harcourt, Brace and World, Inc., 1963.

————. "Response to Hick." *Faith and Philosophy* 14 (1997): 287–88.

————. "Taking the Curse off Language-Games" in *Philosophy and the Grammar of Religious Belief*. Timothy Tessin and Mario von der Ruhr, eds. New York: St. Martin's Press, 1995.

Austin, J. L. "Truth" in *Theories of Truth*, Paul Horwich, ed. Aldershot: Dartmouth Publishing Co. Ltd., 1994.

Basinger, David. *Religious Diversity: A Philosophical Assessment*. Burlington, VT: Ashgate, 2002.

Beiser, Frederick. "Kant's Intellectual Development: 1746-1781" in *The Cambridge Companion to Kant*. Paul Guyer, ed. Cambridge: Cambridge University Press. 1992.

Bell, Richard. "Religion and Wittgenstein's Legacy" in *Philosophy and the Grammar of Religious Belief*, Timothy Tessin and Mario von der Ruhr, eds. New York: St. Martin's Press, 1995.

Byrne, Peter. *Prolegomena to Religious Pluralism: Reference and Realism in Religion*. New York: St. Martin's Press, 1995.

————. *God and Realism*. Burlington, VT: Ashgate, 2003.

Churchill, John. "The Squirrel Does Not Infer by Induction: Wittgenstein and the Natural History of Religion." In *Philosophy and the Grammar of Religious Belief*, Timothy Tessin and Mario von der Ruhr, eds. New York: St. Martin's Press, 1995.

Clack, Brian R. "Wittgenstein and Expressive Theories of Religion." *International Journal for Philosophy of Religion* 40 (1996): 47–62.

———. *Wittgenstein, Frazer, and Religion*. New York: St. Martin's Press, 1999.

Conant, James. "Introduction," in *Words and Life*. By Hilary Putnam, James Conant, ed. Cambridge, Mass: Harvard University Press, 1994.

———. "Putting Two and Two Together: Kierkegaard, Wittgenstein, and the Point of View for Their Work as Authors." In *Philosophy and the Grammar of Religious Belief*, Timothy Tessin and Mario von der Ruhr, eds. New York: St. Martin's Press, 1995.

Cupitt, Donald. *After God*. New York: Basic Books, 1997.

Davis, Stephen T. "Anselm and Phillips on Religious Realism." In *Philosophy and the Grammar of Religious Belief*. Timothy Tessin and Mario von der Ruhr, eds. New York: St. Martin's Press, 1995.

D'hert, Ignace. *Wittgenstein's Relevance for Theology*. Bern: Herbert Lang; Frankfurt: Peter Lang, 1975.

Diamond, Cora. *The Realistic Spirit*. Cambridge, Mass.: M.I.T. Press, 1991.

Ferreira, M. Jamie. "Religion and 'Really Believing'" in *Philosophy and the Grammar of Religious Belief*, Timothy Tessin and Mario von der Ruhr, eds. New York: St. Martin's Press, 1995.

Gale, Richard M. *On the Nature and Existence of God*. Cambridge: Cambridge University Press, 1991.

———. *The Existence of God*. Coeditor with Alexander Pruss. International Research Library of Philosophy: Dartmouth Publishing Co., 2003.

Gellman, Jerome. "In Defense of Contented Religious Exclusivism." *Religious Studies* 36 (2000): 401–17.

Glock, Hans-Johann. *A Wittgenstein Dictionary*. Cambridge, Mass.: Blackwell Reference, 1996.

Griffiths, Paul J. *An Apology for Apologetics: A Study in the Logic of Interreligious Dialogue*. Maryknoll, New York: Orbis Books, 1991.

———. *Problems of Religious Diversity*. Oxford: Blackwell, 2001.

Gutting, Gary. "Plantinga and the Rationality of Religious Belief" in *Philosophy and the Grammar of Religious Belief*. Timothy Tessin and Mario von der Ruhr, eds. New York: St. Martin's Press, 1995.

————. *Religious Belief and Religious Skepticism*. Notre Dame: University of Notre Dame Press, 1982.

Guyer, Paul. "Introduction" in *The Cambridge Companion to Kant*. Paul Guyer, ed. Cambridge: Cambridge University Press. 1992.

Hacker, P.M.S. *Insight and Illusion*. Bristol, England: Thoemmes Press, 1997.

Hallett, Garth. *A Companion to Wittgenstein's "Philosophical Investigations."* Ithaca: Cornell University Press, 1977.

Hanfling, Oswald. *Wittgenstein's Later Philosophy*. Albany: State University of New York Press, 1989.

Harper, Albert W.J. *Discussion and Commentary on Kant's Critiques*. Lewiston, NY: The Edwin Mellen Press, Ltd., 1996.

Hick, John. *An Interpretation of Religion 2nd edition*. New Haven: Yale University Press, 2005.

————. "The Epistemological Challenge of Religious Pluralism." *Faith and Philosophy* 14 (1997): 277–86.

Horwich, Paul, ed. *Theories of Truth*. Aldershot: Dartmouth Publishing Co. Ltd., 1994.

Hume, David. *An Enquiry Concerning Human Understanding*. Austin: University of Texas Press, The Nelson Philosophical Texts series, 1953.

Kaufman, Gordon. *God the Problem*. Cambridge, MA: Harvard University Press, 1972

Kerr, Fergus. *Theology after Wittgenstein*. New York: Blackwell, 1986.

Le Poidevin, Robin. "Internal and External Questions about God." *Religious Studies* 31 (1995): 485–500.

Malcolm, Norman. *A Religious Point of View?* Ithaca: Cornell University Press, 1994.

Martin, Michael. *Atheism*. Philadelphia: Temple University Press, 1990.

————. *The Case against Christianity*. Philadelphia: Temple University Press, 1991.

Mavrodes, George. "A Response to Hick" *Faith and Philosophy* 14 (1997): 289–94.

————. "Polytheism" in *The Philosophical Challenge of Religious Diversity*, Philip L. Quinn and Kevin Meeker, eds. Oxford: Oxford University Press, 2000.

McDowell, John H. *Mind, Value, and Reality*. Cambridge, MA: Harvard University Press, 1998.

McKim, Robert. *Religious Ambiguity and Religious Diversity*. Oxford: Oxford University Press, 2001.

Netland, Harold. *Dissonant Voices*. Grand Rapids, MI: Eerdmans Publishing Company, 1991.

Nielsen, Kai. "Can Anything be Beyond Human Understanding?" In *Philosophy and the Grammar of Religious Belief*. Timothy Tessin and Mario von der Ruhr, eds. New York: St. Martin's Press, 1995.

———. *God, Scepticism, and Modernity*. Ottawa: University of Ottawa Press, 1989.

Palmer, Anthony. "Violations of Nature and the Conditions of Sense" in *Philosophy and the Grammar of Religious Belief*, Timothy Tessin and Mario von der Ruhr, eds. New York: St. Martin's Press, 1995.

Palmer, Donald. *Looking at Philosophy*. London: Mayfield Publishing Company, 1994.

Peterman, James F. *Philosophy as Therapy: An Interpretation and Defense of Wittgenstein's later Philosophical Project*. Albany: State University of New York Press, 1992.

Phillips, Dewi.Zephaniah. "On Really Believing." In *Is God Real?* Joseph Runzo, ed., Houndsmill: Macmillan, 1993.

———. *Wittgenstein and Religion*. New York: St. Martin's Press, 1993.

———. "At the Mercy of Method" In *Philosophy and the Grammar of Religious Belief*, Timothy Tessin and Mario von der Ruhr, eds. New York: St. Martin's Press, 1995.

Plantinga, Alvin. *Warranted Christian Belief*. Oxford: Oxford University Press, 2000.

———. "Pluralism" In *The Philosophical Challenge of Religious Diversity*. Philip L. Quinn and Kevin Meeker, eds. Oxford: Oxford University Press, 2000.

———. "Ad Hick." *Faith and Philosophy* 14 (1997): 295–98.

Price, Jeffrey. *Language and Being in Wittgenstein's "Philosophical Investigations."* The Hague: Mouton, 1973.

Psillos, Stathis. *Scientific Realism: How Science Tracks Truth*. London and New York: Routledge, 1999

Quinn, Phillip L. and Meeker, Kevin, eds. *The Philosophical Challenge of Religious Diversity*. Oxford: Oxford University Press, 2000.

Rossi, Philip J. "The Final End of All Things," In *Kant's Philosophy of Religion Reconsidered*. eds. Philip J. Rossi and Michael Wreen, eds. Bloomington: Indiana University Press, 1991.

Runzo, Joseph, ed., *Is God Real?* Houndsmill: Macmillan, 1993.

Schilbrack, Kevin. "Religious Diversity and the Closed Mind." *Journal of Religion* 83 (2003): 100–7.

Schmidt, Paul F. *Religious Knowledge*. Glencoe, IL: Free Press of Glencoe, 1961.

Senor, Thomas D., ed. *The Rationality of Belief and the Plurality of Faith*. Ithaca: Cornell University Press, 1995.

Sherry, Patrick. *Religion, Truth and Language-Games*. New York: Barnes and Noble Books, 1977.

Snowdon, P. F., "P. F. Strawson" in *A Companion to Analytic Philosophy*, A.P. Martinich and David Sosa, eds. Oxford: Blackwell Publishers, 2001.

Strawson, P. F. "Truth" in *Theories of Truth*, Paul Horwich, ed. Aldershot: Dartmouth Publishing Co. Ltd., 1994.

Thomas, Emyr Vaughan. "Wittgensteinian Methodology and Religious Belief." *International Philosophical Quarterly* 39 (1999), 265–76.

van Inwagen, Peter. "A Reply to Professor Hick" *Faith and Philosophy* 14 (1997): 299–302.

———. "Non Est Hick." *The Rationality of Belief and the Plurality of Faith*. Thomas D. Senor, ed. Ithaca: Cornell University Press, 1995.

Whittaker, John H. "Can a Purely Grammatical Inquiry be Religiously Persuasive?" in *Philosophy and the Grammar of Religious Belief*. Timothy Tessin and Mario von der Ruhr, eds. New York: St Martin's Press, 1995.

Winch, Peter. "Asking Too Many Questions" in *Philosophy and the Grammar of Religious Belief*, Timothy Tessin and Mario von der Ruhr, eds. New York: St. Martin's Press, 1995.

Wittgenstein, Ludwig. *The Big Typescript, TS. 213*. Tr. Grant Luckhardt and Maximilian Aue, eds. Malden, MA: Blackwell, 2005.

———. *Culture and Value*. Tr. Peter Winch, G.H. von Wright ed., in collaboration with Heikki Nyman. Chicago: University of Chicago Press, 1980.

———. *Lectures and Conversations*. Cyril Barrett ed. Berkeley & Los Angeles: University of California Press, 1967.

———. *On Certainty*. Tr. Denis Paul and G. E. M. Anscombe. G. E. M. Anscombe and G. H. von Wright eds. New York: Harper and Row, Publishers, 1972.

———. *Philosophical Investigations*. 3d ed. Tr. G. E. M. Anscombe. New York: Macmillan Publishing Co. Inc., 1968.

———. *Philosophical Occasions*. James C. Klagge and Alfred Nordmann, eds., Indianapolis: Hacket Publishing Co., 1993.

———. *Remarks on the Foundations of Mathematics*. Third edition. Tr. G. E. M. Anscombe, G. E. M. Anscombe, Rush Rhees, G. H. von Wright eds., Oxford: Oxford University Press, 1978.

Index